Moreno's Personality Theory and Its Relationship to Psychodrama

Moreno's Personality Theory and Its Relationship to Psychodrama discusses Dr J. L. Moreno's theory of personality and its relationship to psychodrama from the philosophical, developmental and therapeutic aspects. It provides a theoretical model based on Moreno's personal experiences, combining existential-theological worldviews with a developed personality theory. Giving an integrative and critical discussion and analysis of Moreno, personality theory and psychodrama, Telias invites the scholarly community to revive the interest in Moreno's important work with this book that fills a gap in the theory of psychodrama and sociometry.

The book analyses Moreno's work from six interrelated perspectives: theory and Moreno's biography, the philosophical-theological aspect, the developmental approach and role theory, and psychodrama and sociometry. It begins by exploring parallels between Moreno's biography and his theory of self, examining the development of the concept of Godliness in different stages of life. It then considers Moreno's philosophical-theological perception of the self, Moreno's theory of the development of the self, the significance of the concept of "role" in Moreno's theory and how the personality theory can be viewed through psychodrama.

Giving up to date reflections on Moreno's contribution and writings, this book brings a new perspective and will be of great interest to academics and postgraduate students in the fields of psychodrama, sociodrama, creative arts therapies, existential philosophy and intellectual history.

Rozei Telias is a Psychodramatist, Arts Psychotherapist, Group Facilitator and Mediator. She lectured at the universities of Bar-Ilan and Haifa, and at the academic colleges: Ashkelon and Ruppin. Dr Telias was a Chairperson at the Israeli Association of Psychodrama (retired). Telias established and manages the Institute for Psychodrama, an institute of psychodrama and negotiation training.

Moreno's Personality Theory and Its Relationship to Psychodrama

A Philosophical, Developmental and Therapeutic Perspective

Rozei Telias

Routledge
Taylor & Francis Group
LONDON AND NEW YORK

First published 2019
by Routledge

2 Park Square, Milton Park, Abingdon, Oxfordshire OX14 4RN
52 Vanderbilt Avenue, New York, NY 10017

Routledge is an imprint of the Taylor & Francis Group, an informa business

First issued in paperback 2020

British Library Cataloguing-in-Publication Data
A catalogue record for this book is available from the British Library

Library of Congress Cataloging-in-Publication Data
Names: Telias, Rozei, author.
Title: Moreno's personality theory and its relationship to psychodrama : a philosophical, developmental and therapeutic perspective / Rozei Telias.
Description: New York : Routledge, 2018.
Identifiers: LCCN 2018013409 (print) | LCCN 2018027105 (ebook) | ISBN 9781351021104 (E-book) | ISBN 9781138496613 (hardback) | ISBN 9781351021104 (ebk)
Subjects: LCSH: Personality. | Self. | Drama—Therapeutic use. | Moreno, J. L. (Jacob Levy), 1889–1974.
Classification: LCC BF698 (ebook) | LCC BF698 .T435 2018 (print) | DDC 158.1—dc23
LC record available at https://lccn.loc.gov/2018013409

ISBN: 978-1-138-49661-3 (hbk)
ISBN: 978-0-367-48820-8 (pbk)

Typeset in Bembo
by Apex CoVantage, LLC

This book is dedicated to my family members
My parents: Eliyahu and Matilda Telias
My sister: Pnina Matan
My brother: Menachem Telias
Special thanks to translator Moore Shavit

Contents

Introduction 1

Preface 1
Moreno and existentialism 2
In the footsteps of Marx and Freud: the cosmodynamic man 13
Moreno's therapeutic principles 21
Toward systemizing Moreno's thinking 23
The book's structure 27

1 **Parallels between Moreno's biography and his theory of self** 29

The idea of the Cosmic Man and the myth of the birth and the name 29
The family circle and the environmental circle 32
The development of the concept of Godliness in different stages of life 35
Spontaneity, group psychotherapy and sociometry 44
Theater of spontaneity and psychodrama 48
The women, the muses in Moreno's life: the realization of Godliness and creativity 50
Summary and assessment 52

2 **Moreno's philosophical-theological perception of the self** 54

What is a theological and cosmodynamic perception? 54
The creative act 57
Spontaneity 61
Cultural conservation 77
Warming up 82
Encounter and the interpersonal theory 85
Tele 90

3 Moreno's theory of the development of the self **98**

Spontaneity, creativity, warming up and tele: the developmental outlook 98
The theory of the matrix of identity 103
"Web of atoms": psychological, social, and cultural aspects 114

4 The significance of the concept of "role" in Moreno's theory **116**

The theatrical aspect 116
The social aspect 118
Moreno's interdisciplinary and psychotherapeutic aspect 123
Moreno's and Mead's views: similarities and differences 124
Linking role and personality in Moreno's theory: reasoning 131

5 The personality theory viewed through psychodrama **134**

What is psychodrama? 136
Psychodrama: structure and components 142
Action principle 146
The developmental aspect 153
Role reversal technique 167
Role play and role training 173

6 An integrative and critical discussion and analysis of Moreno, personality theory and psychodrama **177**

Review 178
Epilogue: general assessment of Moreno 181
The death of Moreno – the universal man 184

Bibliography 185
Index 193

Introduction

Preface

Jacob Levy Moreno (1889–1974) was a psychiatrist, scientist and philosopher. The multitude of facets in his thinking is reflected by the three fields he established: psychodrama, group psychotherapy and sociometry. Moreno is accredited for many breakthroughs in psychology, sociology, psychiatry, education and theater. His work served as a foundation for many secondary branches, such as the sensitive group, the modern "human potential exhaustion" movement and action method–oriented coaching groups, as well as role theory as a supportive method in psychotherapy in general and as a means for understanding the interpersonal action in the human experience in particular.

Moreno enhanced human thinking through his creative position concerning philosophy and religion. He was involved in existentialist philosophy and was a key figure in the dramatic and artistic climate of his time. His ideas were influenced by numerous sources: ancient religions, Greek philosophy, classic drama, Christian legends, Asian cultures and his own Jewish tradition. The incessant flow of his ideas and thoughts relating to spontaneity and creativity manifested themselves in cosmological, interpersonal and existentialist matters.

However, most of all, Moreno was considered a pioneer in the development of a group approach to issues associated with social organizations and the driving force in developing a therapeutic approach that considers the individual's social system in a group setting. This group therapy stemmed from his interest both in I-thou encounters and the role dynamics between the self and society. In that context, in 1932 he coined the term "group psychotherapy". Moreno left his impression on various areas in group psychotherapy: family therapy, gestalt therapy and particularly psychodrama. He was the first to indicate the tremendous therapeutic power of action mode reconstruction and role reversal. Psychodrama, in addition to being a powerful therapeutic technique in itself, bears many implications on education, social sciences, behavioral sciences and experimental research with small groups.

Moreno's tremendous contribution to the social sciences, behavioral sciences and group therapy is completely unquestioned. Nonetheless, psychotherapy's position in this day and age is a pale shadow of its days of glory back in the

1940s, when the group therapy movement was established and developed. Over time, the tendency to separate Moreno's methods emerged. In other words, psychodrama and sociometry were separated from their philosophical and theoretical basis. Consequently, psychodrama is erroneously perceived as a therapeutic procedure rather than a method based upon theoretical principles. In other words, in this day and age, psychodrama is praxis without theory, and almost nobody bothers reading the works of Moreno anymore.

Why has psychodrama lost its position in favor of the cognitive approach, which is the dominant approach in present-day group therapy? Why did Moreno lose his prestige as a social scientist? Why does it seem as though Moreno has been forgotten? In this book, the author shall address those questions in an attempt to restore Moreno's standing as one of the most creative, influential minds of the 20th century. Additionally, this work shall attempt to restore the interest in his writings, which demonstrate a fresh, practical approach within the existentialistic movement's framework, proposing a new theological outlook as an alternative to the Nietzschean atheism.

Thus far, no research has demonstrated how all of Moreno's intellectual, philosophical and theological activity is manifested in his praxis. In this book, the author argues that Moreno's therapeutic tools, which he employs in psychodrama and sociometry, are all derived from a broader philosophical, developmental and therapeutic method that relies upon the same principles: spontaneity, creativity, warming up, cultural conserve and tele. The challenge in identifying the point where the theory ends and therapy begins is a consequence of the fact that Moreno, time and time again, uses the same concepts for all three aspects. That, in turn, led to confusion and misunderstanding of his works. Through cautious, close reading of the vast corpus of Moreno's writings, the author intends to demonstrate the way in which the distinct meanings of the various concepts in each of Moreno's areas of thinking may be implemented and to show they do not function as pieces of a puzzle, but rather, each area in itself, and in respect to the other areas, expresses all of Moreno's basic concepts from different points of departure and perspectives.

All perspectives, however, are based upon the concept of "existentialism", which is the framework containing all of Moreno's core concepts, including the psychodrama method. The existentialistic perception shaped and affected Moreno's personal and professional outlook in general and the outlook of humans in particular. The author shall extensively address that perception, because of its importance.

Moreno and existentialism

Existentialism in philosophy

The philosophy of existence seeks to portray man not as a set of static contents, nor as a mechanism of constant patterns, but as an entity that constantly comes into being. It does not matter how true the theoretical fact that a person consists of some given chemicals is, or that he acts out of some mechanistic or pre-determined behavioral patterns. The more fundamental view concerns man as existing in a given time and space. The question is how to raise awareness of that fact and what is to be done about it. Existentialistic psychologists and psychiatrists did not at all reject the learning of pre-determined drives, motives or behavioral patterns. However, as long as they are not enacted in a specific context, there is a risk of losing the meaning of any other detail we may know of a given person.

At the core of this philosophy stands the person as an individual. The only existing reality is the one that the person addresses, granting it its unique meaning to his own life. Any reliance upon general values that society attempts to impose on the individual will be considered a distorted solution and fleeing the true issue of meaning. Existentialism addressed human existence linked to the decline of religious and traditional beliefs and the loss of absolute truths in the modern age. Religion, state, moral values and various ideologies are all considered systems disrupting the individual's freedom and ability to discover his own inner truth. Historically, Danish philosopher Søren Kierkegaard (1813–1855) was considered the first existentialist. Other prominent representatives of the movement are Friedrich Nietzsche (1844–1900), Martin Heidegger (1889–1976) and Jean-Paul Sartre (1905–1980).

Surprisingly, existentialistic philosophy received its great push following World War II. The tremendous destruction spread by the Fascist regimes, which raised the banner of society's and state's superiority over the lone individual, aroused a counter-reaction, which placed man at the center, completely renouncing the importance of society, culture and morals. Existentialism mirrors the moral crisis undergone by western society because of the war, proposing an answer of its own to that crisis. Rather than offering new morals, the existentialist claims that any person must search the unique meaning of his own life by himself (Beith, 1992, pp. 119–120). Existentialistic philosophy addressed important questions, such as man's freedom, death issue and existing loneliness states, as well as modern man's alienation. Loneliness stems from the feeling that a person cannot truly communicate with another. The sense of existence is so unique and idiosyncratic that it may not be shared with another, just as the feelings of existence of that other person may not be shared. Rather than understanding the other's existence, we experience its physical reflection, which bears no real meaning. The person himself, too, is aware that others know him through the mediation of his appearance. The more we become engrossed in our inner loneliness, the more we isolate ourselves from the world, though we may possess vast objective knowledge thereof.

Fear is a natural reaction to life in a world with neither meaning nor purpose, into which a person has been thrown without choice and where he is forced to live. It is a world from which he will be withdrawn violently, by death, without understanding why everything has happened. The alienation in modern society intensifies those reactions among those who live in it. The existentialist compares the person to a screw in machine, immersed in despair and fear, while facing the power of the machine on the one hand and his own weakness on the other hand.

Existentialism is not necessarily nihilist, and its engagement is not limited to describing the suffering of existence. It also attempts to offer a shred of redemption and hope. Human existence and the existence of mind, desire and personal feelings have positive sides, which manifest themselves in absolute freedom, uniqueness and the ability to create. The idea of freedom is the core of the new values proposed by existentialism. Precisely because of the emphasis put on existence's uniqueness, which completely distinguishes man from all other objects in nature, the claim for freedom's meaning is clearer, as compelled by the very fact of existence. Because what renders human existence unique is individuality, enslaving man will be impossible.

Existentialism and psychology

The questions upon which existentialistic philosophy is based became relevant in the area of personality exploration as well, in an attempt to explain psychological questions in existentialistic terms as part of human existence. Existentialistic psychology mainly concerns the meaning of a person's existence and being in this world. It focuses upon the essence of human existence, emphasizing the importance of phenomenology. Phenomenological philosophy, which was founded by Edmund Husserl (1859–1938), proposes a scientific approach that constitutes an alternative to modern science's approach. According to this approach, the empirical observation may not be separated from the scientist who conducts it. The very choice to prefer conducting a specific observation over another indicates that the observation is conducted out of some orientation to the phenomenon that the observing scientist possesses. Hence, phenomenology is interested not in the actual meaning of phenomena, but rather, in the meaning they bear in a person's mind. Thus, it proposes to categorize phenomena by our attitude toward them. The phenomenological method categorizes phenomena by their quality, rather than by their meaning, as opposed to modern science, which measures phenomena by their quantity.

Phenomenology attempts to understand human behavior from the perspective of the person himself. In other words, the scientist attempts as much as possible to set himself free from preceding theories and expectations so as to absorb the experience of the person he is facing as closely as possible to the experience the person himself is undergoing. The object of exploration is the experience itself, the way in which a person perceives the world and himself within it (Beith, 1992, pp. 119–120).

This method is different from the behaviorist approach, which explores the external behavior that is observed and that is different from the psychoanalytical approach, which explores unconscious contents, which are not part of the experience itself. Both behaviorism and psychoanalysis observe a person from outside, as subjected to a scientific exploration, similarly to any other natural phenomenon (Atkinson et al., 1996, p. 529). Existential psychology, in comparison, attempts to explore a person's internal content, that is to say, to explore him from within. The experiencing person is the main subject matter. Human beings are not mere objects of research. Rather, they are to be described and understood in terms of their subjective outlook on the world, as well as their self-perceptions and self-esteem through their own eyes. The key question to which each person is to respond is "who am I"? In order to know how the individual attempts to respond to this question, the psychologist is to act as a partner for the search for existential meaning (Atkinson et al., 1996, p. 529).

Kenneth Spence (1907–1967), one of behaviorist psychology's prominent representatives, wrote the following:

> The question of whether any particular realm of behavior phenomena is more real or closer to real life and hence should be given priority in investigation does not, or at least should not, arise for the psychologist as scientist.
> (Spence, 1956, p. 14)

Spence prioritized phenomena of monitoring, control and analysis of abstract phrasing of rules. Based upon that thinking, several approaches to psychology were founded. However, these thinkers, similarly to psychologists and psychiatrists in the existentialistic traditions, possessed the exact opposite view. They insisted the human science should investigate human beings in their actual reality. Nietzsche and Kierkegaard, who preceded that view, demanded reality should include both the object and the subject, seeking to detach themselves from the illusion that reality may be understood and perceived abstractly and in a detached manner. Likewise, existentialists passionately fought against the tendency to view a person as a controllable object and investigate him in a calculated method, which nearly subdues him. In western research, the common tendency was to turn man into an anonymous unit that will fit the wide collectivism – both industrial and political of the time – as a robot (May, 1958, pp. 13–14). The main characteristic of the mid-19th century was the breaking of personality down to segments. This breakdown was a symptom of emotional, psychological and spiritual disintegration, which occurred for both the individual and society. The split may be identified not only in psychology and the sciences, but also in nearly every cultural aspect of the 19th century: plastic art, theater, etc. (May, 1958, p. 21).

Existentialistic psychology does not present personality theories involving discussion of the development of personality parts and the dynamics between them. Rather, it views a person as a whole entity, not as an object that may be divided (as, for example, "id", "ego", "super-ego") and observed separately. This psychology defines itself as holistic, viewing the person as a whole, as more than the sum of his parts. The followers of this theory claimed that psychoanalytical and behaviorist theory provided only a partial, limited picture of human functioning. Their approach is presented in a clear, extreme manner through Allport's writings:

> [M]ainly in relation to construction and development of human personality, we need to open doors. This is exactly where ignorance and uncertainty are the greatest. Our methods, which suit the investigation of sensory processes for animals and pathology research, do not suit personality research. The interpretation, which is derived from the exclusive use of those methods, is worthless. Some of the theories are partially based upon ill, anxious human beings, or desperate mice's tricks. Few theories are derived from research with healthy human beings; those who are driven not only for survival, but to shape their lives to be worth living.
>
> (Allport, in Beith, 1992, p. 119)

Existentialistic psychologists reject the psychoanalytical approach, as they believe psychology based upon defected, distorted personalities can only yield defected, distorted psychology. They reject behaviorism as well, as being a mindless psychology, which is mostly based upon the investigation of inferior organisms. People are not only driven by basic drives, such as sex or aggressiveness, or physiological needs such as hunger or thirst (Atkinson et al., 1996, p. 529). In their opinion, existentialistic neurosis, namely, mental illness, emerges not only because of a mental trauma repressed, weak ego or life's tension, but because of the individual's inability to find meaning to life. Thus, he lives by an unauthentic model of existence, and his issue is to find meaning in life, transitioning to the authentic model of existence (Frankl, in Ellenberger, 1958, p. 119). Human choice, creativity and self-actualization are the preferred subjects of investigations, and they should constitute the criteria for psychological health, rather than only the control over the ego or adaptation to environment (Atkinson et al., 1996, p. 529).

Another important aspect is viewing a person as possessing free choice and ability to control his destiny. Even here, the opposition of the existential movement to psychology's preceding movements is prominent. Psychoanalysis, on the one hand, maintains that a person is dominated by inner, unconscious forces, whereas behaviorism, on the other hand, perceives a person as an organism dominated by external stimuli. From psychology's outlook alone, the emergence of the third movement may be viewed as a counter-reaction to the other two. As mentioned, those three movements stem from various moral views of the human being and his conduct in the world surrounding him (Beith, 1992, pp. 119–120). This is where the main meaning of the existentialistic psychotherapy movement is addressed. It calls for basing psychotherapy upon the understanding of what turns a person into a human being. This view raises the banner of defining neurosis in terms of factors damaging a person's ability to fulfill his own being. Although existentialistic psychotherapy relies upon scientific analysis as well, it mainly restores the thorough, broad understanding of the human being, namely, the person as a human creature. This view was based upon the assumption of the existence of a "human science" that would not break down the person, his personality, into its smallest parts while exploring and learning it. This approach connects science and ontology.

Existentialistic psychology is closely related to its philosophical origins. It may also be stated that it is not pure psychology, but rather, some no man's land lying between psychology and philosophy (Beith, 1992, pp. 119–120).

Existentialistic psychology is identified with figures such as Sartre, Martin Buber and Heidegger, the latter being of great influence on existentialistic psychology (Beith, 1992, pp. 60, 121). Moreno is absent from the professional literature, despite being a key contributor to existentialistic psychology.

Moreno: theological and dialogical existentialism

Moreno was considered one of the first thinkers of existentialistic-humanistic psychology. He believed that a person was essentially good, bearing human potential for growth, development and creativity. A person's behavior is examined here and now, emphasizing his free will and ability to choose, decide and act.

Similarly to other philosophers and psychiatrists associated with the existentialistic movement, Moreno methodically criticized the existing social order's structure. He thought all old values had been destructed, for good or bad reasons, but no alternative values had been established. The attempt to work with the existing moral order analysis or a declaration of new values seemed to him futile, worthless intellectual gestures. Moreno strove to replace the current institutes, which were rotten and falling apart, with stable cultural and social institutes, which were constructed in a manner more suitable for modern human needs (Moreno, 1943, pp. 299–344):

> The historical situation forced me to follow the long path of radical, comprehensive reconstruction, more than anybody else before me in the western world.
>
> (Moreno, 1949a, p. 201)

By reconstruction, Moreno means the perception of man and divine essence in the modern era.

The winds of secularization in Europe were apparent everywhere. One of secularization's points of climax was Nietzsche's accusation toward mankind of "literally having killed God". This call harshly expresses the sense of meaninglessness and loss in mankind's essence. It is not atheism in its simple sense, but rather, total shaking off of any purpose externally dictated to man. Nietzsche argued that in the modern era, metaphysical God died and God's death led man to nihilism and loss of the freedom of prospects. Hence, human beings are compelled to become human Gods, some kind of a "super-human" (in German: Übermensch).

But what does the statement "God is dead" mean? It necessarily implies that there had been a live presence before; thus it may not be a simple example of atheism, in the sense of absolute, unconditional rejection of divinity (Myerson, 2005, p. 18). Our world is a world where God is dead. Hence, pre-modern values no longer have the value and power of attraction they used to possess. Yet still, in such a world faith becomes important all the more, because there is no absolute moral authority to impose its will upon us. We feel lost, with neither direction nor conscience, in a cosmic, moral vacuum (J. D. Moreno, 1994, p. 105).

In accordance with the existentialistic perception, which views man as a whole entity, and as opposed to Nietzsche's perception concerning God's death, Moreno brings a whole perception of his own regarding the man–God relationship and religion's role in the modern era, despite his criticism of religious institutions. Moreno did not renounce religion and the spiritual and psychological connections deriving from it. Just the opposite: Moreno cautioned against and opposed the secularization and atheism trends that dominated the world, oppressing religious institutions and the concept of divinity. He thought those trends were detrimental to humanity (Moreno, 1949a, pp. 204–205). He took the opposite stance, which views religion's positive side, according to which the concept of God may be perceived as a realistic fantasy, rather than an illusion, as maintained by the other movements. The fact that Buddhism, Christianity, Judaism and other religions succeeded to a small extent as a moral basis for healing society's ailments does not imply the failure of religion's concept in itself. Moreno argued that it was necessary to try religion again; a new kind of religion, whose ambitions and inspirations had been transformed, and its techniques had been enhanced based upon the insights with which science has provided us. Moreno proposed a new religion which, on the one hand, contradicted the common religions, yet opposed the way in which it was presented by the psychological and political doctrines of the time (Moreno, 1953, pp. xv–xvi).

The goal of this new religion was to bring about a new social order and a set of moral concepts which would influence our contemporary culture (Moreno, 1949a, pp. 204–205). This new religion was manifested in finding God through direct encounters between human beings through the interpersonal theory and re-establishment of sociometry, the social science, which is not accurate, but is based upon an actual relationship between the individuals themselves, which he considered an inevitable necessity. Moreno's interpersonal theory stemmed from his religious perception, and one of the important aspects of this perception is a positive outlook on mankind and its consistent emphasis on inquiry and revelation of human, social and political conflicts, as well as personal and familial ones, and their resolution (Moreno, 1943, pp. 299–344; Haworth, 1998, p. 15).

> Two thousand years ago, humanity suffered a highly important moral crisis. The wide mass attained catharsis thanks to Christianity, through the universality characteristic of its methods, with the practical tools, which are

> love, compassion and hope. In our day and age, social and psychological sciences are designated to complete that goal religion intended to fulfill. At present, as in the past, humanity is suffering psychological and social unrest. Catharsis will probably emerge again through tools which will combine universal methods and great practice. One of the most promising methods which [has] been developed in the past twenty-five years, fulfilling those requirements is the psychodramatic method.
>
> (Moreno, 1951, p. 102)

In Moreno's opinion, psychodrama emerged at that time as an answer to the moral crisis. Moreno believed the methods he invented, psychodrama and sociometry, combine universal methods with practical tools which may replace conventional religions as a healing force (Moreno, 1951, p. 103). He thought he succeeded in converting general theological values, such as love, guilt and responsibility, into psychological categories which may be developed and trained through psychodramatic proceedings (Moreno, 1948b, pp. 170–171).

> It may be said that I tried to do through sociometry what religion without science has failed to accomplish in the past, and what science without religion has failed to accomplish. All the cultural and social techniques which I developed in the course of the years have been motivated to serve this purpose.
>
> (Moreno, 1953, p. xv)

Around 1918, the idea of reconnecting religion and psychiatry was perceived as extravagant. It bothered theologians as much as it did psychiatrists. Moreno perceived himself as a lone prophet who formulated his position long before Jung, Jaspers and others, but there are now many who follow him (Moreno, 1953, p. xxxiii). Ever since, humanity has sought a model to guide it to proper conduct. In Moreno's opinion, one of modern man's dilemmas is the loss of faith in the supreme entity, and often in the high moral system as well, as his behavior guide (Moreno and Z. T. Moreno, 1969, p. 21). In an era characterized by such great admiration of materialism, many thought the divinity concept has no worth, and the belief system of those who struggled to create a new man following the October Revolution (1917) made people blind and corrupted their faith. Yet the failure of the divinity concept usually stems from the way in which human beings employ ideas, rather than from the ideas themselves (Sprague, 1994, p. 31). Moreno's initial drive was to provide people with a new vision of God, allowing them to see a flash of the future's universal religion which Moreno was certain that someday would unite all people into one community (Moreno, 1947a, pp. 11–12).

> I could therefore construct a new God values with a certain amount of disregard for past construction. Theology had become to my mind what it

> literally means – the science of God himself, of the supreme value (not of God's creation, the biography of saints, or the religions of mankind.
>
> (Moreno, 1949a, p. 202)

Moreno released himself from the common theological views, wishing to find a new understanding of God as an active entity that covers the whole principle of creativity in the world. Divinity has always inspired human beings, yet it was necessary to clear off a new space for it. That space had always been there, but had never received the proper attention. This is the space of the first-person self and God, a space of subjectivity, the creating actor, of spontaneity and creativity. This is the space of inner divine sources which Moreno viewed as important sources of energy. The subjective dimension does not reject or ward off the old model's neutral, objective and impartial divinity, but paves the way to practicing and training for cosmic love and empathy among human beings (Moreno, 1953, p. xi).

> I postulated therefore that a theory of God comes first. It must be attained first and is indispensable in order to make the life of any particle of the universe significant, whether it is a man, or a protozoan. Science and experimental method, if it be worthy [of] its claim, must be applicable to the theory of God or whatever the name which we give to a theory of supreme value.
>
> (Moreno, 1949a, p. 201)

Moreno believed that when a person loses his life's purpose or meaning, God is out of his existence as well. God is dead when a person feels himself dead deep inside; dead in his other senses, in his physical and spiritual livelihood allowing him to be a whole person. When a person is "alive", God is "alive". God and man work together creatively and mutually in constructing the world (Tyson, 1966, p. 228). Thus, the declaration of God's death might be meaningless. It is very likely that He had never existed, but it is important we be able to create Him in our imagination (Moreno and Z. T. Moreno, 1969, p. 21). Moreno's response to Nietzsche's declaration that God is dead is that he may be easily restored: "We replace dead God by millions of people who may encompass and embody God within their bodies and themselves" (Moreno and Z. T. Moreno, 1969, p. 21). However, as opposed to Nietzsche, Moreno does not believe it takes a supreme man to do so. Basically, each and every one of us possesses the spontaneity and creativity to do the same (J. D. Moreno, 1994, p. 105). The creative part in each person was God. Divinity, in turn, represented humanity's infinite creativity (Haskell, 1975, pp. 148–152). Simultaneously to Sartre, who argued a person must turn himself into God, Moreno declared of himself "I am God", according to the "I-God" principle. Each person is both a creator and created. Hence, he is responsible for the world he created, as well as for everyone and everything in this world (Tauvon, 1998, pp. 29–30).

Perhaps Moreno's self-identification with divinity may be understood by the argument that in order to maintain meaning and value in the modern world, many of us might state "I am God". If in the 20th century there seems to be no God, we may still wish for God to be (J. D. Moreno, 1994, p. 105). Playing God means total involvement in life and fully participating in all of its personal and professional aspects. Any subjective reality of any person is equally valid (Tauvon, 1998, p. 29).

Moreno's interpretation of the concept of God and the way in which he fulfilled the "I am God" idea led him to harshly criticize all existentialistic philosophers in all movements. He claimed that Kierkegaard, Nietzsche, Heidegger and Sartre were philosophers and psychologists, but none of them was an existentialist in the true encounter with life itself. They were everything but *daseinsanalvtiker*. They are more philosophers occupied with book writing than they are action men. Moreno's criticism is not directed to those thinkers' ideas or writings, but rather, their conducting. A talented existentialistic philosopher will never constitute a true, authentic alternative to life and existentialistic experiences.

Moreno believed that being a true existentialist required combining philosophical meditation and life's true encounter and experience, to multiply existential experience by thinking and existence in order for both to flow together, to become one. Although existence and knowledge are not really separate, in his opinion, the attempt to separate them yields odd thinkers. He refers to that phenomenon as creativity neurosis. In order for existentialistic behavior to have validity and meaning, it must involve all subjectivity and existence possessed by the actor (Moreno, 1959, pp. 207–211):

> Just as Kierkegaard drew the picture of the prophet, Nietzsche postulated the superman, a goal which he set for man to attain. Both were existential romanticists. They found representative of their ideal man in the "past", Kierkegaard in Christ, Nietzsche in Zarathustra. Nietzsche and Kierkegaard, far from being prophets or supermen themselves, were frustrated individuals, but they set the imagination of the next generations aflame. The step beyond Kierkegaard and Nietzsche was clearly indicated, it was to fulfill prophetic existence in actu and in situ.
>
> (Moreno, 1959, p. 210)

Thus, challenging Nietzsche and Kierkegaard to follow their own commitment, Moreno says:

> If people are to take up the universal moral responsibility either abdicated or assigned by God, then each person must become God: anything less is inauthentic shrinking-back from this responsibility.
>
> (J. D. Moreno, 1976, pp. 31–32)

Moreno found in other role models, such as Jesus and Socrates, true existentialistic behavior. As seen in Chapter 1, those figures greatly influenced his life.

Jesus and Socrates experienced in their selves and their bodies the authentic encounter and dialogue with true people and life situations. They embodied the therapeutic roles themselves. They did not act according books (Moreno, 1964a, p. 8). While Kierkegaard raised, in Moreno's opinion, the divine's experience to over-subjectivity, with both he and Sartre engaging in the issue of monologue, Moreno identified with Jesus' and Socrates' dialogue. This is the distinction Moreno makes between intellectual existentialism, which discusses the past, and dialogical existentialism, which occurs here and now (Moreno, 1959, pp. 207–211).

Moreno acted out of the basic assumption that man exists in his own world, in a private reality as he experiences and feels it. In a therapeutic formulation, he discussed the protagonist's subjective truth. The idea of being and existing was practiced, embodied and materialized by Moreno and a group of people who established the House of Encounter in Vienna (see Chapter 1):

> What characterizes these truly existential heroes was their actual hereness and nowness of being. . . . Being has no boundaries; it is not limited by birth and death, it includes them. It extends into space and time but it centers in "this" person, in "this" moment and in "this" here.
>
> (Moreno, 1959, p. 211)

At that time, Moreno stated his existential creed:

> The importance of living one's truth in action, the validity of subjective reality. The premise of a living here and now encounter between individuals (including client and therapist); and a deep egalitarianism.
>
> (Moreno, in Fox, 1987, p. 3)

The existentialistic theological-philosophical perspective cited earlier led Moreno to a new outlook in terms of personality development. Moreno is more known for his work related to sociometry, psychodrama and group therapy. It is lesser known, though explicitly stated in his writings, that the main motivation of his general work was philosophical and theological. Moreno did not strive to be a theologian, yet he did include a religious outlook in all of his ideas and thoughts. In many ways, the religious outlook provided Moreno the basic inspiration for his deep views regarding man, God, spirituality and the cosmic process. Historically, in many ways, religion provided Moreno with the basic inspiration for psychodrama's key concepts, his practical work – with the key metaphors and concepts to the human drama in the universe. Moreno converted the conventional theological perspective into human relation sciences. The theological thinking yielded a new psychological perspective, a significant psychotherapeutic method, the development of the modern group therapy idea and the notion that basic behavior takes two.

Moreno's effort to expand the concept of religion beyond its historical and theological sphere, as well as to expand the concept of psychiatry beyond its medical and sociological aspect and limitations, was manifested in the comparison of his view of man and his unique personality theory with Marx's and Freud's.

In the footsteps of Marx and Freud: the cosmodynamic man

Freud perceived man as a psychodynamic person, namely, as a psychological organism to be observed in isolation. Marx perceived man as an economic organism struggling for his physical existence within society, namely, as a sociodynamic person. Moreno's position concerning a positive religion suggested a third plane of personality: man as a cosmodynamic person. Moreno's view is a synthesis of those two perceptions, manifesting itself in the cosmic perception. The latter is based upon the external relationship of a person with his surroundings.

Man within society: Moreno and Marx

Marx (1818–1883) maintained that human history is characterized by a struggle between groups reflecting social classes. Those classes possess two characteristics: one is the grudge between the oppressors and the oppressed; the other is a tendency for polarization between those two classes. According to Marx, the grudge between the classes is an integral part of the basic structure of capitalistic society, serving as the force which moves the wheels of history.

History is not a chain of influences by which a person is affected by his external surroundings, or even by his unalterable personality, or by the interaction between those two factors, as assumed the early materialists. Rather, history is people's struggle to actualize their full human potential. A person's efforts to actualize his potential to the fullest are the efforts to be released from the role of a toy in the hands of seemingly invisible forces, arbitrary and tremendous, namely, to dominate them and himself. This is liberty. A person gains control over his world not by accumulation of knowledge, which is acquired through thinking, but rather through action, work, conscious shaping of the environment and others. This is the first, most basic form of the unity of will, thought and action, of practice. Society's chronicles are the history of creative efforts transforming man, altering his ambitions, habits, perception and his relation to others (Berlin, 1974, p. 10).

Marx investigated the subject from the economic aspect of his life, showing the path leading from the actual suffering due to the struggle for existence, to the subjective awareness of standing, manifesting itself through common ideals and revolutionary activity (Sigad, 1981, p. 7). He began with the idea that man may be defined not only biologically, anatomically and physiologically, but also psychologically. Knowing a person requires becoming acquainted with his actions in general. Marx distinguished human drives, which are a natural, integral part, such as hunger and sex, from drives that are not part of the human nature but a consequence of certain social structures, such as the need for money, which is a true need created by the capitalistic society. However, man has an advantage over the animal, not only because of his bodily needs, but also because of the creative force (Berlin, 1974, p. 101).

For Marx, a person lives only when he is productive and creating. Independence and freedom are based upon the fulfillment of a person's own activity. A man may perceive himself as independent as long as he is a master of himself, not developing dependence relations with others, living on the graces of others.

The whole perception of Marx's self-actualization may be fully understood only in relation to the concept of work. Work is the activity characteristic of man. At work, a person creates both the objects and himself. When the individual cannot control the work conditions, process and outcome, the activity is merely utilitarian and devoid of orientation toward the rational generality. The worker openly expresses himself through it. His nature is expropriated by the objects he creates. Work is alienated. The worker does not provide for his own needs through work, but rather forms means to provide his needs from work. The alienation at work is first manifested by the fact that work is external to the worker. In other words, it is not part of his nature. Consequently, he does not actualize himself through his work, but denies himself through it. The worker does not feel satisfied with his work, but rather, miserable. He does not develop free mental, physical or spiritual energy, but rather, denies himself and destroys his spirit. Essentially, human activity which defines man's humanity loses its human nature, because for an employee, it is merely a means of existence. The alienated work is the outcome of labor division, expropriating man from his overall skill, focusing upon a particular skill. It establishes private property, exchange and objects of exchange, which become external to man, an alien, opposing agent, which dominates him, instead of him dominating it (Fromm, 1961):

> Alienation (or "estrangement") means, for Marx, that man does not experience himself as the acting agent in his grasp of the world, but that the world (nature, others, and he himself) remains alien to him. They stand above and against him as objects, even though they may be objects of his own creation. Alienation is essentially experiencing the world and oneself passively, receptively, as the subject separated from the object.
>
> (ibid.)

Moreno referred to the alienation concept as a manifestation of a mental disorder (neurosis), a thorough, profound process of alienation to reality, comparing his position to Marx's:

> For Marx, for instance, who can be considered as a forerunner of theoretical group psychotherapy, the cause of the neurosis is the economic alienation of man, the fragmentation of man's productivity in the work process. . . . According to Moreno the cause of neurosis is the cosmic alienation of man, his alienation from the essential meaning of the universe, its primary creative processes.
>
> (Moreno, 1963b, p. 120)

Apparently, the philosophical position maintained by each of those thinkers also defined the type of method they supported, as well as the type of actions to be taken in order to find a solution to the problem. Moreno found the solution in developing methods which will permit the training of individual and group behaviors by expressing their spontaneity and creativity. He claimed that behavior's biological and economic neuroses are interrelated and associated with an earlier neurosis of spontaneity and creativity. Marx, on the other hand, believed it was necessary to resolve man's economic alienation first through a social revolution where the working man becomes the main (supreme) figure in a hierarchy of values (Moreno, 1963b, p. 120).

Marx himself argued that the way to bridge the gap between the subject and the object, namely, alienation, lies within praxis. The praxis that forms material life is not a utilitarian act, but rather, an act by which a person shapes his world while fulfilling his essential self. In other words, a man is a consciously social and historical person, who is aware of the fact that by his actions, he shapes history. Work transforms a man's world and himself through activity.

According to Marx, the person's relation to himself becomes an actual objective relation only through his relation to others. When his humanity becomes his object in practice, he views himself as a universal organism, a person, rather than as a defined, distinct individual. It is only in this way that he is free, devoid of enslaving affinities to objects and articles. Because a person's activity within nature and society is performed by physical, symbolic and organizational means, namely, production means, the individuals are to be of equal standing in relation to them. Because private property results in an unequal standing in relation to the various production means, it does not permit the annulling of alienation. Therefore, annulling of alienation requires positively annulling private property, not by its elimination, but rather, by its inclusion within a broader frame of reference. The positive annulling of private property is known as communism.

It is necessary to know not only the individual person, but also the man as the social creature. Yet Marx only saw the social person until he discovered alienation, which is not only man's alienation from his self, but also from any other person. According to Marx, social isolation stems from the utilization characteristic of the capitalistic-economic method. A capitalistic society is the basis for the inability to live together. Therefore, forming a communal society is the way to maintain the dignity and creativity of individuals within society. For Marx, loneliness results from contemporary, historical conditions, which must be altered.

Hence, Marx's goal was spiritually freeing man – freeing him from the heavy chains of economic pressures, thereby allowing him to find unity, wholeness and harmony with other human beings and with nature (Fromm, 1961). His point of departure was that the wage the workers received did not reflect the value of their work. Because they were abused, the workers would unite in one group. That in itself must induce emotional relations between them. "The criterion of utilized economic slaves is to be welded into one dynamic social force" (Moreno, 1963b, p. 121).

This thinking was based upon social analysis as a materialistic-economic process. The economic planning was mainly channeled to the collective of the symbolic membership in the organization. That plan was supposed to operate while ignoring the individual as a psychological energy, and also ignoring society as subject to complex pressure, constantly growing by continuous pressure of psychological processes and the fabric they form. Marx, in Moreno's opinion, was driven by his belief in historical determinism and was unaware of the accumulative influence of interpersonal and intergroup processes. There was little consideration of the psychological factor as a natural human driving force. Consequently, nature, man and society were damaged. Marx's historical mistake, in Moreno's eyes, was that the establisher of scientific socialism did not properly assess the social-psychological forces operating within a group; human beings have a social structure of their own, which requires special tools for investigation and transformation. That insight did not penetrate into Marx's mental perspective (Moreno, 1943, p. 342; Moreno, 1949b, p. 130).

Marx believed economic issues may not be dealt with simultaneously as psychological and social issues. The social issue can wait. There are two types of revolutions. The social and economic revolution should precede what Moreno defined as human society's creative or psychological revolution. Marx attempted to demonstrate that at least in the long run all crucial changes would result from economic revolutions. However, the October Revolution in Russia did not bring about the anticipated change in man's behavior. The change in the economic structure did not yield the change in psychological relations in interpersonal relationships. Moreno found the social-cultural changes lagged behind the economic changes. He thought all theories should be synthesized so as to form an initial fundamental basis for society's psychological planning (Moreno, 1953, p. 11; Moreno, 1949b, p. 132).

For Moreno, Marx's most significant contribution to personality theory was the socio-dynamic person concept, which is dynamically connected to the social fabric.

From psychoanalysis to psychodrama: Moreno and Freud

The psychoanalytic theory maintained that all external experiences and behaviors are embodied in the individual's psyche. People possess instincts of an organic source (Freud, 1915, p. 109). Freud diagnosed what he defined as ego-instincts, which are the somatic system's instincts, which manifest themselves in psychological reactions, influencing the individual's relationship with external stimuli, such as reaction to danger or the presence of food.

According to Freud, there are other instincts as well, which arise from the id, personality's most ancient, primitive part, which acts according to the pleasure principle. Those are manifested in the form of sexual energy and the human need to reproduce and continue the human race. The connection of sex and love led to that instinct's definition as the "libido", or "eros", which is linked to the life instinct. Later on, Freud decided there was another instinct stemming from the id, which is manifested by psychological energy in the form of aggression and the need to destroy. That instinct represents the death instinct, or the drive to destroy, and was later on labeled thanatos (the word for "death" in classic Greek). The death instinct is the drive to restore the inorganic, unorganized state.

The psychological instincts, similarly to the somatic instincts, yield an inner disorder, which requires expression through relief or satisfaction. Those instincts seek an external object into which energy may be released. If, instead of relief, those instincts are returned to the origin and relief does not occur, psychological issues may result (Freud, 1933, p. 128). Freud's psychoanalytical method was illustrated as tending to link life sources with catastrophe and disaster. The key concept in Freud's method is the libido, which, different from Moreno's spontaneity, was associated with anxiety, lack of confidence, relief and negative tendencies. The linkage of human sexuality to perversion was more associated with pathology than with normalcy (Moreno, 1967, p. 9).

Moreno thought that just as Freud did not provide a picture of sexual connections on the adult level and of their interpersonal dynamics, he did not provide a direct positive picture of the creative act as it is experienced at moments of spontaneous inspiration in humans. Freud viewed both from an analyst's point of view. His conceptual system's reference to a creator in situ was equal to the reference to a patient on the psychoanalyst's couch. When asked what creativity was, Freud responded it was sublimated libido. Because he was blind to the true meaning of spontaneity and creativity, he did not realize the libido fulfills only a small role in human sexuality and that the human and non-human worlds were filled with a sufficient amount of pre-libidinal and extra-libidinal instincts, namely, creativity. Moreno opined that the spontaneous and creative forces are much more universal and ancient than libido (Moreno, 1953, p. lv).

> The libido lives on in the sociometric system as a sub form of creativity. The unconscious lives on as a by product of the warming up process.
>
> (Moreno, 1953, p. liv)

For Moreno, Freud's significant contribution to the personality theory was the psychodynamic person concept.

The Morenian theory expanded personality's psychological and economic model, proposing a model which was described as the cosmodynamic person model (Moreno and Z. T. Moreno, 1969). The cosmodynamic person is involved not only in an inter-psychic dialogue and psychodynamic inter-psychic dialogue, but also in a cosmological extra-psychic dialogue, namely, with God, the universal principle of spontaneity and creativity. The cosmodynamic person is an independent agent who is supposed to act in several areas: intrapersonal, interpersonal, familial, social and universal. The person is capable of acting separately within each one and interacting with others. The special dynamic with a person with the cosmos revolves around the universal questions, such as death, birth, creation and destruction. According to this theory, personality theory revolves around three forces: spontaneity, creativity and cultural conservation.

> Very early in my career I come to the position that there is another area, a larger world beyond the psychodynamics and sociodynamics of human society – cosmodynamics.
>
> (Moreno and Z. T. Moreno, 1969, p. 19)

> Freud saw the position of man as the one of a traveler between birth and death. He saw nothing beyond except silence, the cosmos beyond was shattered. Marx saw the position of man as that of a member of human society, the struggle within it as his ultimate destiny; for him too, the cosmos beyond was shattered. I moved man back into the universe. Man is more than a psychological, or social or biological being. He is a cosmic being. Reducing man's responsibility to the psychological, social or biological department of living makes him an outcast.
>
> (Moreno, 1964b, pp. 157–158)

Moreno's self-development theory was mainly in response to Freud's theory. Moreno's openly declared goal was to replace the psychoanalytical theory with a theory of spontaneity and creativity (Moreno, 1974, p. 80). Against the Freudian terms libido, id, ego and super-ego, unconscious and cathexis, Moreno coined the alternative terms spontaneity, creativity and tele:

> These levels of expression suggest a creative theory of personality to replace the doctrine of psychoanalysis.
>
> (Moreno, 1974, p. 80)

> I made the Freudian doctrine the particular target of my attack because it was the farthest developed and the most influential.
>
> (Moreno, 1953, p. li)

Moreno objected to the view which stated that the forces that are active or dominant in human interactions are hereditary. He did not find a way to identify constancy, either. Any constancy will always be preceded by another (Moreno, 1977, p. 102). On the basis of this approach, he rejected the repetition-compulsion principle. According to this principle, as claimed by Freud, there is a compulsive need to repeat previous behaviors from one's childhood (Bischof, 1970, p. 237). Moreno did not deny the importance of the past and unconscious, yet he focused to a greater extent on, and took more interest in, his own attempts to understand and solve relationship-related issues here and now.

Moreno preferred to concentrate upon the individual's spontaneous abilities as a force lying within the individual as an important source of energy. "It may be stated with utmost certainty that the supreme force which dominates the world, namely, the divine force consists of spontaneity and creativity" (Moreno, 1956, p. 117). According to Moreno, this force does not act by energy conservation rules and is not embodied in the individual's psyche alone, but is also present outside of it, in the cosmos. This position contradicts Freud's libido perception, which links the psyche's energy to biological and biochemical processes (the science of medicine), and its amount is constant from birth (Moreno et al., 2000, p. xiv). Spontaneity is associated with a subjective outlook of the person as the actor and creator, which relies upon construction of roles based upon past experience. Spontaneity and creativity are forces that extend human behavior beyond and independently of libido and economic motivation (Moreno, 1972, p. 49).

Simultaneously, Moreno developed a therapeutic approach which was different from the common one of the time. The difference was manifested mainly by the rejection of Freud's psychoanalysis. Moreno's view of psychoanalysis deeply affected psychodrama's development, whose techniques contradict psychoanalytical theory's techniques (Holmes, 1992, p. 9).

Freud and Moreno were both Viennese psychiatrists. Freud was also a neurologist. The psychoanalysis theory he established is based upon an organic-biological view of human nature. Moreno, on the other hand, developed psychodrama and sociodrama from a different philosophical viewpoint, stemming from an existentialistic view of psychotherapy and human relations (Moreno, 1959, pp. 207–217).

Moreno relates of one encounter, probably the only one, he had with Freud in 1912. This encounter demonstrates the difference between psychodrama and psychoanalysis. It took place following a lecture of Freud's regarding the telepathic dream. Moreno reported that Freud approached him, a young student, asking what his occupation was. Thus he replied to him:

> Well, Dr. Freud, I start where you leave off. You meet people in the artificial setting of your office; I meet them on the street and in their home, in their natural surroundings. You analyze their dreams; I try to give them the courage to dream again. I teach the people how to play God.
>
> (Moreno, 1989, p. 61)

In this response to Freud, Moreno did not address the therapeutic dream. He mentioned the fact that helping people dream their lives again was his way of promising them that their lives may improve if they develop their creativity and spontaneity, and even the most outrageous fantasy might be productive, as long as it does not harm others. He noticed that Freud was embarrassed and did not respond. Freud probably considered those ideas megalomaniac, and hence dangerous, but that was part of Moreno's view of psyche's life and the basic difference between him and Freud. It is likely that the difference of opinions between the two were unbridgeable. They were both charismatic, possessing unique personalities, and they were both extraordinary psychiatrists (Z. T. Moreno, 2000, pp. xvi–xx).

Moreno realized that the argument with Freud originated from his behavior as a therapist, as a therapeutic actor.

> I do not think an outstanding caregiver or therapist will look or behave like Freud. I imagine the caregiver as a spontaneous, creative therapist, who is in equal relation with the patient, or in the middle of every group.
>
> (Moreno, 1989, p. 62)

> Freud may lose a great deal of the reputation he has, which was largely built upon his methodical sagacity, but little upon his ability as [a] therapeutic performer. Our epoch, too, will reach a climax with a scientific Christ ending the chain.
>
> (Moreno, 1953, p. xxxiv)

> To my mind, persons like Jesus, Buddha, Socrates and Gandhi were doctors and healers; for Freud they were probably patients. It should be remembered that psychoanalysis grew out of the neuropsychiatric world of Charcot and Breuer. Whereas the origins of my work go back to the primitive religions and my objectives were the setting up and promoting of a new cultural order. It was the conflict between "analytic" and "operational" methods of therapy.
>
> (Moreno, 1953, pp. xxvii–xxviii)

Furthermore, Moreno scorned the fact that for Freud, the couch was the point of departure for therapy. He claimed psychodrama began with his opposition to the couch and the free association technique, as well as with psychotherapy's transformation of a technological position, from the couch's rigidness to the flexibility of the open space, where reality, movement and action are unlimited. Psychodrama is an example demonstrating that: it encompasses all previous technological approaches (Moreno, 1951, p. 108; Moreno, 1953, p. iv). As opposed to Freud, Moreno was willing to meet his patients anywhere, even on the street. Additionally, he demanded therapy occur face-to-face, defending the idea that the patient and therapist are equal in status. He believed in the importance of the therapist–patient interaction, maintaining that their relationships should focus upon the potential of creativity. He objected to the classic medical model, where the therapist places his patient on the couch, making him passive, while he himself is seated behind the couch so that he may not be seen. That state prevents any connection between them. Moreno replaced the patient's position on the couch, placing him facing the therapist instead.

The issue of the therapist's authority and power, which intrigued Moreno, resulted in the psychodramatic method, which he established, proposing several prospects to deal with the issue. For instance, the psychodrama therapist is not limited to offering interpretation only, but also attempts to induce encounters with the patients (Williams, 1989, pp. 186–187). Moreno believed in the encounter's therapeutic potential more than in transference as a therapeutic principle.

Moreno's therapeutic principles

Aside from the difference in therapist–patient relations, Moreno's opposition to psychoanalysis was manifested in three areas, which characterized his theory (Fox, 1987, pp. xii–xiv) and which will be discussed in more detail, as follows: (1) Emphasizing direct encounter between human being, an "I" and "thou" discourse; (2) Emphasizing the person as a role actor and the transition from verbal methods to action methods; and (3) Emphasizing the transition from an individual therapy to group therapy, where the context of the individual behavior is considered but is placed at a broader context.

1 *Encounter means a discourse of "I" and "thou"*. At the core of encounter stand creativity and spontaneity, namely, the encounter is a meeting driving human beings to progress through a spontaneous reaction, yielding an immediate, creative change.
2 A. *Action*. The science of action, as it was called by Moreno, is a key component in the psychodramatic therapeutic method, highly important in Moreno's view of the self and society. The external expression indicating the importance of action is the word "drama", as well as in the name "psychodrama" (drama is the Greek word for action and occurrence). In Moreno's opinion, an action theory addresses, in fact, the interaction between actors and the psychological processes associated with them, such as spontaneity, creativity and warming-up. An action stemming from the source of spontaneity, flowing with it, is a creative action.

As human beings, one of our characteristics is the ability to act. It is this ability which assists us in adapting to the world, manifesting the abilities to express the emotional world.

A science of action begins with two verbs: to be and to create, and with three nouns: actors, spontaneity and creativity (Moreno, 1960b, p. 760).

2 B. *Improvisational Play*. Moreno's experimenting with children's plays in Vienna's gardens, as well as in an improvisational play with professional actors (to be cited in Chapter 1), led him to the conclusion that human beings were born actors, *A person is an improvising actor on the stage of life* (Moreno, in Z. T. Moreno, 2000, p. xiv). Our ability to act is not merely a part structured in the process of life. Rather, human beings may play such a behavior in advance and voluntarily create it. Hence, role play refers to actual behavior expressed based on a conscious decision on the actor's part, or others' demand on him (Kipper, 1996, p. 1). This aspect is an important aspect of Moreno's self-development theory, as he alludes to the fact that this development depends upon the person's ability to constantly acquire a repertoire of roles through which he responds to life's demands. Moreno's mental health concept was based upon an individual with a wide repertoire of roles and the flexibility to present it in the right way, at the right time (Fox, 1987, pp. vii–xiv). Moreno stated psychodrama stemmed from the play principle:

> Play as a principle of cure, as a form of spontaneity, as a form of therapy and as a form of catharsis; play, not only as an epiphenomenon accompanying and supporting biological aims but as a phenomenon "sui generis", a positive factor linked with spontaneity and creativity.
>
> (Moreno, 1950, pp. 1–2)

Freud's opposition of acting out and his hostile criticism of the spontaneity issue and children's play were, in Moreno's opinion, a barrier against psychotherapy's progress by means of play. Freud was willing to analyze and observe children play, but not to interfere in the play and play with them. Freud's psychoanalysis was the natural rival of play technique and play-based psychotherapy (Moreno, 1953, p. xxviii). What was forbidden on Freud's couch became a guideline in Moreno's therapeutic strategy and interaction.

3 *Transition from Individual to Group Therapy*. According to psychoanalysis' perspective, the individual's psyche is the source of his mental issues. Freud referred to the group by a mere hint, considering as the epiphenomenon the individual's psyche. In his opinion, there is no other room for illness anywhere outside the individual, in a group situation, for instance. The reference to the group came from sociology and anthropology, and even here, at the context of status, culture and social hierarchy. From the outset, Moreno was interested in social relations, claiming the structure of large social groups is complex. Therefore, he chose the middle path, focusing upon small groups, rather than on the mass or the individual. The turning point in understanding the psychological processes related to the group emerged upon the publishing of Moreno's sociometry method (measuring interpersonal relations). Sociometry connected psychology and sociology.

> The key to sociometry is that each group possesses the ability for mutual linkage and connection. Those connections form an inner structure which is not necessarily visible. The individual's social world is called [the] "social atom", a term coined by Moreno for the individual's relationship with all past and present significant figures, associated with his psychological experiences. The relations between the individuals connected to the "social atoms" are divided to attraction relations and repulsion relations.
>
> (Fox, 1987, p. xv; Moreno, 1964, p. 315)

The emphasis Moreno put on social connections also led him to the conclusion that social issues are interaction based. Sociometry allows the investigation of the social system's functioning and development, regardless of the individual's intrapsychic conflicts (Williams, 1989, p. 112). The confidence in the group's ability to heal was based upon the belief in the principle that human altruistic love has an infinite means for growth.

The focus of group therapy led to a revolution in psychiatric practice in the mid-1990s. First, the privacy and intimacy which previously characterized the individual therapy were rejected. Second, the therapist's status changed. The therapist would usually be a psychiatrist, and the patient's attitude toward him was transference based. But with sociometric method, the therapist's role was given to the group members, who served as a therapeutic extension for one another, and one group served as the therapeutic extension of another. As soon as the group members became therapeutic extensions, the therapist became part of the group. The fact that the therapist and the patient (group members) are part of the same system alters the therapeutic relationship between the therapist and any individual group member. The focus transitioned from transference (one-way communication) to what Moreno defines as tele (two-way communication). Hence, the importance of the group was perceived as more highly prioritized than the therapist's importance. The therapist is a member of the therapeutic group.

The emphasis on the group work did not stop Moreno from developing methods for the individual's development and growth. However, according to the psychodramatic theory, the development of the self occurs through the group, relying upon the latter as its means.

Toward systemizing Moreno's thinking

The author identifies a true need for theoretical literature which will not only serve psychodrama's validity as a method deserving scientific honor, but will also facilitate in organizing psychodrama's theoretical basis, which relies upon Moreno's personality theory, so that the material will be available to anyone who seeks it. The author undertook this important task in order to attempt to pave the path toward the development of a solid foundation of the theoretical ideas and concepts. The latter, on the one hand, will serve as a foundation for continued development of the theory and, on the other hand, may be available for psychodrama's techniques. As far as the author knows, no study has offered a full phrasing of the theory, with its diverse aspects. The existing studies are limited to specific aspects. The method proposed by Moreno is understood by his overall view, and for that matter, it is necessary to demonstrate the way in which all ideas are interconnected.

This research involves overcoming many obstacles, for although Moreno was a productive author, who wrote dozens of books and hundreds of articles, the connection between his many publications and his contribution to social psychology has never been investigated. The writing of Moreno himself was not coherent, was inconsistent and was generally characterized by lack of ideological order and structure. The professional literature he wrote requires analysis, clarification, explanation and reconstruction, which will clarify Moreno's unique contribution to the mental health field, as well as his unique view concerning human behavior. Such an understanding may be quite useful if we wish to properly assess Moreno's historical contribution to psychology, human welfare philosophy and the world in general.

To this day, nobody has indicated that all of Moreno's intellectual, philosophical and theological activity is embodied within the practice. A well-organized, coherent theory will allow a demonstration of the way in which all aspects of the theoretical model are reflected by the psychodramatic tool and Moreno's self-development. Hence, anyone who implements the classic psychodrama method as proposed by Moreno necessarily implements the theoretical principles, whether consciously or unconsciously, because the method is derived from the theory, and not vice versa. Thus, the separation of Moreno's methods from his philosophy is deceiving and incorrect.

Converting all concepts into a theory that may be empirically studied is the basis which may serve as the anchor for saving psychodrama – theoretically and practically. If the discussion revolves around its effectiveness, a well-organized theory may alter the view according to which Moreno's theory is nonmeasurable, thereby allowing the conducting of researches that will confront his thinking framework, opening a channel for going beyond them. Thus, it will be possible to demonstrate the effectiveness of the models proposed by Moreno and test them for the therapeutic outcomes. As a matter of fact, this procedure is necessary if we wish to lay a solid foundation for a didactic work within psychodrama's framework.

In this day and age, the implementation of psychodrama and sociodrama methods is partial and incomprehensive. The employment of Moreno's methods is not optimal, because although the philosophy is difficult to understand, the method is easy to implement. If we become acquainted with the theory in general, we will be able to exhaust the techniques and more accurately and fully implement the method. Implementing the methods without understanding their underlying philosophy may be compared to driving without any theoretical knowledge. It is technically possible, but practically ineffective and may be detrimental sometimes.

The ideas developed by Moreno, whose importance he identified even fifty years ago, such as training, active learning, spontaneity, creativity and role play, were found very relevant and essential to the challenges posed by the modern world. The revival of those ideas is possible as part of the flowing influence of social psychology from a dramatological viewpoint. It will facilitate to indicate or emphasize the differences and uniqueness of psychodrama's methods in relation to psychoanalysis. This is a valuable leverage for personality's development through the psychodramatic method.

Finally, in order to amend the impression of Moreno and the psychodramatic method, it is necessary to understand Moreno the man. For a long time, the only source for explaining Moreno as a person was no other than Moreno himself, which yielded the reverse outcome, rendering Moreno rather less clearly understood. Moreno should be elucidated and explained from an "outside" viewpoint, namely, to explore and understand his life story, so as to trace his line of thinking and understand what he meant in the psychodramatic research area. It is important to indicate the close connection of his personality and his theory, because not only did the ideas developed by Moreno stem from his personal history, ways of thinking and personality, but when the story of his life did not correspond to the theory he invented, he did not hesitated to alter biographic facts to fit them to the theory in order to emphasize his ideas. The same applies to his name and the place and time of his birth, which he described mystically, contrary to the historical facts. The knowledge related to his life is based upon what he told of himself, but many of the experiences Moreno describes in his autobiography (Moreno, 1989), particularly his religious experiences, have no evidence.

Moreno emphasized that his being a psychiatrist, aside from being a philosopher immersed and intrigued by thoughts concerning practical axiology (the study of values), served him as an inspiration to attempt to form a synthesis. The latter was not only in favor of science, but also for the sake of his mental balance (Moreno, 1951, p. 205). Being a humanist-existentialist, Moreno attempted to understand human nature based upon the way in which he perceived the world and himself within it. He emphasized that human beings in total subjectivity should be part of the connection to scientific research in order to provide the author with an accurate phenomenological description of the occurrences within the human situation (Moreno, 1959, pp. 214–215).

> In psychotherapy, it is particularly difficult, if not impossible altogether, to separate the talent from the therapist's personality. Talent and personality are inseparable, at least at the time of action.
>
> (Moreno, 1959, p. 236)

One of the sources of inspiration for Moreno's perception is Heidegger's perception, and particularly his ideas concerning dasein, or "being in the world". "Being in the world" is the fundamental, transcendental condition allowing the distinction and recognition of all things. Dasein indicates that a person is rooted in the world, as other things are. He does not face the world in opposition to them (Heidegger, 1962, pp. 126–127; Seeman, 1982, pp. 70–83). Heidegger thought the world itself is a phenomenon, namely, a being entity, something that exists just as other things (including human beings) exist. Hence, the world is not a mere accumulation of anything else we experience or encounter. Beyond all objects and people, including "I", there is the world. We have never had an experience or a thought without the world being a part of it (Myerson, 2005, p. 88).

According to Moreno, this perspective yields a call for total, full involvement in life, rather than remaining an observer or analyst (hence, the criticism of other existentialistic thinkers). All the methods Moreno invented, namely, psychodrama, sociometry, role-plays and others, emerged from direct encounters in life, rather than clinical laboratory experiments. At the time when Moreno developed sociometry, he made the following statement of himself:

> The difference between me and other scientists is that I go out [in the] world and attempt to live my philosophy, examining it daily, in my life and my students' and patients' lives, while other authors do the same in the office, behind a desk. I was an experimenter. Experimenters as Buddha and Jesus often seem incompatible, pathological. However, they attempted to lead a life of truth, and preferred imperfect existence to perfect theory.
>
> (Moreno, 1985a, p. 24)

Out of that existentialist outlook of the world, Moreno does not distinguish himself and his creation. He uses himself, or alternatively, his family members, as subjects of experiments:

> The psychodrama of my life preceded psychodrama as a method. I was the first patient of my psychodrama, both the protagonist and the director. With the auxiliary-egos' help, the people surrounding me, I developed surplus reality, a new world which was not developed by the western culture. I also realized I had developed a tool, which was powerful for a social revolution. I was challenging, because not only did I play, I also prompted other people around me to play with me.
>
> (Moreno, 1989, p. 32)

From his own world of experiences, Moreno drew conclusions which he converted into a life philosophy. Furthermore, he was not satisfied with drawing personal conclusions based upon this observation and generalized his conclusions to the whole of humanity.

Moreno perceives himself as the spontaneous, creative person model, which has experienced life through a direct encounter with human beings as cited by his personal theories. The key motives in his thinking – divinity, spontaneity, creativity and man as a role player – complemented one another and were assimilated in his behavior, way of life and the therapeutic methods he invented. The research will indicate that adding fictitious biographic motives is associated with the psychodramatic method in itself. Hence, the method and the person are one entity. Classic psychodrama's history as a systematic method of therapy is mostly and essentially connected and linked to the biographic history of Moreno, its founder.

> I hope that it does not sound immodest, but as psychodrama happens to be my most personal creation, its cradle in my own autobiography may throw further light upon its final delivery. This exception from the scholarly habit of understatement may be particularly excusable because of the way psychodrama developed. It was not a piece of writing which introduced it (which was secondary so), nor a school of rewriters, collaborators and protagonists, but repeated public performance. I started as a conducted of sessions for small or large groups in various places – gardens, streets, theatres, military camps, prisons and hospitals. Indeed such a persistent drive towards self-chosen goals in spite of a nonplussed public opinion must have deep personal implications.
>
> (Moreno, 1964a, p. 2)

Moreno's work is to be examined also in relation to the challenges he established for himself, when arguing a true procedural proceeding may not occur without the healing of humanity as a whole (Moreno, 1934, p. 21). Moreno proposed an idea which was too far-reaching, but its misunderstanding and the opposition it aroused worldwide resulted in concentrating on only a small part from the whole ensemble of his ideas. The author intends to amend the impression left by Moreno and his work, as well as to demonstrate that psychodrama as a therapeutic method is only a small part of what can be drawn from Moreno. Plus, this work is designed to indicate that the other parts should be presented as well, so as to allow the renewed revelation of Moreno.

The book's structure

Chapter 1 demonstrates the parallel between Moreno's life story and the theory he established, based upon the assumption that the method is the person, and that in Moreno's case, the creator is not distinct from the creation. *Chapter 2* discusses Moreno's philosophical-theological perception, addressing the following matters: the development of the divinity concept, which stems from the existentialistic perspective and its connection to creativity; spontaneity, cultural conservation and robot pathology; encounters with interpersonal theory and converting theological perception into human relation sciences; and Tele, which is a healthy, unprojected interpersonal relationships between human beings, replacing the transference concept. *Chapter 3* presents the self's development theory according to Moreno, addressing spontaneity, creativity, warming-up and tele in the developmental aspect. Plus, the chapter addresses matrix of identity theory, with its diverse aspects. *Chapter 4* discusses the importance of the "role" concept in Moreno's self-development theory. It addresses the historical-chronological evolution of the role concept, with its diversity of aspects, its relationship with Moreno's theory of personality and the concepts of spontaneity, creativity and mental health. *Chapter 5* addresses the reflection of the theoretical model through the psychodramatic method. It discusses the way in which psychodrama methods were constructed, the background to their construction and the mode and purpose of their construction. Additionally, it engages in formulating an existentialistic method that emphasizes psychodrama's structure and components as representatives of the philosophical and developmental aspects. *Chapter 6* includes an integrative, critical analysis and discussion of Moreno, personality theory and psychodrama method. The research concludes with an *Epilogue*, presenting a general assessment of Moreno's thinking and influence.

Chapter 1

Parallels between Moreno's biography and his theory of self

Moreno's life story seems to wind down two paths: one, a biographic-chronological path, and the other, a biographic, psychodramatic path, where the imagery and the real meet and merge. Three key motives may be identified throughout the course of his life. The first motive is the search for the Cosmic Man's model; the second motive is the development of the theological-philosophical perception, and finally, role playing as a means to man's self-presentation. Those three motives were manifested in the psychodrama and sociometry method and therapeutic techniques invented by Moreno.

The idea of the Cosmic Man and the myth of the birth and the name

The Cosmic Man philosophy refers to an idea pertaining to the set of traits and characteristics that are universally common, which corresponds to Jung's archetype. Tangibly speaking, universality constitutes an induction from individual problems to general ones. Moreno viewed himself as a voice representing the cosmic dimension, a belief manifested through the myths he established in relation to his place and time of birth, as well as the name he was given.

Place and Time of Birth. Jacob Levy Moreno was born on Saturday, 18 May 1889, at 4 o'clock in the afternoon, in Bucharest, Romania. He was the eldest son of Nissim and Paulina Moreno Levy. His father was absent from his birth, and therefore did not sign Jacob's birth certificate, which is the reason why another male relative signed it.

Moreno was born to a Sephardic-Jewish family, who was a descendant of the *Anusim*, Jews who were forced to convert to Christianity and assume the dominant religion in the country where they lived. His story of his birth is associated with the Spanish-Turkish Jewish community's history, which dates back to the expulsion from Spain. Based upon the limited information about his ancestors, it is known that Moreno comes from a family of educated men, who made a living as businessmen, physicians and lawyers. Even Shabtai Tzvi, "The False Messiah", was known as one of Moreno's ancestors. This background constituted some folklore, which was an integral part of Moreno's upbringing. As he stated, the world seemed particularly mysterious to child he was (Moreno, 1989, p. 15; Hare and Hare, 1996, p. 2).

Moreno: The Myth of Birth. Moreno related his birth as occurring in 1892, on a stormy night, on board of a boat, sailing on the Black Sea from the Bosporus to Romania. It was on a Saturday night, shortly before the closing service. He claimed his date of birth to be inaccurate, since his mother was young and could not precisely calculate it. An air of mystery surrounds the tale of his birth, as he had no birth certificate (however, as mentioned above, officially he had).

There are no identifying details of the boat, either. Was that a Turkish, Greek, Romanian or Spanish boat? "The boat's flag was unknown, thereby inflicting anonymity on my name and my citizenship. I was probably born to be a citizen of the world, a sailorman wandering from coast to coast; from one country to another" (Moreno, 1989, p. 16). This argument reflects Moreno's cosmic view, stating that a citizen of the world belongs nowhere, and yet belongs to everybody. In other words, the Cosmic Man's *locus nascendi* was somewhere on a boat sailing on the Bosporus waters (Marineau, 1994, p. 84). Zerka Moreno, Moreno's second wife and his loyal aide in developing psychodrama, said of her husband: "It may well be said of him that he was not associated with any time, nor any place, family, nation, or any particular species" (Z. T. Moreno, 1994, p. xii).

Moreno's mother never verified the tale of his birth. She altered the tale by stating: "It was a stormy night, as the Holy Sabbath was drawing to a close. You were sailing the boat, yet the latter was my body, which gave birth to you". Thus, Moreno states that the tale of his birth "resorts to the Kingdom of Myths" (Moreno, 1989, p. 16). Formally, Moreno's nationality was Turkish, by virtue of his father's citizenship. Marineau indicates that Moreno's tale of birth bears many versions, with minor variations, but the message conveyed by all is identical:

> This story is an account that incorporates imagination and symbolism with reality. It represents what Moreno will call the poetic and psycho-dramatic truth.
>
> (Marineau, 1989, p. 8)

In Moreno's book, *The First Psychodramatic Family*, his tale of birth is preceded by the following words:

> The stories told in this book strive to be psychodramatically and poetically accurate, as they exist in the minds of the people involved and told by them. They do not strive for historic accuracy. A psychodramatic biography differs in this sense from a historically analytical biography.
>
> (J. L., Moreno, Z. T. and Moreno, J. D., 1964, p. 7)

Why did Moreno choose a travel by sea, of all circumstances, in the year 1892? In the myth he established and nurtured, Marineau reckons this particular date is associated with the religious mentoring Moreno received from Rabbi Bejarano as a child.

The lesson begins with the date 1892, namely, 400 years to the expulsion of the Jews from Spain and the discovery of America by Christopher Columbus. Thousands of Jews were forced to convert to Christianity or were murdered or exiled from the kingdom of Spain, and many of them migrated to the Balkan countries and Asia Minor, as did Moreno's ancestors, who settled in Turkey (Haworth, 1998, p. 18). His place of birth bears great importance as well, as the boat arriving in Spain on its way to Romania may appear as a summary of 400 years of family, social and community history. One does not sail only through the storms and the pain of a mother giving birth to her firstborn. Rather, one is also welcome to share the mystery and uncertainty of a larger group. Four hundred years earlier, Moreno's forefathers were forced to bear the pain of leaving their homeland, facing the challenge of starting anew. Based upon this point of view, Moreno's birth myth relates to his profound identification of the Spanish Jewry.

The idea of Moreno's being a citizen of the world manifests itself even in his adulthood, a time he spent in Vienna, namely, in the years 1909–1923, a time when Vienna was home to many important movements, which greatly influenced the world's history, such as the Nazis, psychoanalysis, communism and existentialism, to name a few. At the time, Vienna University was known as an international center for the educated, particularly the medicine and sciences faculties. In 1909, Moreno started his higher education at Vienna University, at a time when Jewish-Zionist and German-Nationalist students were clashing, as a result of Anti-semitism's intensification he attempted to reconcile the disputes, but to no avail. He stated that he alleviated himself from the political disputes, thereby acquiring a unique standing: nobody knew his true identity. The nationalists would consider him a German, whereas the Jews considered him Jewish and the socialists considered him a socialist. Politically and religiously, he claimed some sort of universal territory for himself. Even his involvement in the Jewish community, which was minimal, times of crises excluded, implies ambivalence.

His connection to the community was essential to him, though not manifested directly, but rather indirectly, through his writing in relation to his closest friend, Chaim Kelmer.

His political philosophy, which was consolidated as he reached adulthood, reflected a view which perceives man as being above politics, partisanships, and sectarianism, thereby corresponding to the Cosmic Person view (Marineau, 1994, pp. 84–85).

The Anonymity Concept and Name Myth. Many believe the name "Moreno" to be Spanish or Italian, yet this is incorrect. The name "Moreno" is common among Sephardic Jews. Its Hebrew meaning is "our teacher", and it is also the Ladino word for "black" (Marineau 1989, p. 12). His father's name was originally Morenu Levy, but was altered to Moreno. Hence, his name was Nissim Moreno Levy. His son, Jacob Levy, gradually altered his name to Jacob Levy Moreno, which was later abbreviated to J. L. Moreno. Adapting the father's first name as his last name indicates their relationship and the desire to take his place. In 1925, when his father was gone from his life for good, leaving nothing behind, Moreno officially changed his name. Thus, by taking his father's name, Jacob was able to present himself as the founder of a new dynasty (Marineau, 1989, p. 67). Thus he writes:

> My relationship with my name has been interesting. My biblical name has been Jacob, while my secular name was Jacques. In early adolescence, a time when my behavior became peculiar, the more I drew away from my family, I also began drawing away from my name, that is to say, the name I was originally given. I searched for another identity, and perhaps sought another name, which would suit my new status, that new identity. Knowing a person's first name and calling him that name implies intimacy, suggested closeness, an equal status, being part of the same tribe. Thus, I did not want to be addressed by my original name. Addressing or not addressing a person by his first name bears deep psychological implication. According to the Laws of Moses, using God's name in vain is forbidden, apparently for the sake of preserving the mystic distance between the dominating God and the little man. Through the process rendering me the prophet, delivering the word of God, I expected people to treat me the way they are supposed to treat God, namely, not to know my name. That was the source of my concept of anonymity. Divinity's anonymity, the self's anonymity, and the anonymity of objects.
>
> (Moreno, 1989, pp. 26–27)

ANONYMITY, AS EXPLAINED ABOVE, CORRESPONDS TO THE COSMIC CONCEPT, AS WELL AS TO INDUCTIVITY

The family circle and the environmental circle

Moreno's first five years of life were spent in Bucharest. At the time, Bucharest was known as "Little Paris" because of the prominent French cultural influence that characterized it.

The family's adjustment to Bucharest was quite rough, as all family members faced economic hardships, which worsened due to the father's financial failures and frequent absences from home. Moreno was a cheerful child and described his childhood as the happiest time of his life. He learned and played, unaware of his parents' drama, which surrounded him. Thus, the family issues had no damaging effect on him at that stage of his life.

As mentioned, Moreno's parents were Sephardic Jews, descendants of the Marranos. Both were rather creative individuals in their respective fields. The mother, Paulina Lancu, was raised by her two elder brothers. When she reached adulthood, she was sent to a Christian convent, since at the time, it was the only structure where girls could acquire comprehensive education. Because of the nuns' pressure to convert her, her brothers decided to marry her off at 15. Paulina was 14 when she agreed to marry the man whom her eldest brother selected for her. One day she was a schoolgirl at a Catholic convent, where she was introduced to the French language and to Christian values and culture. The next day, she was a wife, living on her own, while her husband, who was a merchant, would travel through the Balkan area, selling Turkish working tools (Moreno, 1989, p. 16).

The education Paulina received at the convent instilled a unique perception of religion in her. On the one hand, she had borne Judaism's earlier influence. One the other hand, she bore Christianity's influence later on. She was especially impressed with Jesus' character. She engaged in a variety of fields related to mysticism, such as coffee reading, tarot card reading, fortune telling and consultation with gypsy crystal ball readers. She was known as a wonderful storyteller and also for her command in many languages: German, Spanish, French and, of course, Romanian. Paulina was a very popular woman, involved in the local Jewish-Turkish community life. She was considered an educated woman, relatively so for her time, sophisticated and calm, but did not always know how to distinguish imagination from reality.

Her marriage life was replete with issues, which emerged at the beginning; the husband's frequent business trips resulted in their living separately for the most part, and when they were together, intense tension would arise. As a matter of fact, she raised her six children alone.

Jacob, the eldest, was placed in a special position by her, since they spent much time together, just the two of them. Jacko, as she would call him, was her favorite son. He became her closest aide, replacing his absent father. The father's absence and his eventual leaving for good granted Jacob a special position as the family's eldest son (Marineau, 1989, p. 15).

Moreno's relationship with Paulina was unique. The latter meant very much to him. The young mother was warm and caring. The relationship between the mother and the son became even closer when he became ill with rickets when he was one year old. He suffered several severe fits, lacked appetite, lost weight and was unable to walk. There was fear for his life. No physician could offer any cure. It appeared that he would not survive. Young Paulina cried incessantly, and despair settled in. One day, when she took him out in the yard, a gypsy passed by and told her to cease crying and treat him as she instructed:

> Go and get some fine sand. At high noon, when the sun burns hot, put the baby on the sand. The sun will heal the baby. Pointing her finger at the child, she added this prophecy: The day will come when this boy will become a very great man. People will come from all over the world to see him. He will be a wise and kind man.
>
> (Marineau, 1989, p. 15)

Marineau views this tale as highly important, for it instilled the feeling in Paulina's heart that her son was not an ordinary child. From that day on, she believed God gave her a task of great value, namely, to enhance her child's health, heal him and prepare him for his future journey toward his role in life. This sense of mission, combined with her complex religious faith, was passed down to Moreno himself. Paulina began paying special attention to Moreno, thereby unconsciously laying the foundations for his future megalomaniac dream. Marineau believes this story to be the seed for Moreno's "I am God" idea (Marineau, 1989, p. 14). Paulina accepted the gypsy woman's advice, and several months later, her child recovered and was able to walk. The first part of the prophecy was fulfilled, while its latter part was gradually being created.

Paulina enhanced Moreno's feeling of being the chosen, destined one. This influence was apparent through Moreno's personal style and the charisma he developed throughout his lifetime.

The father, Nissim Moreno Levy, born in Turkey, was a sales agent who failed in all that he engaged. He was described as the one to spark a dispute, an argumentative individual who did little for his family. Nissim was a tough man who possessed absolute control over his family members and cast his authority on his children. He would often work away from home, drawn from his home and family. He expressed little enthusiasm when marrying Paulina, and their relationship began declining soon after they married. They separated for good when Moreno was 14. Nissim remarried in Istanbul, and probably had two other children, though Moreno did not know that for a fact.

In spite of the special relationship he had with his mother, and although he often morally supported her, when the final rift between his parents occurred, Moreno supported his father, opposing his mother and wealthy uncles.

The relationship with his father was extremely complicated. Moreno idealized the father figure. The more his father withdrew from his life, the more he internalized this figure. It was imagination that allowed Moreno to identify with his father and contain him. His admiration of his father was so great that he made him a God-like figure.

Haworth (1998, p. 19) argues that the combination of his father's absence and Moreno's idealization of him evolved into a belief that he himself was his father. Marineau inferred that for Moreno the internal representation of the father was enhanced with a mystic sense, which, in due time, would mix with the representation of God and intensified Moreno's tendency toward megalomania. A psychoanalytical point of view might suggest that by making his father God-like, Moreno, on one hand, formed a connection between father and God, while making the argument, "I am father", consequently leading to the "I am God". The concepts of paternity, creation and divinity led to Moreno's confusion.

The concepts "father" and "God" are symbols of giving birth and creation, components related to the religious-Messianic concept, which will be clarified later on.

In the author's opinion, the God–Father role, along with the father–son relationship issue, constitutes common threads throughout Moreno's course of life.

In 1912, as a student of medicine, he attended a lecture of Freud's addressing the therapeutic dream, as indicated in the Introduction. Later in his life, Moreno would state that what amazed him in his encounter with Freud was the fact that Moreno had never been a "son", other than in the biological aspect. Yet at a very early stage of his life, he had already managed to become a "father" at his home. As a child, he served as a father substitute in his family (Moreno, 1989, p. 61). He viewed his meeting with Freud as an encounter of two fathers, despite their age difference (Moreno was 20 at the beginning of his productive course, whereas Freud was 56 at the climax of his productive work). Freud is the father of psychoanalysis, whereas Moreno is the father of psychodrama.

To the best of our knowledge, Moreno met Freud only once while he lived in Vienna. Their confrontation was addressed several times in Moreno's works, whereas Freud, who probably attributed little importance to their encounter, did not refer to it in any of his works (Haworth, 1998, pp. 15–27). Moreno, however, replaced one "chief" (as he referred to his father) with another, namely, Freud. He projected his feelings toward his father onto Freud, and both fathers let him down, neglected him and ignored him.

Aside from his parents, Moreno was deeply influenced by Rabbi Bejerano, the chief rabbi of the Sephardic Jewish community in Bucharest. The rabbi served as the Bucharest Jewish school principal. When Moreno was 4 years old, he began attending the school and that was where he met Rabbi Bejerano. His knowledge and mastery of the Hebrew language influenced young Moreno, who turned him into some kind of an image of God on earth.

The development of the concept of Godliness in different stages of life

Moreno's divinity concept began developing when he was a small child, within the framework of the family in which he was raised. His upbringing was based on the Bible, but also on Christianity, as his mother acquired her own education at a convent, and thus she introduced him to Jesus' figure. Two figures influenced the child's imagination and patterns of play. The first figure was God, as embodied by his father and Rabbi Bejerano. The second was Jesus, as presented and portrayed by his mother. Moreno himself said:

> I have often been asked whether I have been guided [by] any model through the development of my religious thoughts and behaviors. In the years of shaping, I was introduced to many exceptional behaviors, and was also a sensitive and vulnerable individual. The two earliest events in my life, in relation to my awareness to God, occurred when I was four or five. The first was attending a Sephardic religious school, where I studied Hebrew. The first book to impress me was the book of Genesis in the Bible. When I first read it, I saw before our eyes Adonai, our God, one God. The other [event] was my plays with God.
>
> (Moreno, 1972, p. 204)

As a child, Moreno's plays would always involve God. He repeatedly enacted those plays, receiving full support from his mother. Yet there was one such game that he remembered in particular. When he was a little over 4 years old, his parents went away to visit relatives and left him in the home's basement with the neighbor's children. The children wanted to play and contemplated the type of game they might choose. "I know", said Moreno, "let's pretend to be God and his angels". The children asked, "But who is going to play God?" "I am God, and you are my angels", replied little Moreno. The children agreed, but declared: "We have to build heavens first". The piled chairs, one on top of another, and tied them together until they reached the ceiling. All children helped Moreno climb, until he reached the tallest chair and sat on it. The children began circling the table, using their arms as wings and singing. Suddenly, one of the children asked Moreno how come he was not flying. Moreno spread his arms in an attempt to fly, but immediately found himself on the floor. He was hurt, and his right arm was broken (Moreno, 1964a, p. 2; Marineau, 1989, p. 17).

Moreno realized that the role of God, which he was playing, was an imaginary one, since he fell and broke his arm. Despite his injury, he would not relent. He rose and continued playing. Moreno never ceased to believe that he was God, a unique case, and that God allowed him to be a Fallen God. "That attempt has never left me, and has saved my life thus far. . . . How to contain God, internalizing him, so as to render it an apparent, acknowledged reality. This question has occupied me ever since" (Moreno, 1972, pp. 206–207).

Moreno argued that story was of great significance to him, and he put forth his utmost efforts to verify and prove it.

> All that I have done through the years was to develop, enhance, and fantasize this story. The story's core is undoubtedly true. For me, it was some initial drive, from which all that occurred later on stemmed. From then on, anything was a repetition.
>
> (Moreno, 1972, p. 206)

The following was also written by Moreno in relation to this game:

> The psychodrama of the "Fallen God". This was, as far as I can recall, the first "private" psycho-dramatic session I have ever conducted. I was the director and the subject in one (Moreno stated that in later years, he was often questioned why the psychodrama stage was constructed in the form of three levels and a balcony.
>
> (Hare and Hare, 1996, p. 3)

He responded by stating that the initial inspiration for that structure probably stemmed from the following childhood experience (Moreno, 1972, p. 3):

> It is very likely that the heavens, which turned toward the ceiling paved my way to my idea concerning the multitude of levels on the psychodramatic

> stage, the vertical space: The first level as a level of conception; the second level represents growth; the third level representing coming to term, while the fourth level constitutes the tall balcony where the Messianic heroes are seated. The warm up toward the most complicated role, which is God's role, may imply the warm up process, through which one has to undergo a process of a spontaneous role-playing on the psychodramatic stage. The fact that I fell while the other children ceased holding the chairs might have taught me the lesson, according to which even heavenly beings depend on others, serving as auxiliary egos, whom the client-actor needs in order to play properly. I gradually learned that other children love playing God's role. Children's God-play bears profound meaning. That has maintained my connection to his mysterious plan.
>
> (Moreno, 1964a, p. 3)

It is from the symbolization of this story that Moreno drew his cosmic concepts, as well as his later inspiration as an individual who was about to declare himself God and cause a revolution in the psychological view of the self (Lindqvist, 1994, p. 193).

This story became a legend among the disciples of Moreno, who related it in various versions. According to one version, Moreno's mother approached a gypsy woman to examine her son's arm. The gypsy woman repeated the prophecy regarding the important mission the child would fulfill during his time on earth and recommended him to avoid breaking his left arm as well, because it would be a bad sign. God-plays repeated themselves and were fully supported by the mother.

Marineau wrote that the theme of playing God, supposedly being the omnipotent God, and becoming a father makes sense not only in the religious faith's context, but also guaranteed Moreno a place as the creator of a new dynasty on earth. In his mind, a child views himself as his own God and father (Marineau, 1989, p. 17). This first psychodrama session, which Moreno referred to as the "Fallen Angels" psychodrama, may be viewed as a shaping or constitutive moment within the child's megalomania, and in fact as the first megalomaniac episode. That left in his heart doubts as for the invincible God and also made him wonder about his own power.

In the author's opinion, the fact the Moreno played God is noteworthy, but also the falling, rising and resuming the game, which are even more important, as they, most of all, signify a new response to an old event, implying a spontaneous behavior which resulted in healing. Since it is God who fell, he bears the strength to rise.

Moreno's early years may not be understood without understanding his relationship with his parents and with God. As a matter of fact, his relationships with his surroundings are to be considered from two aspects: first, the family aspect – namely, his relationships with his father, mother, brothers and sister. The other aspect is related to his relationship with the religious world, which may be symbolically viewed as a meta-system (Marineau, 1989, p. 17).

An exploration of Moreno's early years suggests the way in which God-plays affected Moreno the child's further development in adulthood, as well as his philosophical and theological views.

It is at this initial stage that his theological viewpoint may be identified, though in a rather broad sense, as well as the beginning of ideas relating to encounter, creativity and spontaneity.

Adolescence: existential pondering; rebellion; developing the idea of God; expressionism

When Moreno was six or seven, he moved to Austria with his family, where his father was employed by a company in Vienna. Moreno attended a school in Vienna and soon became a prominent, favored student, thanks to his curiosity and intelligence. Though his family had never emphasized its Jewish identity, Moreno had a bar mitzvah in a ceremony at the Sephardic synagogue in Vienna. He was 14 years old when his family emigrated again, this time to Berlin. Moreno did not adjust to his new school and surroundings. Following a discussion with his parents, he was permitted to return to Vienna with friends of theirs. Thereafter, he would never return to live with his parents.

Though he immensely enjoyed himself in Vienna, similarly to his father, he, too, felt as an eternal emigrant compared to the local children. He was both an emigrant and a Jew, and would probably never be a true Viennese. However, the role Vienna fulfilled in Moreno's growth and development is noteworthy. He lived in a city filled with history, with individuals as Freud and Mahler, among others, who brought their new ideas.

Throughout his coming-of-age process and during adolescence, Moreno demonstrated signs of rebellion, which was also targeted against his dysfunctional family. He attempted, in vain, to reconcile his parents' complex relationship, but around 1906, their separation became final. As soon as Moreno lost his father, he became a problem student, going into conflict with his teachers and becoming deeply depressed. He sought answers for spiritual questions that intrigued him concerning life and his role in the world.

Moreno also rebelled against a wider circle. He sought to reassess a society which seemed to him phony and false. The theme of divinity continued developing and consolidating during adolescence, through seeking personal identity, as Moreno was posing challenging, profound questions to himself and those around him:

> Who am I?; Does my body represent myself?; Does it constitute my whole self? Is everything matter, or is there some part of my body, or an embodiment of some other part of me which may be referred to as the soul?
>
> (Moreno, 1989, p. 29)

Those existential ponderings planted the seeds of the encounter concept, stemming from the way in which Moreno understood the Bible, as God's psychodrama where the People of Israel conduct a dialogue with their Creator.

The Encounter concept is one of psychodrama's cornerstones on which Moreno founded all matters related to encounters between humans, and particularly between a therapist and a patient.

Moreno was greatly influenced by Jesus' and Buddha's ideas, particularly the message of unity, friendship and love they both conveyed. The group model – namely, viewing the group as the therapeutic basis in psychodrama – stemmed and developed from those messages.

Moreno now felt he had to reconnect with his so-called mission, yet he was lonely and helpless. He quit school and spent long stretches with himself, meditating and obsessively reading mystic-religious literature.

The two years that followed were characterized by intense misgiving, and were dedicated to attempts to become God himself, or to give significance to the mission he felt God wished him to fulfill. The young adolescent did not know who God was, whether He existed or what he was expected to do on His behalf in order to find answers. One day, he regarded himself as God's servant. The next day, he would perceive himself as an accurate image of God, or even as God himself. The embarrassment he experienced yielded two insights: first, action is preferable to speech; second, experience is more effective than intellectual learning and acquiring one's knowledge from books (Marineau, 1989, pp. 25–26).

At 14, Moreno underwent another religious experience. During his school vacation, he visited his family in Chemnitz. He referred to that experience as "My Epiphany Holiday". While walking down a dark, deserted street, attempting to sort out his mixed thoughts and emotions, he suddenly found himself facing Jesus' statue in the park, illuminated by the moon. A deep desire aroused from within him. He wished that Jesus' statue would come to life and speak to him. He wanted Jesus to move away from the stone and relive his life before his fellow townspeople. Then, he felt the statue was about to speak to him and listened attentively. While facing the statue, Moreno knew he had to make a decision which would determine his future. Inspired by the event, he realized that he was indeed an extraordinary individual, that he was placed on earth in order to fulfill an extraordinary mission (Hare and Hare, 1996, p. 5).

> The question was how I would choose. Was my identity the universe itself, or rather a derivative of a given family or tribe from which I came? I decided in favor of the universe. It was not because my family was inferior to any other, but rather, because I wanted to live by virtue of the greater order, to which any of my family belonged, and where I wished to return.
>
> (Moreno, 1989, p. 23)

The desire to destroy the world in his rebellion period and the resulting depression were now gone, and Moreno wished to establish a new world. He would carry that vision with him in years to follow. Marineau (1989, p. 24) maintains this vision may be considered a constitutive moment in Moreno's "Second Megalomania" period.

Moreno himself addressed the "normal megalomania" concept in the following:

> This is a nasty name. It's really name calling. Actually, megalomania is a natural state of the human being from birth on. Megalomania is nothing exceptional. It has like any other natural states normal and pathological forms. Normal megalomania is just as fundamental to man's spiritual nature as are his lungs for breathing and his blood vessels for nourishing the cells of the body to his physical nature.
>
> (Moreno, in Marineau, 1989, p. 24)

"Normal megalomania" is a key concept in Moreno's self-development theory, which will be discussed in Chapter 3.

Moreno also identified with the expressionist movement, which was popular in Vienna at the time. Expressionism is a movement associated with art of the 20th century, which places the artist, his work and inner views at the core of the artistic work. The movement reflects the artist's emotions and feelings without referring to the external world. The movement called the young generation to rebel against the parents' generation ("kill the father"), demonstrating the new creativity and their morality in order to establish a new world order. The movement's motto was "Let's destroy and rebuild from new perspectives" (Marineau, 1994, p. 87).

Likewise, Moreno's behavior and the values he possessed while living in Vienna corresponded to the expressionism school of thought, emphasizing rebellion and correction. His rebelling God was equivalent to his faith in creation. Rebelling riches and rich people's arrogance while being introduced to the poor elevates the oppressed and deprived souls to the level of God. The dual quality characterizing rebellion and creation was mainly manifested in his raw writing, which expresses despair and disappointment in relation to his parents' splitting up and the loss of his father. From his point of view, the unjust situation was evidence of God's letting him down and abandoning him.

The core of Moreno's story was the rough, cruel chase of his fate and the existential perception which intrigued him in his 20s. The following were the intriguing questions which preoccupied him:

> As far as I remember, I was presented with two alternatives. I was wondering, Who is that man over there? Is he merely a piece of nothingness gone like the rainbow, so as to never return? Or perhaps the self is the most tangible thing that exists, namely, the creator of the universe, the first and last, all-embracing entity? In other [words], [am I] nothing, or am I God?
>
> (Moreno, 1972, p. 198)

Between the two alternatives – insignificance or universality – and through the existential dilemma between nihilism and megalomania, Moreno chose to be cosmos and God. He was guided by the following principle: Why choose the little if it is possible to take the most?

As mentioned, from a logical viewpoint, the existentialistic problem, as phrased by Moreno, is the choice between two extremes: meaninglessness or universality. Moreno proposed to assume what may happen when an individual allows a total existence and what might happen if the same individual totally denies his existence. If futility is chosen, we shall take the direction of suicide or madness. On the other hand, since there is no independent basis or criteria for choosing universality or futility, why not choose universality? This strategy begins with a question regarding ontology (exploring the nature of being), namely, where do I stand in terms of my being? One prospect is the universal self, which bears moral ramifications, as if I am universal, then I am God and I bear responsibility for all human beings. (J. D. Moreno, 1994, pp. 100–101).

> In this mood of pure inspiration, I ran to the house where I lived. It was located in May Valley, in a small town near Vienna. The only sound I heard was voice and words; words coming and going through my brain. I had no patience to sit and write them down, thus I grabbed a red pen, one after another. I climbed the house's upper room, near the tower, and began writing on the wall all the words I had heard and pronounced out loud. I had heard the following; "I", rather than "he", or "you"; I heard "I", which is deeply significant. Saying "he" would be a mistake, as it would transform full responsibility to the cosmic God. Saying "you" would be a mistake, because it would transform full responsibility to Jesus. It is, therefore, "me". It is my responsibility.
>
> (Moreno, 1972, p. 203)

> I tried to put into words in a book which has become known as Das Testament des Vaters (1920) in which the idea of I-Creator and the principle of creativity were proclaimed as the first principle of the universe. All that I know about these collusive things and all that I have done on an experimental level since stems from these days.
>
> (Moreno, 1956, p. 391)

The opening words to the book *The Words of the Father* are: "I am God, the father, the creator of the universe; those are my words, the words of a father". Those words emphasize the dual God–Father relationship, as well as the special role Moreno believed he had been assigned: to act as God's voice.

The Words of the Father was published anonymously, since Moreno believed creativity is an anonymous category (Z. T. Moreno, 2000, p. 1). Anonymity diminishes ego, thus allowing man to unite with the cosmos (Z. T. Moreno, 2000, p. 19). In relation to this, Moreno writes:

> It was anonymous by essence, as those words were not mine. I felt they were channeled through me, and through anyone in the world, with minor

> variations here and there, and therefore, that book was not mine, but the words of God himself. I felt the book's cover should include all the names of the world's people, those who have passed and those who have not yet been born.
>
> (Moreno, 1972, p. 203)

The Words of the Father is a philosophical-theological essay, which contributes to the understanding of Moreno's line of thought. The reason for that is its generalization and brief clarification of the concepts "spontaneity" and "creativity", which characterize all of the ideas Moreno developed later on.

Curiously, Moreno related to Zerka that while he wrote the book, he was not sexually aroused at all. Warming up came from him from an entirely different plane, in an entirely different mental state (Z. T. Moreno, 2000, p. xiv). In the author's opinion, Moreno emphasized that point so as to demonstrate the drive for writing was spontaneous energy, rather than the libidinal energy (the difference between both energy types will be addressed in Chapter 2).

Moreno: the tri-stage divinity development: play, embodiment, performance

Stage One. As a child, Moreno played (in the sense of drama) God. He viewed himself as being God ("normal megalomania"). It may be observed how in his childhood God-plays affected his future course of development as an adult, as well as his philosophical and religious views.

Stage Two. As an adolescent, Moreno perceived the "I am God" idea as the source of creation and spontaneity, an image which suited his emotions and thoughts in relation to himself. He experienced God from within; he embodied Him.

Stage Three. As a young adult, a stage which will be described in more detail later on in this book, Moreno progressed from contemplations to action. He began actively performing. At the performance phase, he declared himself God, Jesus' heir. He used those images as a means of speaking of himself, though he knew they had nothing to do with actual reality.

In 1909, Moreno entered the university and was seen walking down its corridors wearing a green cloak of the type worn by the Austrian farmers. The color green symbolized the expressionism movement, as well as a connection to nature. Everybody began identifying him with this cloak, "the prophet's cloak": "I began playing the role. I did not only want to be a prophet. I also wanted to look like a prophet" (Moreno, 1989, p. 34; Moreno, in Fox, 1987, p. 205).

> Thus I lived the role not only publicly, but also privately and personally.
>
> (Moreno, 1989, p. 3)

Nazism, communism and existentialism

It was in those years when Adolf Hitler arrived in Vienna to study art. The National-Socialist and anti-Semite movements grew stronger from year to year. Fortunately, Moreno was alert and sensitive enough to that. Leon Trotsky had visited Vienna often prior to the Russian Revolution, as did other Bolshevik leaders. There had been communist and socialist movements, which picketed and conducted struggles; they competed with each other to be the most militant (Hare and Hare, 1996, pp. 6–7).

Aside from all those, there was the existentialistic movement, which was active in Vienna at the time and to which Moreno engaged himself. The first few existentialists were easy to recognize by the beards they let grow wild. The beards, as mentioned, signified natural masculinity, yet also posed a challenge to both the bourgeois and communists, as something which grows on its own, rather than not progressing at all. It was a symbol of an individual who freely wishes to go his own way and just be.

The basic principles of the three movements were clear. The Nazis sought to conquer the world for the Germans to rule; the communists wished to conquer the world in favor of the worker class, while the early existentialists emphasized existence itself as holy. The world is already in their hands. They do not need to conquer it. Wherever they notice existential fear, they attempt to preserve it in its natural form.

The first principle of the group was the "all-inclusiveness" of being and the constant effort to maintain from moment to moment the natural, spontaneous, uninterrupted flow of existence. Their second principle was goodness, the natural blessedness of all existing things.

There were the ideas of the "moment" (Augenblick), neither as a function of the past nor of the future, but as a category in itself; the idea of the "situation" (Lage) and the challenge emerging from it; the idea of spontaneity and creativity as universal processes of conduct, countering the clichés of the ethical and cultural conserves; and, above all, the idea of urgency, the urgency of their immediate experience (Moreno, 1989, pp. 47–48).

The existentialistic principles of encounter and direct experiencing of life, "here and now", would later be practiced by Moreno and would serve as an initial foundation for the scientific theories and methods he would develop.

"The house of encounter": converting the religious encounter concept into the existentialistic encounter concept

Moreno had already been introduced to the existentialistic dialogue concept, which was attributed to Jesus, Socrates and the Jewish prophets. The integration of existentialistic principles and the religious influences yielded some sort of a new religious thinking:

> I felt the urge to invent a religion, which will serve the masses. Channeling those forces was rough, and I found my satisfaction in immediate encounter. Did I wish, and did I possess the perfectionism required for establishing

> a new religion? I did, however, possess an uncontrollable urge to attain the goal, and the former granted me the power to do so.
>
> (Moreno, 1989, pp. 34–35)

In order to understand Moreno's own psychodrama, one must view him as an individual who perceived himself as replacing humanity as a whole, as the cosmic-divine dimension's voice. He possessed the idée fixe, according to which an individual did not bear the authority. Rather, he must be a voice representing a group. It must occur within a group framework. The new word must rise from the group. Hence, he went on to search for companions, people who would follow him: good people.

Upon entering the university, Moreno met the person who would become his friend for life: Chaim Kelmer. Like Moreno, Chaim believed that if one gave love, he would receive love and that people are to be helped with solving their problems. Thus the religion of encounter emerged in the world.

Moreno wrote: "We were both carried away by the spreading of religion waves" (Moreno, 1989, p. 41).

Moreno, the man who played God or God who played man, and Chaim Kelmer were joined by three other students. Together, they established a group named *religion of encounter*.

> My new religion was a religion of being, of self-perfection. It was a religion of helping and healing, for helping was more important [than] taking. It was a religion of silence. It was a religion of doing a thing for its own sake, unrewarded, unrecognized. It was a religion of anonymity.
>
> (Moreno, 1989, p. 34)

All group members were committed to sharing, love, giving and partnership, as well as to living a direct, concrete life, which entailed direct involvement with a community founded upon those principles.

Generally, the group as a whole adopted an anonymity policy, following an old Christian tradition of sharing everything in the name of charity, donation and anonymous action (Marineau, 1989, p. 27). Anonymous is an antithesis to possessive behavior and the counterreaction to ego worshiping, a behavior which Moreno considered the 20th century's major plague.

Those early encounter groups were the prototype of the encounter groups that have spread worldwide ever since.

Spontaneity, group psychotherapy and sociometry

Revealing spontaneity and creativity as a divine-like force

At the time, while Moreno was absorbed in mystic experiences and mysticism, he also began taking interest in the world of children, for two reasons: The first reason is associated with his mystic occupation, relating to Jesus' interest in children. The second reason was more practical. Moreno had always loved spending time at the Augarten, a very large Viennese park, where he would play as a child. Around 1908, he began meeting children at that park, relating stories to them and playing games in a way that gave him some idea as to the creativity philosophy's basis and its connection to divinity.

While relating tales and legends, Moreno came across a fascinating revelation: he could not relate to the children the same legend more than once, because he felt committed to them and to himself to preserve their wonder and creativity. Even if the plot was the same, it should be related again in a different version: "It was not necessarily, what I told them, the legends or tales themselves. It was the mysterious atmosphere, which was induced in association with the paradox of turning the unreal into reality" (Moreno, 1947a, p. 4).

Moreno found particularly profound meaning in children's God-plays:

> I allowed them to play God, if they wished. When they missed as I had when I had broken my right arm, I began addressing the children's issues by playing through improvisation, some type of psychotherapy for 'Fallen Gods'.
>
> (Moreno, 1964a, p. 3)

Moreno claimed he suffered from idée fixe, an idea which became an inexhaustible source of efficiency. According to the idea, there is some sort of an immortal, ancient nature, which recurs in each generation. Moreno referred to the initial world (spontaneity) as a quality possessed by each and every human being. He loved the world of embodiment and the kingdom of play, to which he had been introduced through the children's God-plays. He did not intend to ever abandon that world. When he gradually withdrew from the children's world, transferring into the wider adult world, he did so by deciding that the idée fixe would remain his guideline. Thus, whenever he encountered one of life's aspects, the forms and models he witnessed in that chaste, initial world were those he envisioned. "Apparently, those models endorsed me with a life science before experimenting confirmed their truth" (Moreno, 1947a, pp. 3–4).

The earlier experience of playing with children provides many of the insights and principles which constituted the foundation of what would later become the psychodrama method (Rabson, 1979, p. 111).

Discovering group psychotherapy: existential encounter with prostitutes

Upon releasing the children from their parents' restrictions and rigid worldview, Moreno began addressing the other vulnerable groups comprising the human populations on the streets of Vienna, particularly the most vulnerable population, the prostitutes (Moreno, 1964b, p. 154). Moreno described a random encounter with a prostitute who was arrested for her provocative attire. He spoke to her only briefly when a policeman stood between them and took her to the police station. Moreno followed them to the station. Later, when she emerged, Moreno questioned her regarding the sequence of events that resulted in her arrest. The prostitute told him she was instructed by the policeman of the prohibition of wearing such clothes that stood out during the day, since they might attract clients. They are permitted to engage in prostitution only after dark (Moreno, 1953, pp. xxviii–xxix).

In Vienna of that day and age, a small district served as a prostitute ghetto. There they would live, segregated from the rest of society, because of their occupation (Hare and Hare, 1996, p. 48). They were lacking any civil rights and could not obtain medical or legal services. Moreno perceived them as completely defenseless. He did not aim to turn them into more normative women, but rather, to assist them in becoming more united, thereby facilitating them to help each other (Z. T. Moreno, 2000, p. 84).

Moreno began calling prostitutes at their homes in the ghetto, escorted by Dr. Wilhelm Gruen, a sexually transmitted diseases specialist, and Carl Colbert, publisher of the Viennese newspaper *Der Morgen*. They began meeting groups of eight to ten prostitutes twice or three times a week. In the sessions, they addressed the day-to-day occurrences in those women's lives: imprisonments, sexually transmitted diseases and unplanned pregnancy. Over time, their problems and personal suffering became the key aspect in the encounter with the prostitutes. Their personal needs set aside the professional union idea, thereby yielding the first psychodrama group in situ (Moreno, 1964b, pp. 154–155).

Moreno realized that a single person may serve as a therapeutic agent for another person and that group psychotherapy bears real potential. He began employing the term "group psychotherapy" in its clinical sense when he went to work at Sing-Sing prison in 1931. Thereafter, Moreno was called upon to coach at a girls school in Hudson, New York, in 1932, where he began gathering materials for his greatest work, titled "Who Shall Survive" (Z. T. Moreno, 2000, p. 84).

Discovering sociometry: an existentialistic encounter with captives

Moreno did not continue observing the groups of prostitutes, since he was appended to the medicine branch of the Austrian army (Z. T. Moreno, 2000, p. 84). When World War I broke out in 1914, he volunteered for the Austrian army but was not permitted to serve because of the lack of clarity concerning his citizenship, since he had never been able to attain Austrian citizenship. However, as a student of medicine with vast clinical experience, he was hired by the government as a medical clerk (Moreno, 1989, p. 63). Moreno was employed at a department of the Austro-Hungarian Ministry of Interior and granted responsibility for the health of refugees who had spent time at the refugee camp in

Mitterndorf. Here, too, Moreno encountered displaced, helpless people: young and old, women and children. Moreno felt responsible for those vulnerable individuals and wished to instill a sense of belonging in them. Along with the desire and the aim to find a solution for the social problems, another fascinating goal was identified which had not been studied by then. A full community life was established there. The Mitterndorf community consisted of a formal aspect, side by side with an informal and invisible aspect. In order to resolve the tension between both aspects of this pathological community, Moreno began drawing diagrams, curves portraying each home's structure, "sociometric diagrams". Gradually, he developed a method of sociometry, which became a fundamental sociological tool. Sociometry engages in revealing interpersonal relations. It indicates the individual's role in forming his social system.

Moreno returned to Vienna in order to complete his doctoral thesis. He received his degree at the University of Vienna in February 1917 (Moreno, 1989, p. 69). In the years 1918–1925, Moreno served as a public medical clerk in Bad Voslau, a recreation and spa resort not far from Vienna. Additionally, he served as a medical manager of one of the largest cotton-growing areas in town, and was associated with a private medical practice in Bad Voslau and Vienna (Hare and Hare, 1996, pp. 10).

Translating theological perception into the sociometric method

Moreno stated it was important for him, at least as far as his autobiography was concerned, that the universal God model serve as a basis to guide him through the question of being, as well as for the sociometric theory.

According to that model, he constructed the sociometric theory, a conception of a society where everyone's self would be realized and fulfilled. His theological experiences and their analyses provided him inspiration and confidence in shaping areas associated with the secular-materialistic facet on earth (Moreno, 1949a, p. 202). In other words, the perception of divinity led him to a religious-secular perception, which was related to human relations.

> The overall inspiration for the methods and techniques stemmed, directly or indirectly from the divinity concept and the principle of the Book of Genesis, my God conception rendered me highly efficient and creative; all the conclusions I drew from it and its scientific translation were correct. I had no reason to think that my initial assumption was wrong, just because it was unpopular among scientists.
>
> (Moreno, 1953, p. xxxix)

In order to reflect an ideal form of community, namely, the world, Moreno reverted to the vision of the First Day's divinity concept, questioning the image of God's mind embarking on the first day of Creation. Moreno thought one of the plans must have been an axio-normative order of the cosmos. From his viewpoint, sociometry began at the moment he questioned himself as to time and distance between humans (Moreno, 1953, p. xxxv). Moreno's basic assumption was that time and space are the most precious assets in the social world.

Both of these assumptions provided Moreno with a few of the sociometric system's components, namely, proximity, measurement, love of one's neighbor and encounter, along with issues related to spontaneity and creativity.

Moreno insisted that science and religion may be connected and, furthermore, that science's future lies within the merging of religion's philosophy. Those theometrical experiences helped him find a way to bridge the gaps between experiential methods in theological sciences, social sciences and physical and biological sciences. (Moreno, 1949a, pp. 201–202).

Theater of spontaneity and psychodrama

Moreno as a role player: the creative "I" in the surplus reality

Moreno's life has demonstrated the search for stage's essence. Just as he served as the live Cosmic Man model, he also served as a model of an individual who plays a multitude of roles in his life. He attained that position by becoming an actor, an author and a preacher himself:

Likewise, Moreno proclaimed the following of himself:

> That time and for many of the years that followed, I had the sensation that I was the chief actor, the protagonist, in a drama with great scenes and exits, one act climaxing the other, culminating in a great and final victory. It was drama, but it was not theatre. I was my own playwright and producer. The scenes were real, not like those in a theatre. But they were not quite as real as in a simple life. They were of a higher reality. They were created by my imagination with the help of actual people and actual objects in the midst of real life.
>
> (Moreno, 1989, p. 32)

The explanation of Moreno's choice of expressive methods in order to promote individuals or groups lies within the personality of Moreno himself. He established theater and, later on, the therapeutic methods so as to justify his own ambition to play God. He even used to say that thanks to psychodrama, he was capable of controlling and regulating his own "megalomania". His own experience led him to the belief that everybody benefitted from a normal passion to be at the center of the stage. In order to undergo full psychological development and be creative, everybody must find the way to spontaneously perform for an audience.

Translation of the "I-God" idea into the theater of the creative "I"

Following Moreno's suggestion of the creative divinity concept (Moreno, 1920), he came to the conclusion that the following essential step would be practically, tangibly and concretely fulfilling his philosophical ideas, and not necessarily an expansion of the idea on the intellectual level (Moreno, 1953, p. xvi). He introduced the religious ideas, as well as spontaneity and creativity, to the therapeutic play and theater arena because he perceived therapeutic theater as the greatest effort of practicing and expressing the self's image (Moreno, 1956, p. 8).

Choosing the theater realm over establishing a religious cult or a theological system is clearly justified by the political and philosophical circumstances under which those ideas had been developed. Moreno complained that at a materialistic time nobody could play the role of God without being categorized as the lunatic and criticized by others (Moreno, 1947a, pp. 3–4).

Aside from the secularization trend that was spreading among Vienna's psychoanalysts, while the whole continent of Europe was attempting to recover from the total destruction caused by World War I and with Fascism beginning to rise, Vienna constituted the basis for three types of materialism, which were complementary at the time. Moreno thought Marx's economic materialism; Freud's psychological materialism; and technological materialism's atomic bombs, steam freighters and as contradictory to each other as was possible; but even when they were antithetical to each other, all shared one common ground: profound fear, near hatred of the spontaneous, creative self.

The creative, spontaneous self faced opposition, was deeply doubted and was not receiving the proper attention it deserved. That triggered Moreno's struggle against his rivals, restoring the self into humanity's awareness (Moreno, 1947a, p. 4). This is where the theater of spontaneity continues God's work of creating the world by opening a new channel of reality for man (Moreno, 1947a, p. 7).

The myth behind the creation of psychodrama

> As I was walking through the streets and gardens of Vienna, some more than half's century ago (1908–1914), a very anonymous and intensive young man, observing and playing with children, I had a vision which triggered my entire lifework and which gave me a precious anticipation of the great changes which have since taken place in our world. I meditated about the meaning of the universe and about my place in it.
>
> (Moreno, 1964b, p. 153)

This vision led to the conclusion that techniques for life were necessary. There must be methods for life which serve the innermost needs of personality, society and the world.

However, two questions perplexed Moreno and he was unable to let them go:

> 1 How can I communicate with the entire world, with all the people and how can all the people communicate with me?
> 2 How can this be done in the here and now? How can I emancipate myself from the past and create in the moment and for the future, with the people I encounter? Then and there the miracle happened, at least in my fertile imagination, the "encounter" took place: I met all the people and the people met me. I saw them and heard them and felt them.
>
> (Moreno, 1964b, p. 154)

Since he had that vision of creating an encounter of all the people in the world, he sought tools through which that vision could be materialized to become real (Marineau, 1989, p. 95).

Moreno began perceiving spontaneous theater as a means for experimental theology, for fulfilling the spontaneous, creative self. In other words, the theater served as a legitimate setting for experiencing being God.

The transition from theater of spontaneity to therapeutic theater and psychodrama

In 1921, as a young physician in one of Vienna's quarters, Moreno established a theater, spontaneity-theater-style. Originally, work was conducted with professional actors. Moreno adopted some part of the conventional theater's formal structure, integrating it with the evolving spontaneity and creativity concepts, as well as with therapeutic principles. He did not rely on a pre-written script or play; nor were there defined roles. Moreno would simply come up on the stage and stimulate his audience, guiding them toward the matters they discussed. Throughout this experience, he found that the embodiment, and the discussion that followed, yielded catharsis, abating personal concerns and tensions, both among the actors and those in the audience.

Those therapeutic experiences in the theater of spontaneity and the healing of actors having acted out their inner conflicts through the protagonist, other actors and feedback from the audience, as well as Moreno's guidance, yielded the development of the therapeutic tool, which, with the passage of time, Moreno would refer to as psychodrama (Naharin, 1985, pp. 12–15; Hare and Hare, 1996, p. 13).

The women, the muses in Moreno's life: the realization of Godliness and creativity

Moreno referred to the significant women in his life as "muses", the term describing those godly women who fill the poets with inspiration. Since Moreno felt that he was both a man and "God-player", he wished to find a woman who could both be a man's lover, and a God-player's lover. (Marineau, 1989, p. 61; Moreno, 1989, p. 104).

Pia, his first girlfriend, was the first so-called "muse" in his life, thereby replacing his admiration for his mother as a figure who drives him to outdo himself. He met Pia at the time of his adolescent rebellion and melancholy and broke up with her upon his return to Vienna (Marineau, 1989, p. 21).

Moreno's first mature love was Mariana, whom he met upon arriving in Bad Voslau. Moreno saw her in town; he instantly fell in love with her. She became his medical assistant, secretary, lover and mostly, his inspiration. The book *The Words of the Father* was written when Mariana served as the muse.

The relationship between Moreno and Mariana lasted until 1925, when Moreno decided to immigrate to the United States; there he became involved with Beatrice Beecher, a social worker who gave lectures on children's psychology at Mt. Sinai Hospital, New York. Beatrice immediately took interest in his work, and their relationship involved professional collaboration. She worked on the first English translation of "Theatre of Spontaneity" (Das Stegreiftheater), and he demonstrated psychodramatic work with children at Plymount Institute, Brooklyn, where Beatrice was working.

She proposed marriage to him so as to facilitate him in obtaining American citizenship. They married on 31 May 1928 and divorced in 1934, as soon as Moreno became an American citizen.

Moreno continued his search for a muse. He met Florence Bridge, a resident at The Hudson School. Florence was 23 years younger than Moreno (Marineau, 1989, pp. 101–107). She was deeply impressed with Moreno as a prophet and preacher, and particularly with the book *The Words of the Father*. In 1938, they married, and a year later, she gave birth to their daughter, who was named Regina. Though Florence admired Moreno, treating him like God, he was unhappy in this marriage. They were married ten intense, turbulent and unhappy years, until they divorced in 1948 (Hare and Hare, 1996, pp. 16–19).

Moreno continued searching for his muse. He needed a relationship that would be conducive, connecting him to the best parts of himself; a woman who would inspire him, not only admire him. Zerka, the new woman in his life, was the answer to all those missing pieces. In the summer of 1941, a young woman entered his office with three other young women. She sought help for her sister and her son, refugees of Nazi Germany. Of the four women, Moreno focused upon Zerka. He felt it was love at first sight and immediately knew Zerka was the woman he was seeking. He soon discovered her potential, both as a spouse and as a creation partner, and thus developed a relationship with the woman who became his secretary, lover and, most of all, his muse (Hare and Hare,1996, p. 20).

Her immediate understanding of Moreno's philosophy strengthened their bond even further. There was no doubt that Zerka was his inspiration. She served as the moderating and mediating force when Moreno experienced professional conflicts and clashes, and also contributed greatly to the establishment of the institute in Beacon. Gradually, Zerka fulfilled a key role in psychodrama's development, and eventually became a supervisor and mentor in the field. Additionally, she fulfilled a significant role as an interpreter of Moreno's ideas. She held particular responsibility for rendering the method popular in the clinical setting, establishing psychodrama's structure as it is known at present.

Moreno and Zerka married in 1949. At that time, because of their old age, the desire to have a child was unreasonable. However, Moreno did not want Zerka to remain all alone if he died and thought they should have a child. Moreno believed in children and birth, viewing it as a clear sign of creativity, which is nothing less than divinity, and wanted a child who would continue carrying his name. Their son Jonathan was born in 1952, and Moreno finally had an heir for the new dynasty he wished to establish.

Summary and assessment

In this chapter, the author has aimed at demonstrating how Moreno's life story may be related both as a historical truth and as a psychodramatic truth. Paradoxically, the need to construct a myth in relation to his name, place of birth and date of birth did not emerge until his emigration to the United States in 1925. The records available in Europe indicate an accurate reliance upon historical facts (Marineau, 1989, p. 8). The paradox stems from the fact that Moreno created that myth precisely at the time when he decided to relinquish the religious image, with its characteristic terms, which facilitated the understanding of his philosophy, and particularly his God and prophet figure, as a creator and co-creator of the universe (Marineau, 1994, p. 3).

Despite the common interpretation according to which Moreno relinquished his theological ideas and preacher image, including the attempt of Moreno himself to alter his image as a philosopher and preacher to a scientist and author, I shall demonstrate in the following chapters, based upon his explanations and analyses of the theological principles which constitute the foundation of the psychodrama and sociometry, which are supposedly scientific methods, that all was nothing but a false impression.

Moreno stated that the following step in his life occurred in 1925, upon his emigration to the United States and changing his name in favor of the more secular J. L. Moreno, or, alternatively, became a philosopher and a scientist who attempted to continue what he had done in his former religious life by means of psychodrama, sociometry and encounter groups. In the author's opinion, the need to establish a new image as a scientist emerged from Moreno's failed attempt to elucidate and spread the philosophy. The clinical intervention methods, on the other hand, were welcome. Because his religious vocabulary aroused opposition among sociologists and psychiatrists, he chose to shed light on other aspects of his work rather than face the criticism and present justifications and connections between the theology and his own scientific methods. Moreno chose a different way. Once he lived his own myth, he also fulfilled his own philosophy. He embodied the message which he wished to convey. He remade and raised himself anew, thereby stating, "If you did not believe my words and explanation, then believe my actions, in turning philosophy into practicality".

> All my scientific attempts in the field of psychotherapy had strong religious undercurrents.
>
> (Moreno, 1972, p. 214)

In the years 1936–1953, Moreno mainly wrote of the key concepts and methods of sociometry and psychodrama. In 1936, he opened the sanitarium in Beacon, and in 1942, he established the Theater of Psychodrama, a psychodrama institute, as well as the Sociometry Institute in New York City. In 1937, he was a special lecturer at the New School of Social Research and lectured at the Girls' College and Columbia University in the years 1939–1940. In 1951, he established the International Council of Group Psychotherapy, which was responsible for organizing and financing groups and conferences addressing group psychotherapy.

In the years 1954–1960, Moreno travelled around the world and witnessed the spreading of his ideas and scientific literature. "The Third Psychiatric Revolution", as he now named it, was at its climax (thus, let it be commented that the gypsy woman's prophecy from his childhood came true). In his final years, from 1961 until his death on 14 May 1974, Moreno reviewed the history of the movements he initiated, assessing the scope of their influence. Additional articles appeared in anthologies and books, which were translated into various languages. The spread of his doctrine continued (Hare and Hare, 1996, pp. 21–23).

Moreno often referred to the year 2000. He declared that his ideas were ahead of their time, relative to the 20th century, but would be rather relevant and properly serve the following century. The next great challenge would be to epistemologically examine and re-establish Moreno's ideas. Accordingly, the following chapter shall clarify the basic concepts in his philosophical-theological perception of the self.

Chapter 2

Moreno's philosophical-theological perception of the self

In this chapter, the author seeks to argue that Moreno's theory, which was destined to be a theory of personality combining psychological principles, is in fact a philosophical theory that addresses human development to a greater extent than it addresses psychopathology. The philosophical background underlying religion led Moreno to a new outlook. In that sense, he is different from other theoreticians and other personality and psychopathology theories. Moreno's point of departure is not the psychological elements. Originally, the terms "creativity", "spontaneity", "warming-up" and "tele", which appear in his philosophical outlook, are concepts associated with the concept of Godhead, stemming from his existentialistic perception. This Godhead is not psychology. However, in his eyes, it demonstrates the psychological view, which he developed to be psychopathology oriented. Moreno's theological perception also sheds light on his philosophical views, which, in turn, facilitate a discussion of the self in the psychological sense.

What is a theological and cosmodynamic perception?

A theological outlook provides a comprehensive view of a person's life by employing the concept of Godhead. As illustrated here, the therapeutic aspect according to Moreno is merely a part perceiving the individual as a whole. Human beings have always posed existential questions, and for that matter, constructed systems of beliefs, religions, myths and legends to provide themselves with some structures which might give answers to those questions. Religion provided a support system, which was the object of Moreno's revolution and which he conducted by means of creativity and spontaneity (Power, 1975, p. 164).

Moreno's point of departure was that an individual is born into an environment in which he is involved from the moment of birth. Human relationships always require at least two parties. The immediate environment's important role is not argued, yet this relationship's cost is manifested by the narrowing of the cosmos and its influence on human behavior. Simultaneously when interacting with one's immediate environment, there are certain situations in a person's development where he or she takes great interest in cosmic phenomena, which determine his or her place and role within the cosmos, such as birth, death, sex, etc., and which he or she begins struggling and striving to understand once they arise. One would rather control the latter than submit to them. Such aspiration poses an expectation to a psychological force to rise, as well as to assist human, psychological and other aspects of potential to construct and consolidate the accomplisher's system, controlling those cosmic phenomena, and thereby yielding creativity. One may believe that creativity is indeed that psychological force possessing such demands and serves that purpose.

> The principle of theological doctrine holds that any developments are due to the purpose that is served by them. It implies that present activities are not the inevitable outcomes of the past determinants, but rather that the final course of events is their purpose.
>
> (Kipper, 1967, p. 64)

The godhead perception's development

Throughout history, man has emphasized several aspects related to God's nature, which, for some reason seem important to a specific stage of human development. Viewing creativity and spontaneity as a divine dimension has yielded Moreno's Godhead perception. According to Moreno (1942, 1947c, 1969a), the Godhead perception consists of three stages, which portray an evolution from a view of God as distant to viewing God as a close entity.

The First Godhead Model. Namely, "He God"; this was the model that appeared in the Bible. This is a cosmic God who was pictured as an entity distant from the world He created. Separated from humanity, dwelling in the skies, unreachable, unknown, mysterious. The connection to Him was channeled by the prophets and mediators, but mainly forms dependency relations with human beings. He was addressed in the third person only. This is the God who dwells outside the self.

This Godhead type, which served human needs well in the past, no longer did so, resulting in the formation of another form of Godhead, which people addressed in times of trouble.

The Second Godhead Model. Namely, "Thou God"; this appears in the New Testament in the image of Jesus Christ from Nazareth. The omnipotent, cosmic, invisible God was replaced by a simple man, Jesus, who described himself as God's son. It was God embodied by a human being, who was close to other human beings, who could be seen and directly addressed. From abstract and absent, God turned into a personal, real figure:

> The God was a God in the present, a personal God, a spontaneous and intimate God. God, the unattainable Creator of the universe, had grown to be so near and so to add some understanding of man that he was like a father.
>
> (Moreno, 1948a, pp. 95–96)

The exception associated with Jesus was his ability to embody and contain God within himself. This Godhead, however, was embodied by one person alone. Even Jesus Christ's Godhead suited a certain time in history, but no longer does. Moreno believed there was a call for a different, new Godhead model to address the needs as implied by the human living of his time.

The Third Godhead Model. Namely, "I-God"; this places the self as God. Moreno maintained that the forces ruling the world were creativity and spontaneity, and he referred to those forces as God. In this context, God is represented as the absolute creator of the world (Nolte, Smallwood, and Weistart, 1975, p. 72). God, who is embodied by spontaneity and creativity, is no longer a powerful, distinguished entity who dwells in heaven, but some kind of a force that exists in every human being. Thus, this is a so-called cosmic God. Moreno pictured God as acting through every person's creativity (Blatner, 2000, p. 73). God exists within man and embodies himself by man, because a person is capable of acting creatively and spontaneously (Tyson, 1966, p. 228). It is a new, direct interaction with God who comes from within, from our personality through the self (Nolte et al., 1975, p. 73). Moreno adopted the term "I" as a symbolic expression for God. I am God, the creator.

> I formulated in the Testament des Vaters the most radical antithesis of our time by making my "I", the I and "self" of the weak human bastard, the same and identical with I and self of God, The Creator of the world [. . .] The idea of God became a revolutionary category, removed from the beginning of time into the present, into the self, into the every I.
>
> (Moreno, 1947a, p. 12)

The new self could not imagine its birth without being its own creator. He could not imagine any future of a world which had ever been created without him being its creator, personally responsible for that, either (Moreno, 1947a, p. 13; Moreno, 1989, p. 12). The imperative in his book *The Words of the Father* (1920) is "be creative", namely, "be God", which, in turn, means the responsibility of creating human world is man's himself. Since "I-God" is I, and since the rest of the universe's point of view is comprised within my mind, I have no way of escaping responsibility for humanity as a whole (J. D. Moreno, 1994, pp. 99–101).

None of Moreno's ideas have been criticized more harshly than his "I am God" declaration, which was viewed as megalomaniac (Power, 1975, p. 166). Moreno claimed that the declaration "I am God" was universal, stemming from a state of feeling micro-maniac, rather than megalomaniac, and applies to all human beings.

> It is not the I of a lonely, singular person but the I of everyone. But it is the I which matters; it is the I which was provocative and new. And it is the I-God with whom we are all connected. It is the I which becomes the We.
>
> (Moreno and Z. T. Moreno, 1969, p. 21)

The relation between Godliness and creativity

Very early in his life, Moreno began wondering of the source and nature of God. If there is God, who may a person play, act and think in terms of a relationship which is meaningful for divine sources of the entire creation and formation? While the qualities pertaining to the image of God, demonstrating the divine order's supremacy, super-naturalness and wisdom, were the focus of the pertaining discussion, his role as a spontaneous creator, the most revolutionary term of divine functioning in Moreno's opinion, God of the first day of creation was almost always neglected (Moreno, 1964a, pp. 107–108). When Moreno realized that God's state as the creator of the first day in the creation process was neglected, even symbolically, he stated:

> My first concern was the God as he was starting out to create the world, not so much "what" he does but "why" and "how", the Deus Primus or the Creator in situ, this is the God of the first day as against the God "after" the world is created. This is the genesis of God, the creator, rather than the genesis of creation.
>
> (Moreno, 1953, p. xvii)

As mentioned, God's connection to Godhead is related to the creation concept. Moreno started with the idea that Godhead and the creation process are one. For him, "God" means creativity. God is the first creator of the universe, and hence constitutes a model of creative behavior (Johnson, 1974, p. 445). Moreno identified the power of the creator as a God-like force, who is also present within every human being, granting them responsibility for their own creativity. In other words, people share a creative force, the supreme creator (Kipper, 1986, p. 11), which is a philosophy of creation's origin: if I create, then I am like God; creation comes from within me, hence God comes from within me as well. When Moreno declared "I am God", he meant to say "I create". If I create, everybody is capable of creating; everybody can be God and propose his own version of God to others (Moreno and Z. T. Moreno, 1969, p. 21).

The creative act

The idea underlying the term "creativity" is that creative action should be distinguished from the products of such an action. Creative acts represent the means by which spontaneity is manifested through the course of life; hence, one of the creative act's characteristics is its connection to spontaneity, thereby allowing one to keep on consuming energy and facilitating its distinction. Another characteristic of creative acts is their tendency to suddenly, unexpectedly rise to the surface. Additionally, there is a quality to the creative act which has been described as unrealistic. This aspect stems from the observation that the source of inspiration which induces the creative act is not related to realistic thinking or any inhibiting causes. The act rises in order to transform the reality from which it rises (Kipper, 1986, pp. 11–13; Kipper, 1996, pp. 64–65). This idea is manifested through Moreno's view, who believes that the act of creation involves something which has preceded the given reality and all that is beyond it (Moreno, 1964a, p. 35).

Furthermore, creativity brings something new into man's existing knowledge reserve, and in many cases, creation is a relationship which has not existed before (Bischof, 1970, p. 255). God-play is creatively defined as utmost involvement of anything which has not yet been born out of the chaos at the very first moment of being. God created inverse, contradictory roles; thus new things always emerge from their original locus nascendi (Moreno, 1953, p. xvii), and the creative act and the act's locus nascendi are directly related. The true meaning of various behavioral manifestations becomes clear when it appears at their original context (Kipper, 1986, p. 13). Any idea or form has its most suitable, proper place where its meaning is perfectly, ideally expressed (Moreno, 1964a, pp. 25–27). When creative expression is removed from the context in which it was originally induced and placed elsewhere, its meaning changes. By that, Moreno intended to claim that the psychological, physical and emotional transformation the creator undergoes while giving birth to the creation, the original form emerging when the product has not yet been complete but still being created, is not the same process undergone by those who execute the final product for that creation. The creative matrix, the source from which creativity acts, involves the artist's entire personality while giving birth to the creation. In Moreno's opinion, the process of creating those new artistic products bears greater value for the human experience than originally attributed. The first attempts of creating a work of art are just as important as the final product, as imperfect as they may be (Moreno, 1960a, pp. 35–37).

Traditionally, creativity is defined as "bringing something new into being", whether the creation involves a new behavior, construction of a building, a literary work or establishment of a government. It may be new for the individual, but not necessarily so for the rest of the world, or it may be new for the individual and also generally new to the world (Bischof, 1970, p. 258).

Development of the creativity concept

The Waves of Thought addressing creativity were first initiated by philosopher Henri Bergson (1859–1941), who integrated the creativity principle into philosophy at a time when scientists assumed such a concept did not exist in objective sciences (Moreno, 1974, p. 73). In his book *Evolution créatrice* (Creative Evolution, 1907) he coined the term *élan vital* (vital force). This is a hypothetical explanation of an organism's evolutionary development, which Bergson linked with awareness. Bergson believed that life means constant freedom and creation. Determinism's past and future is the brain's outcome, with the brain itself being the final outcome of evolution. The brain is a tool created for a special role, which does not involve capturing life in its temporary flow, but rather to conceive and organize all that's given in space. According to Bergson, the world is incessant creativity, with no beginning, peace or relaxation (Moreno, 1964a, p. 9).

According to Bergson, the Duration (Durée) is constant, incessant, consistent and continuously creative. It was a revolutionary category, since every particle of Duration was brief, and all man has to do is delve into the immediate experience in order to partake of that flow of creativity, that vital force (Moreno, 1975, p. 7).

Moreno thought that of all modern philosophers, Bergson was closest to the matter's essence. He was sensitive enough to creativity's dynamics, which indicated significant progression in creativity-related thinking.

> [I] brought man in his immediate inner experience in contact with evolution [. . .] but this élan vital was in itself insufficient. If his creative evolution should be true it cried for a demonstration for its continuity in the realm of action, or as we formulated it then for the evolution of the "creator".
>
> (Moreno, 1953, p. 8)

Moreno thought that although Bergson's disapproval of the intellectual-mathematical structure was justified, he went too far with the time dimension and measurement of the mechanical moment. His theory does not refer to "moment", but to "duration". With the annulment of those time dimensions, Bergson annulled the creative moment. In such a scheme, no room was found for a "moment":

> But without the moment as locus nascendi, a theory of spontaneity and creativity threatens to remain entirely metaphysical or to become entirely automatic.
>
> (Moreno, 1964a, p. 9)

From Moreno's point of view, Bergson did not bridge between complete, absolute creativity and the person who constructs the time and space in which he lives. The result is, then, that even if these immediate experiences were to have the quality of final reality he claimed for them, they have an irrational status and hence are useless to methodology and scientific progress (Moreno, 1975, p. 7).

Moreno thought Bergson's work remained a biology covered with a mysterious aura. Moreno believed he succeeded in implementing the practice of élan vital, thereby developing the creative act of psychology (Moreno, 1974, p. 76). Moreno expanded Bergson's idea regarding creativity that is constant in the world by emphasizing the current moment's creative act category, as well as by developing the I-creator concept (Moreno, 1953, p. 8). He also indicated the potential of taking a significant part in creativity's personal and collective thinking.

> [T]he principle of spontaneity and creativity – centering around the phenomenon of the creator – is the ultimate source of all existence and of all values. This is the canon of the creator, the widest possible generalization which a mind can visualize.
>
> (Moreno, 1948a, p. 93)

> In the beginning was the Word, said St. John of the Gospel. In the beginning was the dead, exclaimed Goethe's Faust. Let us go further. In the beginning was the doer, the actor; in the beginning was I, the creator of the universe.
>
> (Moreno, 1947a, p. 13)

Creativity's importance

The world is infinite creativity. Creativity is the world's problem, and therefore the problem of existence as a whole; a problem of religion, science, psychology, sociometry and human relations. Yet creativity is not a distinct category – mystic, aristocratic, or theological. Creativity also lies in the bottom and in regression, in the microcosm, as well as in the macrocosm. It lies within both the physical and social atom. It is the eternal form of existence, infinite, yet most temporary, acting here and now (Moreno, 1974, p. 75).

Eventually, the future of any culture is determined by its members' creativity. Dysfunction in creativity, which Moreno defines as creativity neurosis, is a disease tormenting the most basic group: the creative man in the human race. In this state, redefining the creativity principle will be highly important, as will the ability to compare creativity's distorted forms to original creativity.

In Moreno's eyes, creativity is the most important value in the world's and people's psychological development; otherwise, stagnation occurs, which simply means regression. Creativity leads humanity to a constructive response to new circumstances, and not only in adapting to a new condition. As a matter of fact, creativity is the most important factor in mental health, and only the creative person will be able to survive, especially in a technocratic world. Other than encountering new circumstances, personality is required to create them. This is a task one may prepare and train for.

> It is for these reasons that I emphasize the therapeutic technique of spontaneity – creativity. If one accepts the assumption that the more creative the personality, the more problems it can solve, and that the more creative it is the better it can structure and predict the future, then it seems mandatory that we must train for creativity.
>
> (Moreno, 1964b, pp. 158–159)

In order to be feasible, creativity needs stimulants, its main stimulant being spontaneity. Moreno states it is a kind of stimulant which may be accompanied by other stimulants or forces in the universe (Moreno, 1956, p. 372).

In the psychodramatic philosophy, spontaneity is associated with the willingness underlying a given action, while creativity is associated with the action itself. Spontaneity is creativity's constant companion. It is the existential factor intervening in favor of the creative process to be released (Moreno, 1956, p. 359). Being creativity's stimulant, spontaneity is to serve as a mediator enhancing it (Kipper, 1967, p. 63). The search for the distinction which will facilitate the creative act yielded spontaneity's centrality concept and the view of time as a frozen moment, according to Moreno (Moreno, 1964b, p. 158; Moreno, 1960b, p. 9).

Spontaneity

Essentially, spontaneity is a theological idea which was later converted into a therapeutic-scientific term. The analogy between the "I-God" concept, which means "I-creator", and "spontaneity" is better understood through the term's characteristics.

Spontaneity is a fundamental concept in Moreno's personality theory, which explains the motivation underlying a person's behavior, which is manifested as an energy that is subtle and hidden, unless it is expressed through some vector. Spontaneity's presence may be inferred from a person's apparent behavior, which results from it, as an expression of emotions or verbal expression. Additionally, and most importantly, it is an energy which may not be preserved or stored. It must be consumed as a moment's incentive, in the sense of "all or nothing", so as to allow new energy in. The unpreserved aspect of spontaneity, as well as the inability to transfer past energy, as a crucial component in Moreno's existential philosophy, corresponding to the "moment" theory and focusing upon the immediate present, stemmed from the belief that the here and now is the most important time and, psychologically, most significant. The emphasis on the present and the concretization of the moment idea contribute greatly to understanding the spontaneity concept with all its characteristics, serving as the focus of analysis (Kipper, 1986, pp. 11–12).

Kipper believes there is a good reason to assume those spontaneity characteristics validate the fact that it is a theological term. The cosmodynamic source, the fact that energy may not be stored and its role in enhancing creativity all correspond to the philosophical aspect (Kipper, 1967, p. 64).

> We have first to recognize the fact that spontaneity can operate in our mental universe and evoke levels of organized expression that are not fully traceable to preceding determinates.
>
> (Moreno, in Kipper, 1967, p. 6)

The cosmodynamic aspect of spontaneity has not been researched sufficiently, though it has been supposed to shed light on spontaneity's origin and birth (Kipper, 1967, p. 62). Possibly, understanding mental energy's essence in general, and spontaneous energy in particular, may better elucidate the cosmodynamic aspect of spontaneity.

Spontaneity and psychic energy in the religious and scientific aspects

"Mental energy" encompasses all personality expressions, such as joy, optimism, motivation, ambition and hope, granting them one common meaning. A person experiences mental energy in his personality as abundance, whose overall intensity constantly evolves. All personality theories accept the assumption that a mental energy reserve is produced within one's personality. This reserve may decline and then rise again. It is thus questioned from where that mental energy stems and renews itself. The answer to the latter question may come from two directions. The one is related to Freud and psychoanalysis, the other is related to the mystic-religious approach (Shatil, 1994, p. 13).

According to the psychoanalytical approach, the energy stems from a physiological source, namely, a neurological stimulation which accumulates as inclinational tension. When mental energy comes in contact with reality, it dissipates. Shatil (1994, p. 14) explains that according to the Kabbalistic-Hassidic view, which may be found in the works of Ha'ari, Rabbi Nachman of Breslov and Martin Buber, that energy stems from a transcendent source. The pure mental energy is robbed by the evil forces within one's personality and outside of it,

Personality fulfills a key position in psychology's personality theories, always in relation to the formative dimension of its definition as natural sciences' matter or energy conservation principle; thus personality theories in psychology require the assumptions of the energy conservation principle and safeguarding mysticism (Shatil, 1994, pp. 18–19).

Based upon the energy conservation principle, any system consuming energy needs an external innovation source, based upon the three formative dimensions: conserve, use and reversibility. In other words, the natural entity which is manifested in nature as a certain force is capable of metamorphosis, namely, converting itself into a different force or manifestation. The energy which has supposedly disappeared upon the end of the former force's action does not disappear at all. Rather, it continues living, just as a different force or form.

According to the safeguarding mysticism principle's assumption, mental energy is an intrapersonal expression, which may not flow within the interpersonal space or be observed or measured. Freud accepted the assumption comprised in the conservation principle, which maintains the source of mental energy is external to personality itself. He, however, adhered to the mysticism safeguarding principle. His solution relies on the dual meaning of the term "inclination", which implies physical-neurological tension, on the one hand, and primeval wishes on a mental level, on the other hand. There is a constant conversion process, which involves physical-neurological tension, the relief of which has been postponed and repressed, but continues living in the recesses of the mental system, until it rises to the mind level and is thus relieved. Yet the process itself, where physical tension is converted into mental, nonphysical tension, remains obscure. Freud adhered to the assumption concerning the external innovation source of mental energy, while rejecting the transcendental flow of mental energy.

The religious view rejects the assumption regarding the safeguarding of mysticism. Yet it accepts the assumption that a person is always surrounded by an abundance of divine vitality, which is the external, transcendent source that nurtures one's personality. A person is to prepare and train himself to benefit from that abundance. In other words, spiritual or mental energy may flow from outside and renew one's personality system's vitality, while the energy flows on a transpersonal sphere (Shatil, 1994, pp. 13–17). The abundance is absorbed by man on a cognitive level, but it is intertwined with divine providence, which is yielded by this abundance (Auerbach, 1972, p. 469).

In other words, it is some sort of additional transcendent power, which removes some external challenges from a person's path, facilitating him in escaping them. At any moment, reality's existence is due to the constant giving of life from the creator. The latter evokes the need to give and influence. When one influences and gives, one induces the necessary metaphysical conditions for the descending of power and energy from above (Berg, 1984, p. 62).

Religious and scientific influence on Moreno's perception

Religious influence

Moreno supported the religious approach concerning energy in relation to three matters: (1) transcendent abundance absorption, (2) the mind's centrality and (3) an open personality. Similar to the religious perception, Moreno believed in transcendent abundance absorption and energy's transition in the intrapersonal sphere. Spontaneity is not a process occurring within the individual alone. It also involves a flow of emotions associated with another individual's spontaneous state. Naturally, consequently to contact between people, spontaneity will be manifested by interpersonal relationships. Energy flowing through interpersonal communication is referred to as tele (Moreno, 1985, p. 81), a term which will be broadly explained later on.

Freud engaged in the individual's soul only, referring to the mental energy, the libido, whose rate, in his opinion, is constant from birth. In Moreno's eyes, this energy does not serve the individual only, but also encompasses the group and the cosmos, being enhanced with spontaneity and creativity (Z. T. Moreno, 2000, p. xvi).

Scientific influence

The time–space–energy reference framework is common in physical sciences. The concepts "spontaneity" and "creativity" have been broadly accepted by the humanities. Moreno attempted to examine whether those concepts may be adapted to the physical sciences. For that purpose, he examined the energy conservation principle. This principle had become an axiom in physical sciences and a model for the most well-known psychological and social systems, such as the Freudian libido. Freud assumed that if the libidinal energy is not practically channeled in one direction, it is channeled to other directions in order to maintain balance. In Moreno's opinion, Freud never attempted to understand that the unapplied influence disappears, since, similar to other scientists of his generation, he relied upon the physical energy conservation principle, an idea that misled him. If this principle or model is implemented with the energy attributed to spontaneity, one will be forced to believe that man possesses a given quantity of accumulated spontaneity, to which he or she connects throughout the course of life, but it decreases the more he is dominated by cultural conserves. While in action, one draws energy from that reserve, and if not cautious enough, he might use up the whole quantity, or even overdraw it (Moreno, 1975, p. 10)!

Moreno thought that if spontaneity means to be consistently conserved, then two types of energy should be distinguished: one is conservable energy, and the other is nonconservable. Conserved energy may be found in cultural conserves. It may be conserved or consumed when desired and used in different times. Yet there is another type of energy, which is to be consumed as soon as it arises. It must emerge in order to be consumed, and it must be consumed in order to make room for new energy to emerge, as in certain animals, who are born and die during the act of love (Moreno, 1964b, p. 161).

Spontaneous energy contradicted the energy conservation principle, at least in man's psycho-social-cultural world. However, while Moreno examined how spontaneity and creativity may adapt into the universal energy system, he draws evidence from other sciences (Moreno, 1956, pp. 370–371). Respectively, spontaneity and creativity theory do not completely annul the view of energy as an organized system of physical forces; rather than being the origin and beginning of each and every process, as in libido's case, it is the end of the process. Energy reappears as cultural conservation, as the final product; for example, a musical piece's final product, where hidden musical energy is conserved on a disc. Musical energy is not lost. Thus, the energy conservation principle applies in correspondence to cultural conservation; hence, Moreno proposes the following formula:

E (energy) = M (mass) analogous to C (conserve)

This formula is possible if creativity, too, is explained in terms of energy, being the ultimate source of all cultural conserves – the precious equivalent of certain matters in the physical world, such as uranium, which accumulates an enormous quantity of energy. Consequently the constantly growing influence of Einstein's theory of relativity nuclear physics had developed in turn transformed the physical energy concept. It began with the discovery that uranium was radioactive, and gradually, the assumption that the matter may be destroyed gradually penetrated and become common. The very idea that a matter may be produced and converted into energy was a turning point in the way the energy conservation principle was viewed. Energy as understood by Einstein was not only conservable and convertible, but also de-conservable (the antonym of conservation). The physical energy level has reached such a great scope of being precedential that it allows a space for action, freedom and flexibility, which led Moreno to assume another basic principle:

C (creativity) includes E (energy) = M (matter)

It is then that energy and matter will be subforms of creativity (Moreno, 1956, pp. 370–371). Creativity is classified as the primary matter. It is the X-variable, which may be identified by its actions. In order to be effective, he requires a stimulant; spontaneity serves as creativity's stimulant (Moreno, 1964b, pp. 158). X faces creativity's unknown in the world, thereby yielding another formula:

C = X + E (or M)

Moreno thought the adaptation of the spontaneity-creativity principle into the energy conservation system is vital and should not be relinquished as long as the energy conservation principle is independently maintained as an absolute universal validity and, not connected to any human agencies (Moreno, 1956, pp. 370–371). Physicist Max Planck expressed his opinion of this principle by stating:

> My mind absorbed avidly, like a revelation the first law I know to possess absolute universal validity, independently from all human agency; the principle of the [conservation] of energy.
>
> (Planck, in Moreno, 1956, p. 362)

Moreno established his protest against the energy conservation principle's absolutism on the basis of observations of spontaneity and creativity at the context of human productivity. He believed that since this thought was proposed by a social scientist, it was inevitable that it would encounter opposition on the part of those who engage in exact sciences who would reject this thought, claiming it was imaginary, yet surprisingly, Moreno's views were reinforced by physicists as Max Planck, who said the following:

> The principle of the [conservation] of energy, after all, is an experimental law. Accordingly, although today it is considered to be universal and all embracing, its validity may one day have to be restricted – and in fact such a curtailment of its universal applicability has been sometimes suspected in nuclear physics.
>
> (Planck, in Moreno, 1956, pp. 371–372)

Nonetheless, Moreno did not completely abandon the principle of energy conservation. He believed it was a valid principle, as long as it is emphasized to a lesser extent and corresponds to the unconservable energy idea.

> It is truism to state that the universe cannot exist without physical and mental energy which can be preserved. However, it is more important to realize that without the other kind of energy, the un-conservable kind – spontaneity – the creativity of the universe could neither start nor run. It would come to a standstill.
>
> (Moreno, 1964b, pp. 161–162)

How does one attain spontaneous energy in the first place? The answer to this question is far from being clear. Moreno suggested that spontaneity exists as sui generia, a separate kind. Typologically, on the continuum, the spontaneity factor is placed somewhere between innate factors and environmental factors. Still, it belongs to none of those categories. It is an independent area affected by those factors, but not determined by them. It may simply be stated that spontaneity is a human quality whose exact source is unknown (Kipper, 1986, p. 12).

All human beings have been blessed with spontaneity, though they may differ in their level of talent and the ability to employ it (Moreno, 1956, p. 369). Curiously, spontaneity was also characterized as a phenomenon which may be observed. Initially, this characteristic seems to make no sense, since it does not correspond to another characteristic of spontaneity, namely, its definition as energy. May energy be directly observed, in particular, mental energy?

At any rate, a more meticulous examination indicates that those two characteristics are not necessarily conflicting. A phenomenon is observable even if it is not an absolutely tangible occurrence. There is a separate category of experiences, which may be viewed as unobservable, yet real. Love and hatred are a proper example of this. Those phenomena become distinct through mediation of a different expression of an actual, tangible behavior (Kipper, 1986, p. 12). Likewise, spontaneity is essentially a hypothetical structure, which is operatively defined in terms of its discoveries or influences (Rabson, 1979, p. 40).

> No one has ever seen spontaneity. Spontaneity is a hypothesis. It is supposed to manifest itself in the warming process of the creative art.
>
> (Moreno, 1956, p. 372)

Spontaneity: definition and functions

Spontaneity's scientific definition is different from its literal, day-to-day definition. The daily use of that term makes a reference to it as a free expression of emotions, without control, inhibition or prior planning, an automatic, reflexive response (Moreno, 1956, p. 392). At the psychodramatic context, however, the use of the term is different. Moreno defined spontaneity as a proper response to a new situation, as well as a proper response to a past situation (Moreno, 1964, 1941, 1944, 1953, p. 366). The spontaneity concept conserves the concept of action out of neutral feelings and free will, yet contains an element of direction and block (Kipper, 1986, p. 11). From Moreno's point of view, spontaneity is the proper response, not just a free one (Kipper, 1967, 1986).

> It propels the individual towards an adequate response to a new situation or a new response to an old situation. Thus, while creativity is related to the act itself, spontaneity is related to the warming up to the readiness of the act.
>
> (Moreno, 1974, p. 76)

> It is the energy which moves a person towards responding adequately in a situation they have not previously experienced or facilitates the capacity to come up with a new response in a familiar situation.
>
> (Tauvon, 1998, p. 31)

In his definition of spontaneous behavior, Moreno preferred to use the word "adequate", rather than the word "appropriate" or "competent", since the word "appropriate" is associated with obedience and adaptive behavior, while the word "competence" refers to technological effectiveness and mechanical ability. Moreno wished to say that adequate behavior is essentially an autonomous achievement; the individual lives through an enormous number of roles and internal situations, over which his control is exercised (Moreno, 1956, p. 276).

As a matter of fact, reaction's adequacy became the two components of which spontaneity's formal definition consists. It is to be well timed and appear in the proper intensity – not too much, but not too little. The adequacy and novelty aspects pertain not only to the reaction, but to the situation as well. The degree of adequacy depends upon the extent to which one is familiar with the given situation. In a new situation, a person may choose not to react, display an old reaction or display a new reaction. In other words, the unpredictable situation and reaction are spontaneity's precedents. Perceiving spontaneity as reaction to quality assessment serves to identify spontaneity types: (1) Pathological spontaneity, which is a new response that is inadequate for the situation. Psychotic individuals, for instance, are capable of inducing a new response, but it does not suit the given situation. (2) Stereotypical spontaneity, which is adequate for the given situation, yet lacks innovativeness or creativity. (3) High-degree spontaneity, which is a response comprising creativity, innovativeness and adequacy for the given situation. Moreno maintained that spontaneity, by every sense of the word, yields outcomes that are new and serve certain purposes well.

A person's behavior in terms of spontaneity becomes an important criterion in assessing a reaction's quality (Kipper, 1986; pp. 11–12; Kipper, 1967, p. 64; Z. T. Moreno, 2000, p. xv ; Moreno, 1974, p. 76). As a matter of fact, spontaneity is placed on a continuum ranging from impulsive abreaction, through adequate controlled, adequate spontaneity, through creative, efficient spontaneity. It should be borne in mind that spontaneity does not act within a vacuum, but rather, in relation to phenomenon that are already understood, namely, cultural and technological conserves (Moreno, 1964b, pp. 158–159).

Moreno argued that spontaneity in various situations appears in various forms. Spontaneity's added value to a given kind of situation has not been explored. What is pathological spontaneity? What is adequate spontaneity? Hence, it is asked: How may the same concept be both an energy and a standard for the quality of a response? If that is true, can something add quality or features to an energy, based upon their characterization as either pathological, stereotypical or creative (Kipper, 1967, p. 67)? Moreno did not explain the way the situation's adequacy is determined. Nonetheless, in the author's opinion, his ideas imply that adequacy is examined by cultural and social variables. Moreno's statement is logical, but it will raise problems if we wish to empirically examine it.

The here and now and its connection to spontaneity

One of the key concepts which is important to human thought in general is the here and now concept. The moment of being, living and creating. This concept is the stepchild of the universally known philosophical and therapeutic systems because "moment" is a time unit which is difficult to define. The moment has been addressed only in relation to time and space or as a mathematical concept. In the works of most philosophers, time has appeared as a passing point from future to past, the "here in now" seemed to them unstable and thus an inadequate foundation for a system which is both philosophical and theoretical.

In Moreno's work, the here and now concept is associated with the spontaneity concept. A deep faith in humanity's infinite spontaneity and creativity underlies the here in now philosophy. All are considered equal (Tauvon, 1998, pp. 30–45). Moreno believed that he had managed to take that unusual phenomenon and channel it in a way that the here and now would be visible, thus facilitating a clearer, more lucid definition. Constructing such a definition paved the way for a spontaneity and creativity theory, through cultural conservation analysis. Moreno demonstrated the connection between the here and now, immediate action, spontaneity and creativity, as opposed to the common practice of tying spontaneity and automatic response. That first step yielded a transformation in the common thinking concerning the here and now. The next step would be positioning the spontaneous and creative matrix concept as the core of a man's world, not only as a hidden, vague source, but rather as one present on the surface of actual life. That means paving a path which will constitute a constant flow of the spontaneous matrix into cultural conserves, which will carry the spontaneous-creative matrix into the actuality and reality of a person's day-to-day life (Moreno, 1975, pp. 5–10). Moreno believed spontaneity is a quality which requires special attention in order to draw out of it the quality of action and our power as human beings. Whatever a person does *sua spont*, namely, as part of her or his nature, comprises response and responsibility to whatever occurs here and now (Meyer, in Greenberg, 1974, pp. 135–156). In that context, Moreno philosophically illustrates the here and now as follows:

> The meaning of the decision is in this moment, the here and now, even if you have lived through all the instants of the past and will live through all the instants of the future.
>
> (Moreno, 1969b, pp. 139–140)

Spontaneity and psychological determinism

The complexity of the spontaneity concept is revealed as soon as one attempts to trace its linguistic origins. The word spontaneity originates from the Latin word *sponte*, which exclusively appears in this language as the expression *sua sponte* (or with another possessive pronoun, such as *mea* – *my*, or *tua* – your, which means, "out of one's free will" (Meiers, 1947, p. 14). Moreno adhered to the Latin meaning as well (Moreno, 1985b, p. 81; 1974, p. 76). Free will is interpreted as freedom of any external or internal influence beyond one's control. This is the natural tendency of experiencing the self. It prepares the person for a deliberately free action. This freedom enhances the mind's centrality, as well as one's ability to control her or his actions.

The free will concept contradicts the psychoanalytical view (for example, Freud's), according to which there is nothing random in the human mind (Freud, 1938, p. 152). The concept is also contradictory to a view that absolutely denies determinism, as manifested by Bergson's term élan vital. While Freud's determinism allowed no room for spontaneity, Bergson's élan vital allowed no room for determinism, leaving room for creativity only, thereby going to the other extreme. Moreno synthesized both views, arguing that his theory allows room for functional operation of determinism. According to this theory, a person's development may consist of original moments, truly creative and decisive beginnings without any horror vacui, that is, a fear that there is no comfortable past behind it from which it springs (Moreno, 1964a, pp. 102–103).

> In spontaneity two selves – the conscious analytic teller and the unconscious doer – come together so to function as [a] harmonious whole. Action flows smoothly and freely, action and evaluation of action is automatic and hence unproblematic.
>
> (Williams, 1989, pp. 11)

According to Moreno's view, there may be original moments and creative beginnings with no conversation, involving no past fear. This is creativity which occurs here and now. Although the benefit of spontaneity should not be granted to each and every moment of human development, occasionally, there are moments which become those when ideas or experiences come into being (loci nascendi), which drive for experiencing of new roles. Spontaneity is not devoid of past influence. Spontaneity's intensity and scope are influenced by past experiences which inhibit, distract and oppress by arousing anxiety, thereby damaging its flow (Kipper, 1967, p. 64). Plus, spontaneity should be distinguished from impulsiveness, which lacks any creativity expression at all. If the outcome is overemotionality resulting from an impulsive action, it is far removed from what is expected from spontaneous work and is considered a pathology of spontaneity (Moreno, 1975, p. 10). A study conducted by Kipper addressing the relationship of spontaneity, impulsiveness and creativity empirically confirmed, for the first time ever, the argument that spontaneity yields creativity. Spontaneity is positively correlated to creativity, but negatively correlated to impulsiveness. The fact that spontaneity may not be impulsive facilitates in clarifying spontaneity's essence. The former term bears both negative and positive connotations, as it implies both being controlled and being free, uncontrolled. This study positions creativity as one of spontaneity's characteristics. Its conclusions do not completely correspond to Moreno's theory, but they may elucidate the idea he intended to convey while addressing spontaneous situations (Kipper, 2009).

Moreno believed spontaneity and its by-product, creativity, were of such importance that without it, any behavior would become a stereotypical one, robot-like. Spontaneous is the catalyst prompting all psychological phenomena to appear in new, fresh and flexible forms, enhancing it with the temporariness quality.

> This S-function is not satisfied expressing only the self; it is eager to create the self.
>
> (Moreno, 1964a, p. 91)

Spontaneity and mental health

Moreno's theory maintains spontaneity and mental health are positively related. Spontaneity may imply either a negative or a positive connotation. A mentally health individual possesses adequate spontaneity, while maladaptation is viewed as pathological spontaneity (Kipper, 1967, p. 67). Moreno never established any clear theory in relation to psychopathology. His only statement in this regard is the argument that a lack of spontaneity is a pathological state, and he solely presented the "pathological spontaneity" concept. Plus, although he defined spontaneity, he did not define a state where spontaneity is lacking. This sums up his only reference to psychopathology as a whole.

Basically, the more spontaneous an individual is, the mentally healthier he is, and his responses are more adequate, and vice versa. In other words, when a person does not use his reserve of energy (spontaneity) in a proper way, which is in line with reality, he will develop behaviors which will result in a lesser degree of consistency within the self and lack of socialization within a given cultural setting. The illness is manifested by anxiety, which is a function of spontaneity. If the response to a present situation is adequate, spontaneity is considered whole, and anxiety will dissipate. As spontaneity declines, anxiety will expand; as total spontaneity is lost, anxiety reaches its highest degree, namely, the point of panic (Moreno, 1953, pp. 336–337). Under such conditions, one is not capable of creating a new existence, which is necessary for his ambitions (Moreno, 1947a, p. 128). With apprehension blocking or inhibiting constructive relief, neurosis may occur (Howard, 1963, pp. 1–7).

Apprehension lives on, regardless of traumas and frustrations which may emerge in one's life. Traumas emphasize or intensify apprehension, but never induce it. Apprehension stems from the individual's separation from the rest of the universe. The individual finds himself withdrawn from vital relationships; the once loved and familiar world becomes uncanny, and the withdrawal results in a sense of helplessness and death (Moreno, 1964b, p. 163).

It may be concluded that according to Moreno, a vast range of cognitive and mental pathology may be described through the anxiety and failure of spontaneity development concept, or some sort of an addictive clinging on to the old solutions, as though they represent safeguards for the rest of our lives (Moreno, 1987, p. 47). A healthy person will demonstrate high spontaneity, whereas a sick person will demonstrate low spontaneity. The opposite of spontaneity is not "nonspontaneity". Rather, there are two equivalent scales; one describes spontaneity, and the other describes a lack of spontaneity. Both scales rank those qualities from lowest to highest. There may be a state of high lack of spontaneity, which is considered pathological, and there may be a state of high spontaneity, which is considered a healthy state. The general relationship between the scales is inverse: one cannot be both spontaneous and nonspontaneous in the same situation and at the same time. In certain situations, a person may be spontaneous, and nonspontaneous in others; hence there is no scale without spontaneity (Kipper, 2009). Theoretically, the matter may be summed up by stating that individuals who have achieved high spontaneity are expected to be more tuned to the present, namely, to be very attentive to the given moment. Individuals who focus upon the past are characterized as individuals with recurrent habits and behaviors (Kipper, D. A. & Christoforou, A., 2006, p. 32).

Training for spontaneity

Moreno argued that spontaneity appears as the most ancient phylogenetic agent which penetrates into human behavior, probably more ancient than memory, intelligence or sex. It is present in the no-developed fetal stage, but bears unlimited training potential (Moreno, 1947a, p. 7). When spontaneity is examined in relation to other human mental functions, such as intelligence and memory, the sense for spontaneity seems least developed, which Moreno justified by stating that in the cultural conservation age we have developed, a person employs memory and intelligence to a greater extent than developing and training spontaneity.

> The sense for spontaneity, as a cerebral function, shows a more rudimentary development than any other important fundamental function of the central nervous system.
>
> (Moreno, 1947a, p. 40)

The amount of spontaneity available to man in this world is rather small, but it is enough for survival. The incapability of coping with the instability characteristic of the here and now, the ability to correspond accordingly and the innovation encouraged man to develop intelligence, memory and cultural and social conservations. The problem is that spontaneity may not be accumulated. One may either be spontaneous at a given moment or not (Moreno, 1974, p. 80). This rule may justify the inferiority a person experiences while facing unexpected situations (Moreno, 1947a, p. 40). Unexpected situations are situations where memory or intelligence is not sufficiently developed to facilitate proper coping with various life situations.

One of Moreno's first discoveries was that spontaneity may age and be consumed if a person does not consider her or his own development. Lack of inner control may constitute a distraction when a new act's spontaneity emerges. Another discovery was that one may be trained for spontaneity, regardless of its low intensity in the outset (Moreno, 1947a, p. 7). The greater part of the human mind and its pathology may be attributed to insufficient development of spontaneity, and consequently, to an inability to mobilize or recruit sources of creativity. Hence, the prospect of "training" for spontaneity is a hope-inspiring quality, which requires exploration by scientists, educators and therapists. (Moreno, 1974, p. 80).

Until Moreno's time, spontaneity was conceived as a factor which should not and may not be induced through any techniques. Moreno believed training and enhancing a person's spontaneity was possible by means of psychodramatic techniques, which had been established to serve that purpose (Kipper, 1967, p. 64). Apparently, spontaneity training as a concept does not make any sense. How may one train in order to develop spontaneity and still argue that it is an innate skill?

If spontaneity were possible to acquire through training, then its parts subjected to improvement and those determined by virtue of innate skill should be identified. The traditional resolution of this tension, maintaining that it all has to do with the individual's potential, does not clear the difficulty, since spontaneity is an integral part of the human being and is not conservable; nor is it storable. Furthermore, it is difficult to understand how one may train for spontaneity and how the latter may be developed, with the definition of spontaneity as energy to be employed here and now. Plus, if spontaneity begins as a constitutional factor, why should we consider the cosmodynamic principle in this etiology? Which of the two is unnecessary? While the cosmodynamic motivation concept suits the theory's essence, the constitutional explanation is a typical example for deterministic thinking. The latter undoubtedly encounters the theological doctrine of direction to future goals. Kipper thinks it may be assumed that it is not spontaneity that one trains for, but some mechanism skilled to induce spontaneity, and the two are, of course, not identical. He believes training is associated with the warming-up concept, which will be elucidated in due course (Kipper, 1967, p. 67). In Kipper's opinion, the answer to those questions, which Moreno himself did not address, is the transformation of the spontaneity characteristic from "energy" to a "state of readiness for action":

> A positive, emotional and attributable state of mind coupled with the readiness to act freely.
>
> (Kipper, 2010)

These states, as Kipper maintained, may be acquired through practice.

Furthermore, the "states" are not automatically aroused. They are not preliminarily present; they do not come into being by virtue of a conscious wish, but rather, by virtue of the individual's readiness and preparation for free action. This readiness expands the more the warming-up enhances the awareness of spontaneity. This whole process recurs time and time again, regardless of the proximity of two consecutive situations (Moreno, 1964a, p. 37).

Thus, in training for spontaneity, Moreno means, in fact, to say that one may be warmed up by means of an external training, thereby arousing the spontaneous states within the individual and employing them for the present need.

Readiness for spontaneity training may be based upon the action theory in the context of a baby's development, which will be addressed in Chapter 3. This theory maintains that the baby learns through experience and action aimed at obtaining those things he needs. His learning is directly related to action, and his actions are need based. If, for instance, hunger arises, the baby will attempt to satiate his hunger by obtaining food. Thus occurs active learning as to how to obtain food. The active experience at its best occurs at the moment of birth and immediately afterwards, diminishing throughout the course of life, hitting the bottom sometime at the end of one's life. In the course of life, one turns to her or his reserve energy, but to a diminishing extent the more he is dominated by cultural conserves. When the child comes of age, the learning and need fulfillment processes occur through knowledge acquisition, not through active experience, and regardless of immediate needs. From this point on, Moreno maintains, two centers develop: the act center and the content center. Those centers develop separately, operating in parallel, never meeting.

> The material learned does not reach the act-center of personality. A shut-in memory develops and prevents the integration of the factual knowledge into the active personality of the individual.
>
> (Moreno, 1964a, p. 139)

However, Moreno believed that an adult who acts upon a moment's incentive, having no reserves from which he may draw energy (at least not consciously) while being forced to cope with new situations, is similar to the situations with which a baby is forced to cope early in his life (Moreno, 1975, p. 11). Here, in Moreno's opinion, the spontaneity training method should be implemented in order to restore the active learning method for the adult as well. A person has not been trained to rely upon spontaneity's reserve of energy. He possesses no alternative to facilitate him in producing the same quantity of emotions, thoughts and acts exactly as demanded by the new situation, since the surplus may tempt him to hoard the energy, thereby coming full circle toward cultural conservation (Moreno, 1975, p. 10). Hence, the human organism must be like a reserve of free spontaneity, so he is constantly prepared and able to present the variety of immediate, quick and useful prospects (Moreno, 1975, p. 14).

Moreno's training for spontaneity idea may be fruitful in itself, since if we succeed in making people more spontaneous, they will be mentally healthier. In the author's opinion, however, the attempt to convert the adult's passive learning into active learning, similar to the baby's way of action, is deficient and may not be completely right. It is easily evident that the baby's active learning is possible because his behavioral range is small. The problem lying within an adult's active learning stems from the fact that intellectual strengths, as well as memory and intelligence strengths, are already present. Any attempt to neutralize them through the play experience is contradictory to any outlook of developmental psychology. Thus, theoretically, it may not be stated that the learning ideal is a proper form for action. Moreno's statement has never been examined in light of developments in statistics and psychology, which addressed processes and stimulus–reaction mediators, such as cognition, though according to Moreno spontaneity precedes cognition, memory and the unconscious.

Perhaps under certain conditions spontaneity may be employed in situations where the other elements are developed, and the emphasis shall be put on active learning rather than experience and memory. If, for instance, an individual's past was traumatic, then rather than relying upon it, one should experience the here and now. Furthermore, in the author's opinion, an active, recurrent expression of certain situations eventually becomes an integral part of personality, even if no attempt to neutralize intelligence or memory occurs. In such an expression, catharsis occurs, as well as integration, rather than purification involving relief and abreaction. If spontaneity indeed yields mental health, then it is clearly personality's healthy part. In order to be healthier, one must work on the less healthy parts. The psychological processes involving spontaneous behaviors are shame, fear and anxiety lest one fails or looks stupid. People are to be rid of those so as to facilitate their spontaneous acting. That may be achieved through training for spontaneity.

Spontaneity: discussion and critique

Since the end of World War II, interest in the concept of spontaneity has grown in the area of education, and from there, has expanded to all types of arts: singing, music, dance and painting, as well as to psychodrama and the fields of religion and politics. The extensively growing implementation of spontaneity has brought about a revolution in terms of understanding the concept's practical and actual meaning. For Moreno, the concept has undergone development and evolution of meaning until he managed to generally consolidate a general perception of the concept, as well as of the other complex ideas it represents.

> Spontaneity and "spontaneous" have finally come to mean value – a human value. Spontaneity has become a biological as well as a social value. It is today a frame of reference for the scientist as well as for the politician, for the artist as well as for the educator.
>
> (Moreno, 1975, p. 7)

Traditionally, spontaneity has been discussed by philosophers such as Bergson and Charles Peirce (1839–1914), but not by psychologists and not in the context of psychopathology. Moreno argues that in psychological literature, spontaneity and spontaneous behavior are present, though negligibly, since psychologists viewed them as immaturity, childishness, life lacking awareness and a dangerous emotional relief. Moreno was credited with being the first who, on the one hand, turned spontaneity into a key concept in classical psychodrama's theory, representing a general philosophical perception, and, on the other hand, to a specific therapeutic mediator.

From its philosophical aspect, the "spontaneous person" idea mirrors a way of life, as well as a general outlook on life, which appreciated the advantage lying within living "here and now". As a therapeutic mediator, spontaneity is supposed to be a healing element, which should, hopefully, enhance openness, reducing inhibition and suppression, thereby improving the individual's personal welfare and emotional healthy (Kipper D. A. & Christoforou A., 2006, p. 24). This duality, consisting of a general outlook on the one hand and a specific therapeutic mediator on the other hand, caused a certain degree of embarrassment in relation to spontaneity's meaning and the ways in which it is manifested (Kipper, 1967, 1986, 2002; Kipper and Hundal, 2005, p. 119). In the philosophical sphere, for instance, Peirce defined spontaneity as follows:

> What is spontaneity? It is the character of not resulting by law from something antecedent. I do not know what you can make out of the meaning of spontaneity but newness, freshness and diversity.
>
> (Peirce, in Moreno, 1974, p. 80)

Moreno acknowledged the fact that Peirce, the founder of pragmatism, was the key pioneer in the concept of spontaneity's shaping and development, instigating its leap forward. He believed, however, that his ideas had remained abstract and metaphysical, and did not succeed in attaining the degree of concretization to which Moreno was able to bring them. Creativity and spontaneity, the complementary concepts, are not abstract elements, but rather, practical functions among human beings, fulfilling a role in human relationships and interactions (Moreno, 1956, p. 631).

As far as Moreno was concerned, the weak point in Peirce's work is his view of spontaneity as a generalized response to generalized situations, rather than as being materialized and real. Coincidence and spontaneity were the same in his eyes. Moreno argued the way in which he suggested training for spontaneity entailed practicing spontaneity. It could not be conceded in order to verify the theory (Moreno, 1972, p. 209). For Moreno, spontaneity was a bridge safely connecting ontology and science, since it constituted the ultimate means, more than any other concept he knew, to clarify all the world's living and nonliving phenomena. Moreno maintained Peirce was an observing philosopher, rather than a playing philosopher. He did not attempt to change the world. He merely attempted to understand it. Yet society may not be understood as long as no attempt to evolve it occurs. Thus, Peirce's view remained amorphous. Moreno, on the contrary, brings the therapeutic players of the great religions, which, in their time, penetrated human nature by acting and fulfilling spontaneity themselves. A psychodramatic analysis revealed that those are the strategic seeds of a profound action underlying the religious therapist's external inspiration, being connected to an action strategy in the therapeutic theater (Moreno, 1964a, pp. 9–10). With such conceptual guidance, it is relatively easy to establish analogous concepts in all areas of sciences, yielding a monistic worldview addressing social phenomena. The religious therapists indicate that human beings do not behave as automats or robots, but contribute in varying degrees, demonstrating initiative and autonomy. Zerka Moreno argued that nobody before Moreno put forth such a consistent effort to prove that spontaneity and creativity are special functions of the human brain, and, unfortunately, those qualities had not been properly appreciated and acknowledged by western cultures as were intelligence, memory or motor control, and particularly behavioral adaptation and conformity (Z. T. Moreno, 2000, p. xv).

Not only did Moreno think spontaneity may be practiced and concretely demonstrated, he also maintained that role playing is the ultimate way of prompting spontaneity. Initially, many misinterpreted the latter assumption, as though Moreno was attempting to say that spontaneity manifests itself only in cases where a person is in a state of action. Moreno clarified that point, claiming that spontaneity may lie within a person even when he thinks, rests or feels (Moreno, 1975, p. 12). Yet the argument according to which spontaneity may operate subtly does not facilitate the understanding of the ways in which it manifests itself. Spontaneity's definition posed a challenged in the early days of psychodrama, and that challenge is still valid now. Although spontaneity as a concept is intuitively understood, it is difficult to define it empirically. The problem partly stems from the fact that spontaneity was described as energy which may not be conserved and may not be observed, since it is not apparent (Kipper and Hundal, 2005, p. 120). Spontaneity's multitude of characteristics and the various definitions Moreno attributed to it pose even greater challenges to understanding the concept. Moreno's initial definition – namely, spontaneity as an energy driving for action in a conscious, pure mode, which has not been contaminated by other elements – is less tricky in itself, yet later on, Moreno modified it, turning spontaneity from representing a drive (energy), which yields various types of response, into the responses themselves (Kipper and Hundal, 2005, p. 128). According to Christoforou and Kipper (2006), spontaneity is a psychological state of mind, or a quality of willingness, which predisposes the individual to respond in a certain way, as well as willingness to respond to external and internal motivating stimuli. In that sense, they follow Moreno's original view, according to which spontaneity is an energy which triggers a response (Kipper and Christoforou, 2006, p. 24).

Cultural conservation

Spontaneity and lack of spontaneity are interrelated. As far as the lack of spontaneity is concerned, the theory addresses the following two concepts:

1 Cultural Conservation: The finished product of the creative process is the cultural conservation which comes from *conservare*. It is anything that preserves the values and morals of a given culture (Moreno, 1974, p. 77). Those outcomes contain dormant creative qualities, which maintain the energy conservation principle, emerging when a linkage to spontaneity occurs. There are technological cultural conservations, such as books, paintings, films, records, rockets, bombs, etc. There are also human conservations, which are a key factor contributing to personality's development or regression, such as behavioral models which are determined and fixed in advance (Bischof, 1970, pp. 259–261). Moreno argued that human beings are granted certain roles which are fixed as a conserved form, thereby causing a lack of action. That role conservation may assist or damage personality's development through day-to-day behavior (Moreno, 1974, pp. 81–82).
2 Robotic Behavior Pathology. The word "robot" originates from the Czech word "robota", which means labor. Moreno coined the term zootechnical animal, deriving from the Greek word zoon (animal) for robots, since he did not only refer to labor, but also to the destruction they imply (Moreno, 1953, p. 599). Those robots represent forms of existence which are completely different from other proceedings of creativity, with which humanity is identified. The robot is lifeless. He is able to issue much of the same thing, but has no ability whatsoever to create anything new. Continuing the cultural conservation's line of development, the robot appears from the great loss of spontaneity and creativity. Paradoxically, since the robot is a human invention, it actually poses danger to creativity and spontaneity because the person does not set his hidden creative energy free so as to create new things (Moreno, 1974, pp. 80–83). Robots pose a threat to man's existence

> and survival, because they lessen man's ability and power as a creator, on the one hand, and his ability to control them, on the other hand (Moreno, 1964a, p. 44).

Cultural conservations oppress spontaneity and creativity. Spontaneity and creativity themselves are highly important, and once they become conserved, by definition, they lose their relevance to the world (Moreno, 1960b, p. 13). The risk of cultural conservation lies within its finality. Cultural conservation has become highly valuable and placed into a constant pattern or form. As such, it has become a public property; thus any outcome of a creative action which may be conserved and employed again, and is accessible to the wider public, is considered cultural conservation. That was the consequence of generally accepting a value system which admired final outcomes and perfect works. Those perfect ideas are linked to the concept of God himself in his second status following the creation of the world (Moreno, 1975, p. 8). That second status, as opposed to the initial status representing the sources of creativity and divinity, is the reason for a person's modern separation from his God (Moreno, 1948a, p. 96), from the sources of creativity within him, and their turning into cultural conservations.

The risk lying within cultural conservation is its finality. First, there are "technological conservations", such as the Bible or Beethoven's Ninth Symphony, which become objects of admiration in their own right. Those conservations are a complete, final product, and their modification or changing arouses reluctance to change them. Second, the satisfaction drawn out of cultural conservations is a habit hard to break. Cultural conservations are a source of security, and there is a tendency to idealize them, which results in behavioral fixation (Moreno, 1974, p. 82).

> The world is full of old-fashioned "lovers of [conservations]". It is the hardest habit to break, even including drug addiction and coffee. The [conservation] is so comforting and maternal; it gives security to the weak, the sick and the old, and reassurance to the isolate[d].
>
> (Moreno, 1956, p. 392)

As opposed to Moreno, Sorokin did not view "creative conservations" as passive, petrified and completely lacking creativity, but just the opposite, as highly dynamic catalysts, which drive other phenomena in the world, both in relation to themselves and as hosts (Sorokin, 1956, p. 380). It is possible that creative conservations, such as Plato's philosophical system, Buddha's theological perceptions and Shakespeare's Hamlet, incessantly dictated the changes that followed them; for hundreds of years, they controlled the thoughts and behaviors of thousands of human beings, as well as social and cultural phenomena. As a matter of fact, those cultural conservations are probably the most "radioactive" mediators, namely, mediators which may be converted into energy in the world known to man.

> If the creative "[conservations]" are the final product of the preceding creative élan, the "[conservations]", in their turn, are the greater catalysts of subsequent creative élans.
>
> (Sorokin, 1956, p. 380)

This is the reason, in Sorokin's opinion, why any theory attempting to illustrate cultural conservations as static, petrified and devoid of any creato-active stimulus, or of any further development and evolution of themselves (in the form of other creative achievements deriving from them, representing the change, their "variation"), or their inability to move and change billions of other phenomenon, clearly seem irrelevant to the author (Sorokin, 1956, p. 380). Moreno responded to that criticism in the following words:

> Multiplications do not make a [conservation] less or more of a [conservation]; it is in cold storage, dormant energy [. . .]. Conservers by themselves without an intervening factor do not become creative.
>
> (Moreno, 1956, p. 383)

Aristotle and Plato idealized cultural conservation, as did many western philosophers thereafter. More than the creators themselves, we admire their conservations until they become as sanctified as the Bible, Beethoven's music or the pyramids. The inspirations arise through cultural conservations; the fact they nurture the imagination of each new generation of people should not cause any embarrassment or confusion with the matter in discussion. In themselves, the final products, the cultural conservations, are eternal and lacking any spontaneity (Moreno, 1956, p. 386).

However, the advantage of cultural conservations are noteworthy as well. They fulfill an important role in the development of culture and human society, because of their constant form. First, they may be relied upon as a source of guidance and direction in coping with uncertain situations, which pose a threat in a world that constantly and thoroughly evolves (Moreno, 1975, p. 16). Second, they are responsible, to a great extent, for the immortalization, continuity and development of the world's cultural heritage. They serve as the past's archive and therefore are to be revived repeatedly in order to replace the existing cultural conserves. Finally, cultural conservations are the guards and developers of the human creative ego. Without them, a person will not possess the spontaneous creative ability. When they are employed properly, they grant continuity to spontaneous creation's behavioral models (Bischof, 1970, p. 259), contribute to stability and serve as a function for constancy, thereby fulfilling an important role in adaptation (Moreno, 1975, p. 16).

A world without cultural conservations, where creative actions are incessant and eternal and that is purely creative is a world without meaning and stands in contradiction to the type of world in which we live (Moreno, 1956, p. 388).

Man, robot, and cultural conservation

Our human world is becoming extensively full of robots, and it seems that there is no end to their new forms and development (Moreno, 1953, p. 599–600). Man needed to create the robot in order to survive. If the human world had contained abundant creativity, the robot would have probably never come into being; it could have been part of the creating man, rather than being an object external to him (Moreno, 1974, p. 82).

Spontaneity and roboticism are two opposite ends of the same scale. The area they create is a reference framework to any type of action, work or appearance: maximum spontaneity on one extreme, and zero spontaneity on the other, with a multitude of spontaneity degrees in between them. This scale is also a moral scale, with the one end's ideal is the cultural-technological conserve and the other end's ideal is the totally spontaneous creator.

Robots may be loved or completely despised; however, they possess no ability to respond independently. In other words, robots are like individuals who have lost their spontaneity (Moreno, 1953, p. 68). Those robots possess extraordinary conditioned response abilities, but they lack the sophistication lying creative inspiration and spontaneity that are characteristic of the human spirit, as well as the mutuality required to respond to unexpected situations. Conditioned responses yield only one model of behavior, while the warming up involved in preparing the person for action and constructing the action allows an infinite number of responses. Personality is not bound to encounter new situations only, but also to create new situations. The behavior of uncreative individuals resembles robots in many ways. They fail to survive in a world where the situations constantly evolve, since they do not respond accordingly (Moreno, 1964b, pp. 158–159). Yet the stronger the cultural conservations become and the more extensively they are spread, the greater their influence; and the more attention is paid to the completed, perfect product, the lesser the extent to which people feel the need to deal with the present and the need to create in the here and now (Moreno, 1975, p. 8). Thus, it is not surprising that the "here and now" category has had little room for development and expansion in a culture like ours, which is replete with cultural conservations and admiration of sanctified morals and values (Moreno, 1964a, p. 106).

In Moreno's opinion, the lack of a relevant "here and now" concept has disrupted any attempt to establish a theory of spontaneity and creativity and its connection to cultural conservation. He found a manifestation of that in the works of Bergson and Nietzsche. Bergson's and Nietzsche's references were pertaining to cultural conservation's viewpoint and framework. Whenever they were required to address a given work, the gods and the heroes (Napoleon, Bach) became the basis for their theory. The fact that cultural conservations were of such a high degree makes no difference to the cultural conservation. From a creative matrix's point of view, all conservations, whether of a high or low degree, are placed on the same sphere. Replacing old cultural conservations with new ones, or variation from one cultural conservation to another, does not make any difference in man's position in the struggle with daily reality and may not facilitate the development of a human society where the real ruler should be man.

Cultural conservation is a concept through which the dynamic significance of the here and now may be demonstrated; thus he becomes a frame of reference:

> This situation called forth, as if to rescue, the dramatic opposite of the cultural [conservation]: the category of the moment.
>
> (Moreno, 1975, p. 8)

Spontaneity and the here and now mentioned earlier in relation to cultural conservations were challenged by Moreno in terms of the way in which they perceive interpersonal relationships and intersocial relationships. The purpose was to refrain from oppressing one's creativity at the here and now. We are to reassess those conservations which serve us, to keep on employing them, but to dare modify and enhance, and perhaps even to abandon, those which have become ineffective, or perhaps even detrimental (Blatner and Cukier, 2007, pp. 294–295).

From cultural conservation's viewpoint, creativity may be categorized into two different spheres: freely flowing creativity and conserved creativity, which fills the world with cultural conservations, which maintain it in its frozen state, inactive and dormant (Moreno, 1974, p. 77). The fact that cultural conservations are characterized by lack of spontaneity does not impede their ability to serve as a warm -p toward future spontaneity.

Cultural conservation may serve as a springboard for developing new spontaneity, which will lead to creativity. Just as there is a direct chain from existence to spontaneity, from spontaneity to creativity and from creativity to cultural conservation, there is an inverse chain, namely, from cultural conservation to spontaneity, from spontaneity to creativity and from creativity to existence. Moreno refers to this process (Moreno, 1956, p. 386) as creative circulation. The Bible, for instance, is an indication for such a creative activity. Some people view the Bible as something to follow without question, a sealed product where nothing is to be changed. Others perceive the Bible as the source of formation of new religions, which, in turn, have become cultural conservations themselves (Artzi, 1991, p. 25).

Moreno believed cultural conservation is negative when it prevents new spontaneity and creativity, bounding man, but when it conduces new spontaneity and creativity, then it is positive, becoming a well that never runs dry (Z. T. Moreno, 2000, pp. 9–10). One way Moreno suggested for dealing with cultural conservations is the development of a cultural system consisting of spontaneity and creativity, appearing in the here and now. Cultural conservations are to be consistently revived, replacing the old value system with a new value system, better adapted to the time in which it occurs (Z. T. Moreno, 2000, pp. 9–10; Kipper, 1986, p. 13). In Moreno's opinion, if 1 percent of energy is channeled toward the cultural abilities at the moment of creation itself, rather than toward constructing machines and robots, then humanity will embark on a new cultural era, a culture that doesn't fear the existing machines and robots or those awaiting to be constructed. This struggle against the robots calls into action not only the individuals and small groups but also the masses. Moreno referred to this war within ourselves as "the creative revolution" (Moreno, 1960b, p. 10).

Warming up

In Moreno's personality theory, creativity and spontaneity are tied to the term "warm up" in a connection that is impossible to annul (Rabson, 1979, p. 40). Warming up yields spontaneity, which, in turn, yields creativity, whose final product is cultural conservation (Bischof, 1970, p. 253).

Moreno did not develop any motivation-related theory, but sufficed with the general observation, according to which human beings possess some type of propellers, which he defined as "hunger for action", namely, as an innate passion to act. This passion is nurtured by consistent forces tagged as warming up. Warming up is the process preparing people to begin demonstrating spontaneous, creative behavior (Moreno, 1985b, p. 190; Kipper, 1986, pp. 11–12). All spontaneous actions originate from warming up.

Warming up is a psychological and biochemical process through which a person becomes motivated to embark on a certain action. Almost any human action begins with warming up. Inability to warm up is considered a pathological phenomenon, as is autistic behavior or a catatonic state. Warming up and spontaneity are intertwined and thus are engaged in a cause–effect relationship, though it is unclear which preceded the other. The greater the spontaneity, the shorter the warming-up process, and personality becomes more effective in coping with various life situations. An effective warm-up may lower emotional anxiety (Bischof, 1970, p. 244). Overly warming up may result in regression in behavior. On the other hand, low-degree warming up is not sufficient and leaves us without spontaneity and creativity (Z. T. Moreno, 2006b, p. 277).

Proper warming up in intensity and pace is one which ends when it reaches the climax while in action, and the action, in turn, is considered satisfactory. When one acts while not being spontaneous, this will cause the action to be unsatisfactory, and might even be detrimental. It may be stated that the actions allowing one to diminish the defense mechanism and regulate the "hunger for action" are actions which by their accomplishment gives rise to our satisfaction. Those actions are always associated with spontaneity and creativity. Usually, extreme states of very high or very low degrees of warming up result in an unsatisfying action (Artzi, 1991, p. 25; Kipper, 1986, p. 83; 1967, pp. 69–71). In the author's opinion warming up as a biochemical mechanism is to be distinguished from warming-up techniques, whose source is external, as therapeutic methods. As an innate mechanism, warming up is pre-conscious, but as artificial warming-up, as in psychodramatic, it may be consciously regulated, thus influencing the innate warming-up process.

The pace refers to the swiftness with which the warming-up process goes into action. In extreme states, warming up ranges from rapidity to slowness. The rapidity, intensity and continuity of the warming-up process are estimated by the severity and intensity of the situation that the individual faces, on the one hand, and by the urge for instigating a change, on the other hand. The more unsatisfactory one's present is, the greater the need for instigating change will be. Even though one may not be aware of her or his dissatisfaction, the passion for changing the situation will still come to the fore. The intensity and continuity of the warming-up process are positively correlated to the desired goal of changing one's present. The rapidity of the warm-up process does not indicate the scope of satisfaction with the present. Sometimes, it is precisely a slow warming-up process that is necessary or even a general warming-up process. A warming-up process which is not acted out may indicate a serious aspiration for a better future.

> This is also in accord with the teleological doctrine accepted in psychodramatic philosophy, the need for a more satisfactory future is equally important as the disappointment with the present. And both dictate the manifestation of the warming-up process.
>
> (Kipper, 1967, p. 71)

How does a person win a warming-up ability to begin with, and how does this mechanism work? The warming-up process arises through starters, which are responsible for instigating the beginning of spontaneous behavior. There are three types of starters. All of them are interrelated:

1 **Physical Starters:** These starters stem from the body's actions, for example, the pace of motions such as walking, running and breathing. From a developmental point of view, these starters are the first to develop, and they dominate during the earliest time in a child's life, even prior to birth. The physical starters tend to come into action in cases of danger and emergency (Kipper, 1986, p. 84).
2 **Psychological Starters:** These starters are more complex, and refer to actions influenced by psychological stimuli and catalysts, such as fantasies, dreams, aspirations, fears and feelings of guilt. The psychological starters' development begins as soon as the child is able to tell the self and the environment apart. The environment includes both objects and people; hence psychological starters are also known as interpersonal starters.
3 **Social Starters:** These starters include influences by social and group norms. All starters may arise through an internal stimulation, self-initiative, or external stimulation.

As stated, the different starters operate a system of interactions. Physical starters may psychologically warm up a person, whereas psychological starters may physically warm up a person. People tend to develop warming-up habits, and many prefer a specific type of starters for given actions. For example, some will prefer to go for a walk before they begin writing (Kipper, 1986, p. 84).

Aulicino believes that just as it is proper to discuss the two types of spontaneity, it is also proper to discuss the two types of warming up. It is noteworthy that Moreno used the term "spontaneity" not only in relation to a specific type of action (a proper response for a new event and a new response to an old event), but also to the readiness to demonstrate such an action. A general state of readiness for connecting to an action is examined by assessing the conditions of the situation, which will bias the action toward propriety. From that viewpoint, it is worthy to think in terms of two warming-up states: one is a general warming-up state, which will occur when the individual becomes aware of the prospect that a new reaction is required in unexpected situations (physiologically, the organism becomes prepared for the unexpected with the increasing of adrenaline flow and it becoming more rapid, etc.); the second warming-up state is placed in a specific context. Action has a frame of reference which has to be intentional and meaningful (Aulicino, 1954, pp. 152–153).

Kipper (1967, pp. 67–68) thinks the warming-up concept is not sufficiently estimated, since it is overshadowed by the concept of spontaneity, because the warming-up process is sensitive to external, environmental influences and may be externally manipulated. On the contrary, spontaneity may not be externally manipulated, and in that sense, it is more autonomous than the warming-up process. In the author's opinion, the way in which Moreno presents the spontaneous energy, as a nurtured energy which exists externally to the personality as well and may be converted, facilitates to manipulate spontaneity, too. Spontaneity begins from within, but does not end there.

To sum up, it may be stated that the warming-up process functions as the carrier of intangible, invisible spontaneity, serving as the foundation for spontaneity's progress.

> The warming up process is [an] "operational" manifestation of spontaneity [. . .] Spontaneity can be measured by the dynamics of the warming up process.
>
> (Moreno, 1953, p. 337)

The terms "spontaneity", "creativity", "warming up" and "cultural conservation" indicate the psychological forces within every individual as promoting or inhibiting the inherent human potential. However, in addition to that, Moreno called our attention to the human nature, offering a framework of reference which grants meaning and dignity to human encounter.

Encounter and the interpersonal theory

The term "encounter" originates from the German word *Begegnung*, which contains the root *Gegen*, meaning "against". The word encounter, deriving from the French word *rencontre* is the closest in meaning to *Begegnung*, which means an encounter with a rival or a friend for facing-off purposes. This is the discourse of "I" and "you". In the encounter's core stand creativity and spontaneity; thus, encounter is a meeting between human beings, where they are driven forward by a spontaneous response, which yields an immediate creative change. The encounter is a direct encounter, including communication between people in varying degrees of intensity, in speech, gesture, by a hug and a kiss, becoming one (*una cum uno*). Encounter is a relationship consisting of both a positive and a negative connection. It is an improvised encounter occurring at a moment's drive, here and now (Moreno and Z. T. Moreno, 1969, pp. 25–26).

Moreno argued that if we wish to meet others and truly get to know them, we should learn to see ourselves through their eyes, and they should see themselves through our eyes (role exchange) (Moreno, 1969a, pp. 8–9). Role exchange during encounter is an action where the person attempts to experience and feel the other. This is an encounter with the other's different stance, while maintaining one's selfness (Moreno, 1960b, p. 15; 1972, pp. 210–211).

Moreno used the term "encounter" many times in many of his works (Moreno, 1960b, p. 15; 1969b, pp. 25–26), but the clearest definition was given in 1914, when he published in Vienna the first in a series of poetic writings titled *Einladung zu einer Begegnung* (*Invitation to Encounter*), which is certainly the first publication addressing encounter, a term which would be a core concept in the existentialistic movement. Moreno's series of publications in the years 1914–1938 indicated that the theory and therapy of an interpersonal relationship originated from that encounter-related insight, directly stemming from it.

The journal *Daimon*, which Moreno edited, published in 1918 a dramatic dialogue by Moreno, titled *Invitation to Encounter*. In that article (page 6) appeared the term interpersonal communication. The term interpersonal relations, which was used by Robert Macdougall in 1912, took on significance in Moreno's book titled *Who Will Survive?* (1934) and in the journal he published starting from 1937, *Sociometry: A Journal of Interpersonal Relations*, the first journal to use that combination of words in its title (Johnson, 1974, p. 445).

The general assumption concerning Moreno is that the interpersonal relations theory is a consequence of psychiatric thinking, although in fact, psychiatry was third in order of importance in that thinking:

> First came religious and ethical thinking which provided the most rigorousness operational definition of interpersonal relations it can be found, for instance in my dialogues (1918); [. . .] culminating in sociometry; psychiatry came last. The theory of interpersonal relations is born of religion.
> (Moreno, 1953, p. xxxi)

Johnson presents four key contemporary viewpoints, which are in dialectic relation with one another, regarding the way in which psychologists understand religious behavior. First, there is the conflict theory, which views a person as a deeply problematic and complex personality. A person desperately struggles to solve conflicts, reaching a reconciliation and compromise stance of productive adulthood. That was Freud's outlook, who offered psychoanalysis as therapy in order to merge the unconscious conflicts and life's painful crashing up against them. Freud viewed religion as a compulsive neurosis, attempting to ease the internal apprehension and guilt stemming from the Oedipal complex through coming to terms with the father figure.

The second is the collective theory, which also originated from the conflict idea, but views conflicts as trends complementing one another into a full picture of mutual support when they combine into a broader wholeness. That was Jung's (1958) view in his psychology of the collective unconscious. For him, a religious drive is the penetration of mental energy from the collective unconscious, whose mysterious significance is to be discovered within universal symbols or archetypes appearing in many cultures and races in order to guide and inform the individual while struggling with his fate to fulfill the hidden strengths of being and his existence.

The third theory questions Jung's collectivism idea, which hides the individual uniqueness, while also rejecting the view according to which a person is driven by instincts and past's determinism. Allport (1950, 1955), for example, thought that a person's direction of growth should be forward. A person's role is to progress and overcome the obstructions which stop and inhibit his coming into being. Hence, in order to move toward maturity and effective behavior, new motives are necessary to replace their precedents. A mature religious behavior operates by conscious orientation toward proper purposes, facing the future (Allport, in Johnson, 1974, p. 444).

The fourth view is the interpersonal view, which finds the person's special nature in his encounter with others. Moreno's interpersonal theory contradicts each of the three other theories (Johnson, 1974, p. 445). Moreno believed that if a person is not complete as an individual, neither does he exist in isolation, nor does he find his fulfillment in the mass, and through drowning into the collective. Moreno finds the person's special nature in his encounter with others; hence he found another alternative, an interpersonal technique of communication (Moreno, 1953, p. xxxi)

Psychiatrists focus upon the individual's inner dynamics, and sociologists focus upon the mass as a collective, without attributing any importance to the individuals within it; the absence of the other "player" prevents the encounter and direct, nonabstract communication between people (Moreno, 1953, pp. 64–68). Moreno thinks the revolution unexpectedly started with him, a neo-theological individual who was inspired by life's deep conflicts, but thought that they required a creative solution in the religious area. He was not satisfied with the religious institutes, which were occupied in maintaining past tradition, and was more impressed with the dramatic dialogue of Jesus and Socrates.

> It is what interpersonal dialogue addresses as I confronting thou in the decisive relation of the present moment.
>
> (Johnson, 1974, p. 444)

In 1923, Moreno wrote:

> The personal situation is not only an internal event, it has also a relation outside of himself, to the situation of another person, out of the interpersonal relations of two different individuals, the conflict may arouse interpersonal situations.
>
> (Moreno, in Hehnevajsa, 1960b, pp. 712–713)

And in 1934, he wrote the following:

> A and B are actually two pole of one movement reflecting and changing each other.
>
> (Moreno, in Nehnevajsa, 1960, p. 713)

The interpersonal relations theory is based upon the primary dyad concept, which suggests that an encounter of two actors, where the concrete situation, and the direct communication constitute the preliminary event of all interpersonal relations (Moreno, 1953, pp. 164–168). Moreno assumes the encounter is also the true foundation of the therapeutic process; encounter, rather than psychoanalysis' transference, is the basic principle underlying all forms of psychotherapy (Moreno, 1959, p. 234).

The encounter idea encompasses the seeds of two concepts, each placed at opposite ends of the same scale: spontaneity and cultural-technological conservation (Moreno, 1953, p. 68). That may be demonstrated through a book's author and his reader. The face-to-face encounter with people is basic and direct, yet the book triggers an infinite dilemma by distinguishing the person from the author, as well as the person from the reader. Every author's dilemma is to communicate through a book with a reader who is not there in the immediate situation. The missing component is the other, whose absence does not allow an active struggle or interpersonal communication (Moreno, 1943, p. 309). The cure for this dilemma was an "invitation to encounter", namely, actualizing the encounter and making it real.

Moreno called for returning the original encounter of the interpersonal relations to the pre-writing and pre-book times, an era where the preacher (the author's equivalent) had no choice but to encounter his sermon's audience face to face (Moreno, 1959, p. 212).

Moreno implemented the spontaneity in the interpersonal relations principle through his idea concerning encounter. There is a combination of an authentic desire to directly connect with others, with profound consideration of the other's viewpoint (Blatner and Cukier, 2007, p. 295).

The interpersonal theory emphasizes the need to enrich, improve and enhance the individual through the face-to-face connection. When the communication is face to face, the other person's entire being conveys some message to you, while your whole being conveys to her or him a message that penetrates into her or his life. The true human interaction occurs when one person meets another while being at the action's origin (*status nascendi*), and in full responsibility for the situation and the immediate state. Moreno argued the encounter was a true category of reality. It is more than a mere intellectual plan as a basis for interpersonal relations:

> The meeting was a category of realization and on a different plan from intellectualized derivations as interpersonal relations.
>
> (Moreno, 1947a, p. 119)

Moreno's interpersonal theory continued developing in philosopher Martin Buber's work. In the years 1918–1920, Moreno and Buber collaborated in the literary, existentialistic and expressionistic journal titled *Daimon*, with Moreno serving as the chief editor, and Buber serving as deputy editor. The articles written by both of them, addressing the person-to-person encounter appeared side by side. It is unclear to what extent they influenced one another and what roles each of them fulfilled in interpersonal theory's history, yet they jointly flew down a stream of fruitful inspiration pertaining to it and the man–God encounter.

God's I-thou concept was the keystone of the main interpersonal concept as documented in the two men's publications in the years 1920–1923. In 1920, Moreno anonymously published his books *Words of the Father*, which contained a direct dialogue with God. Buber's book *Ich und Du* (1923) was translated into English in 1957 and was titled *I & Thou*. (Johnson, 1974, p. 446).

According to Johnson, Buber acknowledges the idea initially developed by the German philosopher Ludwig Feuerbach (1804–1872):

> The individual man for himself does not have man's being in himself, either as a moral being or as a thinking being. Man's being is contained in community, in the unity of man with man – a unity which rests, however only on the relation of the difference between I & Thou.
>
> (Feuerbach [1843], in Johnson, 1974, p. 448)

Buber relied upon theological perception and insight in terms of the man–God relations, and similarly to Moreno, he believed that true life lies in the encounter and face-to-face relations, that encounter is a life involving a dialogue, where one man addresses (also in speech) the other. In those dialogue relations, the man I meet is not the experience's object (it), but becomes a Thou, its direct and main object. When I encounter Thou, the present life experience comes to life. When "Thou" speaks, "I" considers his side within the relationship. The full, true present occurs in an encounter comprising life and mutual relations (Johnson, 1974, p. 448). In order to avoid a sense of alienation, the emphasis must be put on the I-Thou relations, rather than the I-it relations (Holmes, 1992, p. 6).

A person does not become whole when he is alone, or stands in relation to an object, but only in relation to another person. Buber claimed the smallest human unit is not one person, but two, namely, I-Thou. I may not be "I" unless I stand in relation to "Thou" (Kellermann, 1986, p. 34). The whole self is an opposition unit, resistance where tension and conflict arise due to personal existence's basic duality. Buber refers to that as Inborn Thou, which from birth one has always been superior to one's uniqueness (being alone). Entering the relationship and accepting the tension stemming from that duality are the key to conflict's being and life experience (Johnson, 1974, p. 448).

> A man becomes "I" through "Thou", and without it, he cannot exist. A person who lives with himself alone is not a person. The attachment instinct bears more power than attributed to it by those who support the libido concept. It is manifested by the passion to experience the world as a person who emerges to approach us, chooses us and knows us, who becomes happy because of us, just as we become happy with him.
>
> (Buber, 1963, p. 23)

Buber was a pioneer in the I-thou anthropological philosophy, while Moreno was occupied with his work on interpersonal relations in psychiatry and social sciences (Johnson, 1974, p. 446).

Moreno considered the interpersonal therapy the solution for existential and universal problems of alienation, despair and loneliness. For that purpose, he proposed sociometry and psychodrama as a means for amending human relations. The psychodramatic theology is based upon a doctrine comprising reconciliation and proper relationship with the self, since the person's view of himself or herself becomes a source of action. Self-love is the basic component of self-actualization, and it renders the person responsible. All that applies to the individual also applies to the structure of a relationship, which is also known as "group life". Nobody can live alone, separately from others. Drawing away from a proper relationship results in loss, and a sense of belonging is important for one's emotional health. Loss induces a large vacuum. Every person holds her or his own existential vacuum and his despair. Yet a person possesses the ability to freely choose – one may choose creative life or destructive life.

This theology is related to the way in which a person is perceived with faith and the conception of a person as a creator or as an initial instigator (God). It defines the way in which we act in order to bring our origins of being into the lives of people, assisting them to overcome feelings of frustration and failure. The theology of interpersonal relations views life's dynamic quality as a process for attaining identity, driving people's lives toward fulfillment. Its purpose is to assist a person in day-to-day life, selecting a process which will facilitate him in achieving his goals. Relationship's theology is founded upon the promise that whatever a person does is important for him, for his fellow human beings, and as for his God. It includes fulfilling the potential lying within him, as well as actual achievement. It bears the element of being, consisting both of the element of being and the element of becoming. Accepting the potential that lies within a person, as well as fulfilling the true scope of his nature, poses a challenge (Oman, 1974, p. 151).

Furthermore, a basic component of Moreno's original philosophy and classic method states that it is not sufficient for psychotherapy to address the inner world alone. External conflicts and personal pathology are outcomes of interactions with the outside world, namely, the family and society as a whole (Haworth, 1998, pp. 20–21).

Many philosophers and theologians, both religious and secular, recognized the mutual dependence of human beings, as well as the results achieved through friendship between human beings, and concluded that the richest, most creative life occurs when people live with others who allow them express themselves to the fullest. Buddha, for example, following a long, thorough study of the social reality, concluded that friendly behavior toward others bears crucial significance. In Jesus' ethics, one may find an emphasis on the importance of friendliness and the implication that all human beings are brothers and sisters. Early in the 20th century, philosopher John Dewey (1859–1952) expressed an idea concerning the unity of humanity's mutual act: the acts in which we express our perception of the ties which bind us to others are its [i.e. the community's] only rights and ceremonies (Dewey, in Zeleny, 1956, p. 185).

Moreno's hypotheses seem to resemble the hypotheses common among many philosophers, both modern and ancient; thus, there is no novelty to them. However, the interpersonal theory, which stems from an axiological origin, paved the way toward a new science of human relations: sociometry. In sociometry, the religious element is implemented in the sense that everybody should be creators, thereby fulfilling the Christian idea of brotherly love, while the scientific element is employed, because sociometry may measure interpersonal relations, and psychodrama may amend them to reconciliation

Tele

Personality development theory is associated with the relation and interaction among human beings. Moreno proposed the term "tele" as a mechanism of human attachment, claiming it to be encounter's scientific equivalent (Moreno, 1960a, p. 17).

Basically, tele is a term substituting the transference's role in psychoanalysis as a healthy attachment between people. It is manifested through a true, rather than projected, relationship (Moreno, 1959, pp. 6–10). This concept is significantly inter-related with the concept of encounter. Encounter is a human face-off where the tele process is active. At this context, tele encompasses the meaning of I-Thou within a relationship, while transference probably expresses the I-it relationship. Psychologist Rollo May wrote in 1967 that transference may be perceived as encounter's distortion or falsification (Kellermann, 1986, p. 33). Moreno defined tele as follows: "By definition tele means the simplest unit of feeling transmitted from one individual toward another, a feeling which is projection into the distance" (Moreno, 1934, p. 432).

Kahn defines tele in this way:

> It is the basic bond that lies at the root of all two-way communications. It refers to a bond of perception, a bond of affect and a bond of love or object relationship.
>
> (Kahn, 1964, p. 30)

Prior to the 1930s, when psychology was mainly of individualist orientation, it was commonly thought that emotions arose exclusively for the individual and were not related in any way to what another individual might feel. Moreno maintained that one-way projection of emotions is unreasonable in terms of sociometry, and instead argued that there is a flow of bi- and multilateral emotions radiating one toward the other's private world among several individuals, thereby yielding the emotional-social structures (Barbour, 1994, pp. 114–115). The tele process is an objective system of interpersonal relationship. This is an important force determining the way in which human beings treat and relate to each other. Moreno argued there is an enormous number of attractions and repellence variations among individuals, requiring a common ground of a social and physiological basis (Moreno, 1960a, p. 40). Those emotions operate in different directions; repellence, attraction or indifference. According to Moreno, tele is the overall sum of a relationship's emotional aspects (Moreno, 1953, p. 314).

Because emotions are transferred from one to another, projected to the distance through space and time, Moreno chose the word tele in order to explain that phenomenon. The word's origin is the ancient Greek word *telecephalon*, namely, "from afar" (Barbour, 1994, p. 2; Moreno, 1953, pp. 311–315; Kellermann, 1986, p. 33). The term represents the capability and ability to feel a relationship between people without words; it is an invisible bond which keeps people and groups together (Tauvon, 1998, p. 34).

Moreno used the term "tele" in two senses; one sense refers to the general category of interpersonal relations, including repellence, attraction and indifference, and is associated with the choices and preference idea. The other sense refers to the human interaction (Blatner, 1994, p. 285).

Choices and Preferences. In Moreno's opinion, as mentioned, tele is a natural human tendency to accept choices and make preferences (Moreno, 1934,

p. 285). Tele constitutes an expansion of the preference concept, and is linked to symbols, images and emotions. This is the imaginary aspect of an instinctive process, similar to what Jung defined as archetypes. Preference is an elemental psychological function which refers to an ensemble of physical actions, such as eating, playing (music), artistic creation, etc. Simultaneously to the physical preferences, emotional preferences exist in the bonds between human beings. Just as a person feels revulsion or affection as extensions of biological feelings within himself (like or dislike of a certain type of food, clothes, etc.), affection and lack of affection also take place between the self and others, be it individuals or groups (Bischof, 1964, p. 365; Northway, 1967, pp. 46–47):

> Thus tele becomes the flow to and from the affectivity between individuals.
> (Moreno, 1956, p. 62)

Human Interaction. Anywhere interpersonal dynamics occurs, be it positive or negative, there is interaction between people, which turns the tele phenomenon into something far more complex than mere preference. Interaction is a key component in the tele concept, reflecting the human ability to feel or imagine how others feel about a relationship. We do not see them as they are, and not as we ourselves are, but the way they appear in relation to us (Moreno, 1956, p. 15). One's personality is much more than a reactive factor. A person possesses the ability to induce his own reactions. In that sense, there is the common action with other human beings, as well as the ability to react to them. Beyond the physiological system, a person may function on the philosophical level without any external stimulation (emotions such as anger, sadness, joy, etc.). Because those functions are tele's pioneers, tele's meaning significantly exceeds mere sensitivity to others (Bischof, 1970, p. 241).

> Tele has a built-in self-starter, the self energizing characteristics of tele may therefore initiate a feeling tone within the individual, even before anything [has] happened to cause a reaction from another person.
> (Bischof, 1970, p. 241)

Some individuals are bound to each other by harmony and mutual emotions, such as love, that are characterized by a high sensitivity to mutual interaction and satisfactory gestures (Moreno, 1947a, p. 68). They often do not need to look at one another, as they communicate through special senses, supposedly by what Moreno defines as medial understanding (Moreno, 1947a, p. 68). In order for tele to be an interaction, the individual has to be capable of appreciating the other person's realistic qualities. This capability is known as telic sensitivity.

The degree of sensitivity greatly varies from one individual to another. A tele relationship contains more than empathy and counter-empathy; the ability to understand and penetrate the world of another individual lies within tele sensitivity (Bischof, 1970, p. 241) – it is the smallest emotion unit measurable.

Tele and transference

Preferences, choices and interactions describe, in fact, the dynamics occurring between individuals and groups. According to the psychoanalytical outlook, the dynamics between individuals are demonstrated through the therapist–patient relationship. Freud discovered the patient projected onto the therapist unrealistic fantasies, defining the phenomenon as "transference". According to Freud, transference is the tendency to generalize and interpret actual relations based upon past experience with similar personas (Freud, in Moreno, 1959, p. 4). Those are behavior models which were acquired in childhood but suppressed, and are now re-embodied unconsciously in current relations (Tauvon, 1998, p. 35). Transference is a subjective, psychodynamic experience. It stems from the individual, and is based upon a fantasy which implies psychopathology. The process is projective and one-way, going from the patient to the therapist (Blatner, 1994, p. 289; Moreno, 1953, p. 311). Later on, Freud discovered that the therapist is not free of personal involvement, and referred to that phenomenon as counter-transference, indicating the therapist's emotional reaction toward the patient (Holmes, 1992, p. 45; Freud, in Moreno, 1959, p. 5). Zerka Moreno thinks that the term "counter-transference" expresses an erroneous implementation of the transference concept, since transference is always a one-way process, involving projection from one party to another. Transference is always subjective. At best, there may be two simultaneous transference cases between two individuals (Z. T. Moreno, 1966, pp. 231–232).

Moreno thought the terms "transference" and "counter-transference", which are common in psychotherapy, do not properly express the psychodynamics and processes taking place within a collection of people bounded by traditional or emotional ties. On the one hand, the term "empathy", too, which was defined by German philosopher Theodore Lipps (1851–1914), namely a two-way emotion toward another ego's private world and as such a psychological phenomenon, is incapable of explaining the multitude of emotions' interactions (Moreno, 1953, p. 318). Though empathy is a realistic process and a positive factor, it does not include the mutuality element. Moreno took the terms "empathy" and "transference", uniting them under a third, broader term, namely, "tele".

Moreno acknowledged that the transference phenomenon was a real one, but only as a limited part of an interpersonal relation. Simultaneously to transference behavior, the emotions arising within the patient are partly based upon current, true information regarding the therapist, and he also intuitively assesses the kind of person he really is (Moreno, 1959, p. 5):

> The tele relation may be considered the general interpersonal process of which transference is a special psychopathological outgrowth. Consequently, underlying every transference process projected by a patient are also complex tele relationships.
>
> (Moreno, 1964a, p. 231)

Moreno rejects the counter-transference idea as well. As far as he is concerned, it is merely an interpersonal relation where a two-way transference occurs. Thus, it concerns two individuals of different backgrounds and expectations, as well as conflicting roles. Eventually, either transference relations fade out, or they become a tele relationship. The tele establishes an integration of interaction between two branches: pathological transference and empathy. They are distinguished from tele, but in life, they blend (Bischof, 1970, p. 243). Therefore, tele is:

> [A]n objective social process functioning with transference as a psychopathological out growth and empathy as esthetic outgrowth.
>
> (Moreno, 1953, p. 311)

Moreno preferred defining emotional relationships between people, including between a therapist and a patient, as tele relations, rather than transference relations. In his opinion, the term "tele" expresses the true basis for the bond between human beings (Moreno, 1969a, pp. 3–7). Tele, as opposed to transference, is not a projection from the past, but an experience which consists of reality-based components, of emotions individuals have toward each other, their interactions in roles and situations they share at the here and now (Z. T. Moreno, 1966, p. 233). Tele relations express two-way, egalitarian relations, characterized by collaboration, appreciation and maintenance of uniqueness within the relationship. This is a spontaneous process, where people accept each other for who they are (Moreno, 1934, p. 160; 1959, pp. 6–10).

Moreno argued the relationship between the patient and the therapist is a special case of a universal phenomenon. A similar process may also occur between two lovers. Following an idealization period of transference between the parties comes the moment where the two become sober, and then a tele relation comes to being. Additionally, he believed tele was the frame of reference for all professional methods and psychotherapies, including psychoanalysis or group therapy, as well as methods unrelated to psychotherapy, such as faith healing (Moreno, 1959, p. 234).

Allport objected to that view, claiming that defining a therapist–patient relationship as the relationship of lovers is unreasonable. Any healthy relationship depends upon tele's presence, but a therapeutic relationship is different and special because the patient's distress pushes aside the therapist's inner needs. Since the patient needs support, love and security, it is more likely that he will be the one to do the transference. Allport was not sure whether or not Moreno, in his definition of tele, had considered the terms "role perception" and "role adjustment". He thought Moreno had tended to underestimate the importance of essential difference between pre-determined social roles (formal roles) between a therapist and a patient (Allport, in Moreno, 1959, pp. 15–16). In the author's opinion, Allport underestimated the importance of nonformal roles, which are not predetermined, between a therapist and a patient. In tele relations as a basis for psychotherapy, the influence of the therapist's personality on his formal role should be clarified.

Moreno responded to Allport's criticism with the argument that the therapist's formal role is known. He must be trained and skilled in the art of psychotherapy, and his responsibility is to provide the patient with treatment. Nobody expects the patient to treat the therapist. It is true that a therapeutic relationship may be described as any game containing rules that apply to its participants. The game is conducted under the conditions of several rules known in advance and formally outlined, and the same applies to psychotherapy. The therapeutic relationship consists of the following four agents: (1) the therapist in the professional role; (2) the therapist as a private person; (3) the patient in the sick person's role; and (4) the patient as a private person. In order for the treatment to be effective, it is important to integrate all four roles. The transference is not directed at the therapist, but rather, at the role which the therapist represents in the patient's eyes, such as a fatherly role, or the all-knowing smart figure. The therapist, on the contrary, may perceive the patient in complementary roles, such as the son's role, or the role of the ignorant, dependent individual (Moreno, 1959, pp. 7–9).

Moreno's explanation raises the question whether tele refers to the human personality or to the roles one fulfills. The answer to this question calls for a discussion of the connection of tele and transference to formal and nonformal role relations.

Tele, transference and formal and nonformal role relations

Since tele expresses an emotional distance, partly based upon an assessment process, it may be inferred why there is some tele associated with formal and nonformal roles. From a sociological viewpoint, people treat each other through formal role relations. Formal relations are determined by cognitive roles, which, in turn, express transference relations, since they are not based upon presently active emotions. On the contrary, from a sociometric point of view, tele is based upon spontaneity and nonformal role relation styles (Blatner, 1994, p. 287). Tele relations may significantly evolve when role relationships evolve (Nehnevajsa, in Moreno, 1956, p. 62). Nonformal role relations are determined by emotions. On the one hand, one may admire a certain person's talent (cognitive process), but the two may not necessarily be affectionate toward one another. One the other hand, one may be attracted to somebody even though our good judgment warns us about him. In nonformal role relations, the process of choice occurs between people equal in standing, regardless of their status. Hence, Moreno thought a therapist's position and a patient's position shared some symmetry, and therefore the emotions being transferred between them are based, eventually, upon tele relations (Moreno, 1969a, pp. 3–7).

From this, it may be inferred that the same individual may possess two types of tele; therefore, assessment of others is necessary; how do I act toward the person I am facing, professionally or personally? Since an assessment process takes place, it may be assumed that tele is not merely about emotion. The attitude is emotional, but assessment is cognitive. Moreno emphasizes only tele's emotional aspect (according to the definition), and in the author's opinion was wrong in that. A tele relationship should be two-sided, namely, both emotional and cognitive.

The connection between tele and formal roles which are not part of the self's component may account for the reason why projection- or transference-based relationships may not be compatible for a decent theory which allows the self's manifestation. Additionally, the association of tele and role relationships yields the conclusion that tele is a social concept. Transference and empathy are psychological phenomena operating in the personal aspect (Moreno, 1953, p. 316).

Tele is a social phenomenon, first because it represents many modes of interactions, and second because it is viewed from the viewpoint of the social wholeness, rather than from the viewpoint of one person or another. Transference and empathy may not provide a satisfactory explanation for the appearance of unity and social configurations (Moreno, 1953, p. 311).

Tele: criticism

Moreno presented tele as the key factor for the formation of a society and human beings' realistic assessment of one another. Moreno's explanation of that two-way emotion between people, which is far-projected, seems like metaphysics from a social sciences point of view. How may one explain things known to exist that yet are invisible? In the author's opinion, the concept of tele should be bound to the explanation concerning the essence of mental energy as presented earlier this chapter as part of the discussion of spontaneity. Mental energy was illustrated as a complex of emotions, and according to the religious explanation, which Moreno supported, it involves emotions transferred from one person to another. Hence, it is asked: Does tele represent the same energy external to the individual's mind, which functions on interpersonal levels? Is tele the manifestation of interpersonal spontaneity?

Moreno himself thought tele was an abstract concept which may not be directly observed, but still exists, and is quantifiable and measurable. Tele may be measured only through discovering tele sensitivity by means of a sociometric test. Its existence became experimentally valid, which proved, without doubt, that it operates in association with attractions and revulsions among group members (Z. T. Moreno, 2006b, p. 283). It was a key advancement in social psychology, since it provided a means for employing tele and demonstrating its existence (Lindzey and Byrne, in Barbour, 1994, p. 2).

Furthermore, it was revealed that tele and empathy may be subjected to training and learning (Moreno, 1953, p. 317). Moreno himself writes:

> Tele is an abstraction; it has no social existence by itself. It has to be comprehended as a process within a social atom. But it is possible to classify it according to the equation of its social expansion and its social effect.
>
> (Moreno, 1953, p. 317)

Thus, tele functions on the level of will, social passion, choice and behavior within a relationship. It bears an effort-related aspect, as well as a cognitive aspect.

In the concepts addressed earlier, Moreno presented all personality components, which interrelate to form a special psychological dynamic, as will be demonstrated in the next chapter.

Chapter 3

Moreno's theory of the development of the self

Moreno's self-development theory attempts to implement his psychological concepts, namely, spontaneity, creativity, warming up, tele and the moment's time, into human developments. Those concepts are manifested in all aspects of personality's development, from genetics to birth, through the familial, to the social roles a person plays.

Spontaneity, creativity, warming up and tele: the developmental outlook

An infant comes into a complex world. At this stage, the brain is not sufficiently developed. In the first few weeks following birth, he or she is in a state of chaos. The brain centers, language, the coordination of muscles and walking have not yet developed. Even rocking, breathing, crying and urinary elimination have not yet been formed. The infant is transitioned from a cellular dimension into an unlimited dimension, from a closed place to an external environment, which is illuminated and full of colors, voices and sights; from the limitations of one position into a society comprising thousands of unlimited positions and directions.

In order for the infant to survive in the new world, his reactions must be ready on the spur of the moment corresponding to the states he encounters. The gap between the infant's physiological readiness and the life conditions outside the womb turns on the fact that he has been born and survived to be a near miracle. At that point, neither is the infant ready nor is he capable of caring for himself, similarly to most animal cubs. This neediness induces the interaction between him and those around him.

In that light, the following three questions are raised:

1. What is the mechanism which enables the infant's survival and motivation?
2. What is the mechanism that facilitates the infant in instigating interaction with other individuals?
3. What ramifications does this mechanism bear in terms of the inner world?

As stated, the infant's anatomic readiness in the final month of pregnancy does not provide a sufficient justification to the fact that he was born alive, or survived afterwards. There must be some factor which enables the infant's survival and interaction with another. That factor was titled "spontaneity" by Moreno, who claimed that without it, the fetus would not be able to survive (Bischof, 1970, p. 254).

As elucidated in the Introduction, Moreno referred to spontaneity and creativity as initial, positive phenomena, which contribute to personality's organization and expression. The spontaneity factor usually comes into action due to "act hunger". This process is portrayed in the following way:

> The self-initiated behavior of man and its most frequently used definition emphasize the factors of adequacy and novelty of human responsiveness.
> (Rabson, 1979, p. 40)

Basically, Moreno states that spontaneity prompts an adequate reaction to a new situation, or a new reaction to an old state. Another definition maintains that spontaneity is a reaction adequate for a new event (Moreno, 1934, p. 42). Both definitions neither are complete nor accurate. In the author's judgment, it will be more accurate to state that spontaneity is induced by virtue of the warming-up forces, and it is only then that it prompts an adequate reaction. Prior to birth and immediately afterwards, the infant demonstrates initial abilities and skills that are driven by his inherent spontaneous and creative forces. Those forces are active in other stages of personality's development, yet their dramatic manifestation appears at its best during infancy. In the author's opinion, the infant is not more spontaneous or creative than an adult. He is simply forced to exploit the sources of energy (spontaneity) more frequently, as he deals with more new states than at any other time in his life due to the numerous skills that he is acquiring for survival's sake. The transition from the world inside the womb to the new world results in a feeling of emptiness and anxiety. Returning to the womb is not a possibility, thus calling for the need to adjust to a new state. The warming up for the new state facilitates spontaneity's emergence. Throughout the act of giving birth and soon thereafter, the maximum level of the spontaneous action's warming up is achieved, allowing the infant to survive and live (Moreno, 1953, p. 336).

Warming up's somatic expression is characterized by many foci and organs which serve as physical starters. According to Moreno, every warming-up process occurs in its own organic locus. The oral organ is also represented by the mother's breast, or the bottle's nipple, and the infant's proximity to the source of milk. In that sense, the hands, feet and other body organs and areas may collaborate or form mutual communication with the original oral organ. The final outcome is that the warming-up process may be well placed outside the body itself, being channeled to other places, objects or people (Bischof, 1970, pp. 246–247).

As for adults, the warming-up process is categorized as physical and mental starters. For the infant, the categorization into two separate starter types is still not possible. The infant's mental starters at birth are invalid. The infant warms up through the physical starters and sensory-motor motions. The warming-up process begins at birth itself. At the act of birth, the initial movement toward emerging from the womb is the infant's initiative. He must help himself to be born. In the state of birth, the physical starters are in motion even before the act of birth itself. In order to be gradually prompted, the infant employs his physical starters within the warming-up process, until he has broken through the womb. Life begins with independent physical starters, which are incomplete, such as breathing. In order for a minimal warming-up process to occur, he needs immediate help, which he received from the mother and the staff assisting at birth.

The infant is capable of self-motivation to a certain extent, both in his efforts to be born and in life roles, such as "the eater", "the sleeper", etc. However, his efforts will be in vain if the assistants (mother, nurses and doctors) do not come to his aid. Immediately afterward, the infant recognizes the external forces which facilitate the independent physical starters, or, in Moreno's words, the auxiliary egos, who are the self's extension. The auxiliaries contribute to the shortening of warming-up time. The shorter the warming-up time, the better the infant's spontaneous act will be, because warming-up time is inversely related to spontaneous abilities. When the infant is assisted by the auxiliaries, the mental and interpersonal starters develop as well.

The infant's forgetfulness and "act hunger" syndrome

The evidence for spontaneity being the infant's main motivation factor is based upon the fact that other factors, such as memory and intelligence, are not yet developed, but rather, are in the initial formation process. Memory does not exist in the initial infancy stage. Under those conditions, the spontaneity factor is an active mediator in favor of the infant, long before intelligence and memory become available to him. When the infant grows a bit, things begin changing. He gradually shows the first signs of remembering people and objects that are intimately familiar to him, such as his mother and the foods he eats, yet he easily forgets. His memory span is rather narrow, thus the impressions of actions and events are weak and quite rare. In cases where there is no registration of experiences and events, no remembering shall take place. Subsequently, if no remembering has occurred, one is unable to forget and no suppression can occur. Moreno's explanation of forgetting is based upon a warming-up process preceding spontaneous actions. Relying upon his experience with psychodrama patients, Moreno realized that the patient was totally immersed in the process of action, as an active actor, and no part of his ego observes from the side, registering and assimilating the events. Similarly to a psychodrama patient, an infant is an improvising actor. Throughout the warming-up process, which precedes a spontaneous action, every part of his being is involved in the actions. No part is out of the action, which occurs on the spur of the moment.

The infant doesn't permit any part of its being to function in any reference except that of the moment – the immediate situation (Moreno, 1964a, p. 65). The number of new experiences with which the infant must deal is far larger than the number of experiences which an adult is to encounter. The need to acquire several basic skills, such as eating, walking, speech, etc., stimulates a learning process in many senses, which differs from the adult's planned memorization or learning. The infant is unable to distinguish the absorbed information from the action towards which he has been warming up. This is the basic reason for the fact that both dimensions, namely, future and past, are not developed or appear as traces of something unknown, at best. Therefore, learning out of memory does not yet occur for the infant, and he mainly learns from immediate action.

Throughout the growth process, lacking any experience to rely upon, the infant is so close to processes occurring at their status nascendi that the distinction between a state and a reaction is artificial. The infant encounters new states and experiences and is constantly challenged within a spontaneous learning process, which resembles no other time in life. Because of these continuous new experiences, for the infant, creation and existence are the same. The act hunger, namely, the longing for an action which is an innate quality and always lies within, is so great within the infant, and incessant, that he employs all his energy (spontaneity) for the action's sake, and to a lesser extent for memory's sake (his auxiliary-egos remember for him).

> The act hunger syndrome concluded that the organism of the child is driven by a hunger for action.
>
> (Z. T. Moreno, 1975, pp. 55–45)

In later developmental stages, where intelligence and memory have sufficiently been materialized, they dismiss the spontaneity factor and swallow it up. Spontaneity becomes a forgotten function as the child grows older (Moreno, 1964a, pp. 79–80).

Infant's lack of dreaming and the unconscious

Moreno distinguishes the time when the infant demonstrates forgetfulness from the time when functions of dreams, memory and intelligence are enhanced. Forgetfulness is linked to an infant's lack of dreaming. The infant's development process ranges between two worlds. The initial world is divided into two phases. The first phase is the all-identity period, where no distinction of people from objects occurs, the self included. The infant perceives them as many duplicated, undifferentiated, varied and complex copies.

> The matrix of identity suggests that unity and integration come first before there is differentiation.
>
> (Moreno, 1987, p. 131)

The second period is the time when people and objects become distinguishable and separate. There is still no differentiation or distinction between reality and imagination, life and death, mirror images and the real.

Accordingly, Moreno suggests that the infant, in fact, does not dream during that time, although there is no empirical evidence for that. The forgetfulness period was described as a time when the infant neither is able to register nor to remember past events. Considering Moreno's statement, this fact limits the ability to dream during sleep. Moreno rejects the prospect of dreams arising through past events in an all-identity time. Even the possibility that a dream arose consequently to a state that caused sudden fear within the infant at the spur of the moment is rejected. All dreams observed and explored on the psychodramatic stage, as well as those explored by other authors, referred to a time when the self, people and objects are differentiated.

The emergence of dreaming ability is associated with the declining of the infant's act hunger intensity. The dream hunger grows as the act hunger declines. The dream hunger will become gradually more valuable when the child experiences the gap between fantasy and reality. The infant lives in one temporal dimension: the present. The past temporal dimension develops later on; thus concepts like guilt and the unconscious may develop only when the concept of time has emerged. If the night dream indeed appears in the final stage of the psyche's development, then the theory of unconscious in itself may no longer rely upon the main justification for its existence. In Moreno's opinion, the unconscious may not be viewed as the source from which personality-related mental phenomena and contents may be drawn.

The appearance of tele

Moreno rejected the presence of the unconscious at the early infancy stage and focused more upon social forces facilitating the organization of personality. Those forces are different and distinguished from the environmental forces. The tele phenomenon development elucidates that point more methodically (Moreno, 1951, pp. 377–378).

The infant's psychological dimension develops simultaneously to the development of neural, physical, visual and hearing components of the cerebral cortex. This is also the time when the tele component develops. The sight and hearing senses allow the infant to outline the social dimension's contour. It is then when the infant either becomes attracted to people and objects, both real and imaginary, or retreats from and is repelled by them. This is the first social reflex, which signifies the appearance of the telic factor. This is the core of the dynamic underlying the attraction-repulsion model and emotional experience. The tele demonstrates the degree of attraction between different people, which results from spontaneity, or alternatively, the social forces surrounding the individual later on.

The previous chapter elucidated that tele, by definition, is the smallest emotional unit transferred from one individual to another, and is far projected. As for the developmental aspect, tele is defined as an interpersonal experience, which evolves from one person to another, and from a person to an object from birth on, and gradually enhances the ability to engage in interpersonal relations as well as in a sociometric structure (Moreno, 1953, p. 642; 1960b, p. 39). The tele phenomenon functions in all dimensions of para-semantic and semantic human communication (Moreno, 1951, pp. 377–378). When tele begins in the human system, he is a psycho-organic level of emotional expression, and over time, when the human mechanism matures, the tele's sensitivity becomes psycho-social, possessing the highest ability of expression (Bischof, 1970, pp. 241–242).

The theory of the matrix of identity

Moreno believes that any human action is examined from its status nascendi. This concept is associated with two other concepts: namely, "locus" (place) and "matrix". Those are the three components of which any action consists (Moreno, 1947a, p. 17):

> By respecting Moreno's sense, it may be noticed that the term 'locus' determines the place where something was born. Status nascendi is where the temporal dimension, the moment in which it occurs. So, the term 'matrix' designates that something is in its maximum specificity.
>
> (Bustos, 1994, p. 65)

The development and organization of personality by means of social forces occur in various social structures, to which Moreno refers as the matrix of identity. A person develops his life in consecutive matrices – genetic, identity related, maternal, familial, social and cosmic.

Genetic matrix

The genetic matrix is the first system structure where the self begins to form itself. The mother's womb is the locus, and the matrix is the ovum from which the fetus grows, and the status nascendi is the pregnancy (Moreno, 1964a, p. 52).

The profound mother–infant connection begins at the fetal period, where one body lives within another. Psychologist Michael Balint described the womb as a place where the infant is not subject to formative boundaries; the environment and the infant cross the boundaries between them. They coexist in mixed harmony

(Balint, 1968, p. 66). In that process, the infant is nurtured and is introduced to many processes in the mother's unconscious through genetic codes, thereby opening a new dimension of biological independence (Zuretti, 1994, p. 214).

Birth

In correspondence with Moreno's spontaneity theory, the infant does not come in to the world without actively participating in the act of birth. The physical separation from the mother does not result in a psychological separation. The psychological bonds last longer. From the moment of birth, the infant begins relating to others. He moves, cries and sometimes smiles and seeks the closeness of those around him. That is facilitated by the motivational forces, which are linked to the basic needs, including food, sleep and contact with others (Holmes, 1992, p. 55).

Spontaneity is the source upon which the infant relies in order to satisfy his basic needs. Additionally, auxiliary egos are available for support purposes, namely, people and objects through which he establishes his primary social setting. The latter setting facilitates the infant's initial socialization process, as unconscious as he may be to the process.

> The infant lives before and immediately after birth in an undifferentiated universe which I have called matrix of identity.
>
> (Moreno, 1964a, p. iii)

> The matrix of identity is the infant's social placenta, the locus in which he roots. [ ] According to our hypothesis, a mental operation like all-identity must have preexisted in the infant before operation like identification can take place.
>
> (Moreno & F. B. Moreno, 1956, p. 143)

Matrix of identity

The *matrix of identity* is considered the primary world in which the infant grows and develops. It bears various characteristics which are differentiated from the secondary, final world. The *primary world* provides the human infant with a social setting which provides him with confidence, direction and guidance. In terms of psychological development, this is the egocentrism stage, where the infant is unaware of people and objects other than himself. This primary world serves a structure in which the infant experiences his existence as the center of the world. Moreno defined that time as "normal megalomania". This phenomenon also refers to Moreno's perception of man as more than a mere biological organism, reflecting the cosmic aspect to his perception (Z. T. Moreno, 1975, p. 55).

The primary stage, where the infant begins organizing the self, is the stage when his self is an inseparable part of the mother's self. The infant feels as though the mother is his own extension, and together they form a whole unit. That stage may be constructed as a maternal matrix. The infant lives in a world where there is no clear definition, nor offering of any guidance, thus there is no experiencing of the self. Since the infant bears no verbal communication skills at that stage of his life, the child's experience, the feeling of the self, the people and the objects surrounding him are channeled through the mother or anything representing her.

> [T]he body and the self of the infant do not as yet exist for the infant. There is no self, no person separated from the infant. There is an identity.
>
> (Moreno, 1952, p. 244)

English psychologist Donald Winnicott (1989) uses the term mother–infant unit, thereby attempting to say that an infant is not to be viewed and understood on its own, but rather, always as part of the dyad he forms with his mother. The mother establishes a nonverbal communication based upon a two-way empathy, otherwise known as tele. According to the tele theory, telic sensitivity development is closely related to the matrix of identity and cerebral cortex development.

> Telic reciprocity proposes that a and b are an interactional co-operational unit; that they are two parts of the same process although occasionally at different points in space and time. Telic sensitivity is therefore a two-way process – sensitivity of the parts "for one another".
>
> (Moreno, 1964b, p. 164)

At this stage, the infant's dependence upon his mother, or any caring figure, is total, and his actions involve food intake, urination and defecation, which are uncontrollable at this stage. When the infant is hungry, he is provided with food. When he is in pain, an attempt is made to ease his pain. Thus, the infant learns trust. If his needs are consistently fulfilled, then the infant's development will be a healthy one. If the mother does not respond properly to the child's needs, then good mothering may not occur. In those cases, the infant feels there is no consideration of his true needs. In response to such upbringing, the infant will began to develop a false, forced self and shall attempt to adapt to the world while hiding the true self's emotional needs. The infant learns to look at the world as a place hard to figure out, feeling that he cannot be understood or figured out by others. Consequently, he lacks basic trust toward others.

The matrix of identity, the initial social matrix, grows and expands gradually the more autonomous the infant becomes. In other words, partially independent starters begin to develop. When the starters collaborate, as in the case of eating, urination, defecation, moving the body parts, etc., the dependence upon the auxiliaries will decline. As a matter of fact, birth constitutes an opening for the ever-expanding independence-oriented processes through the course of life, and the dependence upon the mother, family and cultural imperatives gradually declines over the years.

The self: an internal structure of role relations

The establishment of the first social matrix through human auxiliaries and objects, as well as the external adaptation through motivational forces (spontaneity and tele), still does not provide any explanation for the self's internal structure. Moreno did not offer any topographic mapping of the psyche, as Freud had, who discussed ego and superego.

Moreno identified three categories of roles comprising the self:

A **Psychosomatic Roles Category**. The role of the eater, sleeper, the nursing one, the sucking one, which fulfill the fetus' primary, biological needs, providing him with the body's sensation and experiencing, and are associated with physical activity. Those roles were genetically assigned, and by essence, were destined to allow the infant to survive and adapt to the environment and new people who are responsible for providing food, comfort and protection. Their dynamics are characterized by dependence and passivity, and they are mostly learned in relation to the mother figure.

B **Psychodramatic Roles Category.** This induces a sense of psyche and is associated with imagination and fantasy – father, mother, son, teacher, etc., as assimilated within us, but do not necessarily meet reality. Those are active roles, which involve work, self-confidence, the ability to achieve and practice attaining power and a sense of autonomy and activity, and they are mainly learned in relation to the father figure.

C **Social Roles Category.** The father, mother, son, teachers who induce the sense of society. Those are general rather than personal roles, which are linked to social and cultural conventions. Those are roles that are bound to friendly relationship of brotherhood, through which the child learns to act, compete, cope and share, as well as to defend himself against any type of aggression toward the self.

(Tauvon, 1998, p. 39)

Body, psyche and society are the forces mediating the self's various parts and the whole. The various role categories begin developing gradually, and an interaction system between them begins to form. The roles' quality, namely, the way in which one acts them on the outside, is influenced by environmental, social and psychological reasons. Frequently, imbalance has been observed between the role categories, and even within each group in itself. That imbalance results in a delayed emergence of the experiential, practical and actual self, or, alternatively, amplifies the self's disorders. When the role categories form, their unity may be identified and experienced, and hence be defined as the "self" (L. Clayton, 1975, pp. 144–146 ; Landy, 1993, p. 33; Moreno, 1964a, p. iii).

In Moreno's terms, the self is a set of roles, but this calls into question how those roles come into being in the first place. What are the foundations of human dynamics? Role construction is paradoxical, because at birth, the infant is a nonverbal actor, whose cortex is still almost entirely undeveloped. The infant does not have a world of his ow, where he can function, thus he is forced to construct or shape his own world based upon weak, small zones surrounding the body. Moreno presented the term zones to refer to areas serving as physical starters for the purpose of warming up (Moreno, 1964a, p. 56).

Those zones may be either operative or nonoperative. Each zone's significance lies within the fact that it was formed to perform a vital function for the infant, thus causing the infant to focus upon that given function. Whenever an object approaches the visible zone, a warming-up process occurs, and the zone's nervous/muscular system fulfills a leading role. Each warming-up process tends to be limited to a certain area as its source of action. However, the zones which have been the first to become sensitive through those warming-up actions are not exactly attached to the infant's skin. In fact, there is no oral or anal zone, but rather zones of which the mouth or anus are integral parts. In this sociometric sense, the zone is the area where the mouth, for instance, the mother's breast nipple, the milk and the air connecting them are auxiliary parts. Whenever those components reach a focal point, the zones appear.

> Every zone in the focal point of a physical starter in the process of warming-up to a spontaneous actuality state – such state or states being components in the shaping of [a role].
>
> (Moreno, 1964a, p. 57)

> In addition to being a zone, related to a given organism, it becomes the locus nascendi of starts warming-up towards objects and persons. It becomes the focal point of the spontaneous act itself.
>
> (Moreno & F. B. Moreno, 1956, p. 398)

The warming-up process with a given zone's set of starters tends to separate and isolate it in the practical aspect, more than what may be apparent through the physical state. The specific warming-up's focus appears in order to cause the infant to channel energy in relation to what occurs in one zone of his body, enhancing his attention toward the immediate action. As the infant grows, the practical, actual experience becomes more complex. He is capable of warming up to wider zones of his body, thereby encompassing additional zones. The separated zones will merge among themselves, to expand to wider zones of the body. It is noteworthy that different zones may be simultaneously operated and collaborate with one another, as do the mouth, throat and neck; they may also draw away from and repel each other.

Because the infant is weak and not mature enough, he needs auxiliaries who become part of the warming-up process. From the infant's point of view, those auxiliaries appear as an extension of his body and are essential for the infant to be able to properly act within the world (Moreno & F. B. Moreno, 1956, pp. 398–399). In light of this, behavior within a role, according to Moreno's view, is manifested first and foremost through psychosomatic roles (Bonney and Scott, 1983, p. 49). This role may be demonstrated through the role of the eater, which is the first, elemental psychosomatic role the infant fulfills. All the other roles evolve or revolve around that core. They are inferior to it, secondary, or at least greatly influenced by it (Bischof, 1970, p. 250).

The role of the eater

The role of the eater is usually perceived as an action performed by one person involving the simultaneous operation of both body hemispheres, such as the right and left hand holding the knife and the fork. This distinction occurs, because the infant's role of the eater is a bilateral adaptation action, which is carried out by both the infant and the mother. Yet in the first days of his life, the infant experiences those means as though they co-exist within him and as if they are his. Or, alternatively, he experiences his existence as joint to theirs, or being part of them. He is still not aware of the difference between both types, those that are his and those of his mother's.

Thus, assuming the infantile role of the eater consists of two functions: role giving, which, on the outside, is acted by the auxiliary ego (the mother), and role receiving, acted by the infant who receives his care from the mother. The mother is warming up toward the infant by several consecutive actions. The infant, in turn, by the very fact that he receives the food, develops some level of inner consistency. This interaction's outcome is predictable, and is gradually formed among the parties involved in the role construction process. This is a two-way warming-up process, aimed at one goal: to satisfy the child's hunger. The physical strain of organic adaptation is intertwined with the mother's mental adaptation (auxiliary ego). Observing infants breastfeeding indicates that the infant spontaneously completes the feeding once the point of saturation has been reached. Sometimes, due to a deficient warming-up process and lack of spontaneity, the mother is anxious, believing she does not provide her child with sufficient food. In such a case, she may try to extend feeding time beyond the infant's point of saturation, or, alternatively, to abruptly cease the breastfeeding session. There is also a reverse state, where the infant resists the rhythm dictated to him by the mother, which does not suit his needs. If such a negative process indeed occurs, it will result in a disorder which will manifest itself in deficient warming up in the role of the eater (Moreno, 1964a, pp. 56–60).

According to this view, the mother becomes the infant's first auxiliary ego, and this interaction yields the psychosomatic roles.

> This co-being, co-action, and co-experience which in the primary period exemplify the infant's relationship to the persons and things around him,

> are characteristics of the matrix of identity. This matrix of identity lays the foundation for the first emotional learning process of the infant.
>
> (Moreno, 1964a, p. 61)

This emotional learning is the beginning of personal identity. The image of construction and joint action process in assuming the role of the eater reveal a process of emotional learning, which is sometimes described as "imitation". The latter is a concept which is usually expressed as a one-way path toward role relations. The child imitates and copies the other's behavior. The mother's role is a cultural role (conserved). The child does not learn the role of eater from her, and it does not involve imitation or assimilation of the other's role. Rather, he constructs a role ex nihilo. Tele, nonverbal interaction indeed exists. It is the interaction that facilitates role construction, though the mother's role is a conserved role. In other words, the mother (auxiliary ego) assists in shaping the roles of the child himself by gradually allowing him a greater degree of independence. The mutual infant–mother communication process is the nurturing matrix of the first role acted by the infant (Moreno, 1964a, p. 63).

In the author's opinion, this action is referred to as a "role", because it involves an action which is a unit of behavior within a social context, which is linked to other people and objects. The primary roles are formed before they are connected to verbal symbols and before any social experience or history have been accumulated (Bonney and Scott, 1983, p. 49). Mead (1980) stated that the self may begin its development only from the stage when the language and social awareness develop, thereby allowing assuming the role of the significant other. Moreno, as opposed to Mead, argued that the spontaneity factor may revive an action even when there is still no self or language. The tele allows the interaction with the other even when there is no awareness of the social world yet. The action of roles already exists out of the sensory-motor stage act, which is based upon the child's need to move and become involved in action. The child repeats his actions, imitating himself and attempting new actions. Such playful activity facilitates in acquiring the psychosomatic set of roles (eating, sleeping, etc.). Those, in turn, allow the infant to feel his body. Through the physical sensations, the infant's physical self begins to form.

The psychosomatic set of roles is acquired at the stage where the infant is totally dependent on his mother for his survival and existence. If that dependence is spontaneous and holding, the child will learn to accept his dependence upon another, side by side with assuming personal independence as an adult. If the dependence on the mother involves anxiety and the needs of care and nurture remain unfulfilled, then the infant will face physiological and psychological distress, which will be linked to sensations of neglect and loneliness that will be transferred to other relationships, where avoidance of containment and acceptance will occur. The psychosomatic roles exemplified by infant–mother relations define an interaction model, which may appear in different times through the course of life (Moreno, 1961, p. 520; Landy, 1993, p. 33).

As the infant grows but is still in the matrix of identity stage, his attempts to become independent materialize. Over time, he will renounce some of the actions, which are the mother's part, and will begin to develop autonomous actions, leading to biological and mental independence.

The second real world: a bridge between reality and fantasy

At some point, the transition from the primary unrealistic world to the realistic, final world begins. The boundaries of the former world are broken, yielding a separation between the self and the world. The infant finds himself struggling with the second, unfamiliar second world, which also entails the sense of loneliness, as though he has been robbed of all abundant sources of spontaneity and creativity, which were his lot in the former world. He was not involved in constructing that new world, nor in its creation. He simply awoke into it. In the second world, he is forced to share the world with many other "self's" like him.

The transition from the first to the second world, in fact, begins the personality's organization, also altering the socio-dynamics in the infant's world:

> Following the second stage development, personality usually reacts to two types of actions; realistic and unrealistic. In Moreno's opinion, spontaneity dominates the rapid transition from one universe to another. Without the spontaneity factor, the individual does not always distinguish reality from fantasy. There are two courses of warming-up processes which arouse spontaneity; the one towards the realistic actions, while the other is geared toward unrealistic actions. The deeper those courses are etched, the more difficult the transition from one course to another will be. A deficient warming-up process may damage the emergence of spontaneity, and the infant will face difficulties in transitioning from one universe to the other, as well as to properly react to real states and objects at a spur of the momenting.
>
> (Moreno & F. B. Moreno, 1956, p. 407; Moreno, 1964a, pp. 72–73)

The infant gradually outgrows the megalomaniac stage, where he was the center of the all-identity world, moving on to the stage where he possesses an identity which is separate from other people and objects. That late stage leads the child to the awareness of two types of experience, namely, subjective and objective. The infant realizes that whatever he thought and felt to be his universe (fantasy) is different from the way others feel and think of the universe (reality). The shattering of the primary universe illusion usually results in some type of a traumatizing experience. The infant becomes aware that he is not the whole universe, finding himself in the second world, an individual among many. In order to overcome the shock, the child attempts to bridge the fantasy universe and the realistic universe by fulfilling some of the fantasies. As a matter of fact, the infant lives in both worlds simultaneously, namely, realistic and unrealistic, developing two emotional courses of action.

If the infant's basic needs are properly fulfilled, then he will learn of both worlds, balancing and uniting them as he relies upon the spontaneity factor. If spontaneity is improper, both universes will not be able to merge in a balanced, compatible manner. Then, a regression into the subjective, egocentric and megalomaniac universe occurs. Such regression may lay the foundations for personality pathology, which may be manifested by intrapersonal and interpersonal disorders and social deviation. From that moment on, each individual lives somewhere on the continuum stretching between both universes, attempting to maintain the balance between them, where spontaneity is manifested (Moreno, 1975, p. 55; Z. T. Moreno, 1989, p. 85; Williams, 1989, pp. 221–223; Moreno, 1964a, p. 72).

Because no individual may permanently live in a totally imaginary or realistic universe, reality functions by establishing intermediate values dictated by society. Moreno clarified the dialectic conflict between the individual's desire and society's desires through the development of two additional role categories, as will be illustrated later on.

Moreno described the infant's first role as megalomania, believing that the Prescription of either conserving or continuing the primary role's inner core means to repeat it. As long as the bridge connecting fantasy and reality does not exist, the realistic components and fantasies merge into one large role. The other roles evolve or revolve around that core, being either inferior or secondary to it. The core of his personality is supported by continuous reference to his own self, or by repeated doses, as Moreno phrases it (Bischof, 1970, p. 250).

Aside from the rather large, key role of the supreme self, which is acted by the infant, first at the normal megalomania period, at some point of his development, he must learn all the other roles which society demands from him, as well as the new roles he claims for himself. The personal roles may contradict society's demands, or society might ignore them, particularly when they are acted on the fantasy level.

Beside the bridge connecting reality and fantasy, two new role categories appear. Upon separating the imaginary world from the realistic world, the social universe gradually reveals itself, and the fantasy world breaks away from the psychosomatic world within the matrix of identity. Psychodramatic roles appear in response to the fantasy world. Those are roles which Moreno defines as follows:

> The personification of imagined things both real and unreal – God roles and ghosts fairies and hallucinated roles.
>
> (Moreno, in L. Clayton, 1975, p. 146)

The fantasy or psychodramatic performances are free of social, extra-personal imposition. Until the infant expresses his own desires, he lives simultaneously in both universes. In fact, he develops two emotional manners in his world: the one is realistic and the other is unrealistic. Those modes may operate independently, without ever crossing, and sometimes the original status is merged, or re-merged, because of the child's deep need to reintegrate himself with the cosmos.

This aspiration may result in a clash between both courses, as well as induce blockage and suppression of spontaneous flow. Both courses constantly struggle within the person's psyche. There is an attempt to maintain the balance between the modes in which spontaneity attempts to reach its utmost expression. As soon as the psychodramatic roles are established, they drive for an expression which may be manifested on a positive level, namely, employing the psychodramatic role toward social benefit, and on a negative level, social incompatibility. Psychodramatic roles are much wider and more dominant than social roles.

Whereas psychodramatic roles develop in response to fantasy, social roles develop in response to reality. Those are roles that call for correspondence between the infant and other people, objects and goals in true situations, outside himself. The social roles developing in later stages rely upon the psychosomatic and psychodramatic roles as primary forms of social experiences, which will serve the individual in adulthood (Moreno, 1964a, pp. 57–63; L. Clayton, 1975, p. 146).

The author thinks role learning in the primary stage is to be distinguished from role learning in the secondary stage. In the primary stage of role learning, which occurs within the matrix of identity, there is no imitation or assuming the role of another, but rather, functionality that is related to a role involving another. If the infant wishes and needs to eat in order to physically exists and the other person responds to that by feeding him, he has then facilitated his survival. In a situation where one person needs another, a role is yielded. Functionality causes the role to be yielded or to survive. Through nonverbal interactions, as well as through behavior's functionality, physiological roles are established without previously serving as social and psychological roles to interact with. The role is experienced through active learning, at the here and now, rather than through memory or intelligence. Such learning is experienced and assimilated into the self, but may not be studied, whether repeated or memorized, since it is experienced at a stage that precedes both the establishment of unconscious and conscious. The interaction between the role construction process in relation to personality formation on the one hand, and the social context on the other hand, integrates the role experienced into personality.

Once the maternal or paternal roles have been integrated into the self, they are difficult to embody on the outside in later years because those roles are formed and experienced consequently to shared infant–parents experience. At this time in life, the infant still does not distinguish the self and nonself. He does not experience those roles as someone else's but rather, as though they are part of him, as a complementary part of assimilation and adaptation to the external environment. It is easy for a child to act the mother or father under spontaneous activity's circumstances. The spontaneous energy perishes at a spur of the moment, and thus may not be employed another time while verbally instructed to perform the role, such as "act the mother". Furthermore, they are not stored in their memory. Moreno claimed that spontaneous, active learning induces integration with personality, whereas conceptual learning may be remembered, studied and perceived, but not integrated. Acting a role out is task oriented, whereas embodying a character is personality oriented, hence experience and role should be distinguished from one another (Moreno, 1964a, pp. 173–174).

Additionally, the role is a behavioral model which the person develops based upon his life experience in order to adapt to a given situations. In other words, in daily life, we embody roles for a specific reason (Dayton, 1994, p. 21). At the role's primary stage, the child needs the mother and father roles for his existence. When he matures, those roles become negligible, irrelevant and are not as functional as they were in the primary stage; his expanding universe absorbs a repertoire of social roles, which are more essential for his development.

At role learning's second stage, the social roles are learned and rapidly expand, since the child may symbolize the basic, primary language, linking that symbolization to the primary gestures, movements and sounds. Role assumption occurs through conditioning, perception, assimilation and a cognitive process. By now, the unconscious and conscious have developed, thus learning by repetition or memorization is possible. Plus, the "I" and "you" are now distinguishable; thus, the other's role may be assumed through imitation and assimilation. In terms of development, role assumptions continues when children assimilate roles of significant, generalized others (Landy, 1993, pp. 34–35).

Social roles (policeman, doctor, etc.) are not integrated into the self; hence they are easier to embody on the outside. They may be symbolically represented and explored more freely. Since roles appear in clusters, the mother's role may include a set of feminine roles, such as the father's wife, caregiver, etc. The same applies to the paternal role cluster as well. Conceptually, there is a transition of spontaneity from those role clusters to other roles, such as from father to policeman. Children who correctly assimilated the original role are capable of maintaining the new aspect of the role separately from their deep, old view of it and are capable of objectivizing and embodying the role in its new version. For other children, such a revelation may be more difficult; they are incapable of defining the role within its immediate social context. They are deeply dependent, internally at least, and sometimes externally as well, upon joint action with the mother, as in the spontaneous learning stage. Those children are considered less mature and spontaneous, and the development of their self is distracted.

The social matrices: family and external social systems

The self's inner structure development through a set of roles continues in the various social matrices to which the individual belongs. The social matrix represents all social systems with which the individual is associated. Each system may be understood in itself, without referring to the other systems, but since they operate hierarchically, their relationship is complex. In a social setting, there is a web of relationships which is constantly under development. They will be established or formed in accordance to the needs displayed by different social settings, in different times, and that, in itself, constitutes the human social structure.

The individual learns and develops behavioral patterns within the family matrix. The family is the smallest social structure to which a person belongs. The family learns the social models and connections, upon which its behavior is based, within those social systems. The familial association to wider systems external to the family, such as social, political and religious systems, associates and influences the individuals as much as it influences the family as a group. The dominant, representative figure of that growth time is the father, who symbolizes the authority figure. The father figure corresponds to the position of autonomous activity and connection to the outside world, though it is a cultural statement, rather than naturally determined behavior.

The nuclear family is perceived as most important not only because it regulates cultural and biological continuity, but also because it constitutes a means for instilling the generally accepted values to each individual. It places the individual in the social structure, determining its position within it, since through that structure he acquires statuses, roles and norms determined by force of association. The family provides the child with an environment where he trains for his psychodramatic and social roles established by other social structures. They will be the closest plane in which family members will construct and establish the roles through which they will be included in the wider social setting. This dynamics induces the appearance of the active roles clusters, which are characterized by self-confidence and ability to achieve goals. Most people are members of a family and are associated with it either biologically or legally. Being part of a family refers to the individual's ability to function successfully or unsuccessfully. Any change in one of the system members may result in an imbalance within the whole system. Proper integration allows the individual to develop within wider social settings. Thus, in Moreno's opinion, as far as the individual's development of the self is concerned, all interrelated systems, as well as the mental universe, should be taken into consideration (Holmes, 1992, p. 20; Bustos, 1994, pp. 64–69; Moreno, 1964a, pp. 174–176; Zuretti, 1994, pp. 216–218).

The individual, the nuclear family and the wider social systems are operatively intertwined. Those connections are formed between roles which allow drawing maximum satisfaction out of the given setting. Whereas spontaneity defines the unique mode and personal way in which a new way of learning may be acquired through roles, environment fulfills a highly important part in that process.

"Web of atoms": psychological, social, and cultural aspects

Each individual is a dynamic organism, which is bound by a complex web of ties with various people and societies. The individual is involved in a hierarchical system of both roles and emotions; there is a sense of mutuality and a total inventory of mental emotions and physical starters arising within them. This is a stable system, yet it frequently changes The relationships between the individual and other people may be emotional, cultural or social in their orientation. They involve feelings of repulsion, attraction or indifference. The whole set of interpersonal structures stemming from various choices concerning a certain individual is known as the "social atom" (L. Clayton, 1975, pp. 146–147).

The term "social atom" stems from the Greek word *atomon*, which means the smallest part, something that may not be divided. The term was introduced to scientific jargon by philosopher Democritus (370–460 BC). He used that term to refer to the smallest particle in the physical world. Moreno borrowed the term from the physical world, assimilating it into the social world.

The social atom is the smallest social unit, which may not be divided. It is also viewed as the smallest structure of human society. It is the special model of interpersonal relations, which develop from the day an individual is born. As a small child, the individual absorbs the systems surrounding him, the relationships between the parties involved and their roles. He interprets the information he has absorbed to his knowledge, and the information is assimilated within the recesses of the self's formation.

Thus, the self's developmental perception according to Moreno begins as early as pregnancy, continuing through an incessant proceeding of belonging to various matrices, which constitute the foundation for the familial, social, worldwide web. The development from a simple organism to a higher complex, separate and more complicated being is facilitated through constant acquisition of role repertoires. Accordingly, the following chapter shall address the role theory and its connection to the personality theory in various aspects.

Chapter 4

The significance of the concept of "role" in Moreno's theory

The previous chapter emphasized the notion that Moreno's view of the self's development may not be understood without connecting it to the term "role", with its various aspects. "Role" is a key concept in Moreno's theoretical system, directly linked to his view of the person as a role player. In itself, the concept "role" has undergone many metamorphoses been and differently interpreted, depending upon the professional approach behind the investigation. Theater professionals adhere to the theatrical aspect. Personality authors tended to focus upon the individual and his choices of self-expression, according to his role; sociologists emphasize role assignment according to the social class to which a person is bound, while anthropologists portray roles in various cultures and traditions supporting those roles and supported by them. Moreno, as will be demonstrated here, supported an interdisciplinary psychopathological approach. Understanding the historical evolution of the term "role" will elucidate the various interpretations, on the one hand, and emphasize Moreno's unique view and its connection to the personality theory, on the other hand.

The theatrical aspect

The term "role" originates from an old French word which penetrated into medieval French and English, deriving from the Latin words *rotula* (small wheel) and *rotua* (wheel). In ancient times, this word was used to describe a wooden paper roll, around which a tightly stapled parchment was wrapped so as to avoid its crumbling or breaking apart. Later, the word was used to describe an official volume of papers which belonged to the courts, such as in France, or to the government, as in England, such as memoranda or lawsuits.

The small parchment which served the actor while learning his part was called role in medieval French, and only later, the word would refer to the role itself, directed at nonprofessional actors who would publicly present the church's messages.

In old Greece and Rome, the theater roles were written on rolls and read by the prompter to actors who wished to remember their lines by heart. The word part (partitura) indicates the part the actor plays in the play. The term person is linked to the term "role" (or "roll"). A person is somebody who plays the parts without identifying with them, that is to say, a mere person, with no special qualities. When he possesses some nature or quality, the term personality applies.

The original meaning of the word personal in ancient Latin was a mask. That word served the Latin language deriving from the translation of the Greek word *prosophon*, which means the actor's mask. The word "persona" evolved later on and received a meaning that was reversed to its original one, again, because of the Catholic Church. In the fourth century, Catholic theologians argued for the Holy Trinity's formulation. One of the church's founders, Tertullianus, proposed the notion of three personas, namely, the Father, Son and Holy Spirit, and throughout medieval times, the term "persona" served as a referral to Jesus playing the role of God on the earthly stage, namely, as a representative of God.

"Persona" was defined as a mask by those who prefer to define personality in the sense of semblance; the emphasis on appearance, rather than the inner structure's organization. However, in ancient times, too, that term bore other meanings, one of which was the actor behind the mask, namely, the true complex of internal and personal qualities, thus even in classic Latin, the term bore meanings, some of which preceded the "semblance", while others preceded the "inner structure" concept.

Hence, the terms person, role and persona originated from theater's history. The role referred to a character as a certain type of a person more than to the person himself.

In the 16th through 18th centuries, with the appearance of what we think of as the modern stage, the roles assumed by the actors again received the same significance they bore in medieval times. The actors embodied the roles as a social mask, with an emphasis on the specific type of person embodied, rather than on the person in general.

In the 20th century, simultaneous with the development of psychological realism, the roles coming to life were of deep psychological complexity. The roles which appeared in masks allowed the actors to exaggerate them, taking them to the extreme, thereby yielding characters such as Mother Courage, Hedda Gabler and Nora Helmer – realistic characters that were given psychological depth. Yet at that point, with all the psychological depth within the character played by the actor, the performing artist embodied a role and acted upon the playwright's and director's instructions. He did not express his emotions, but the fictional character's emotions. He does not experience emotions, but rather, absorbs, conceptualizes and analyzes them. He methodically examines them, embodying them as a professional artist on stage. According to this approach, the actor and the role are separated by an emotional barrier. Constantin Stanislavski (1863–1938), a theorist and drama teacher, established a natural, emotional psychological play method, as cited in his books *An Actor Prepares* (1936) and *Building a Character* (1949). He broke down some of those barriers and thought that not only was the actor to know how to analyze and understand the character he was playing, he should also understand, discern and question himself to what extent he is able to find within himself, his feelings and life experiences similar experiences. This exploration allows both proper, reliable shaping of characters and the actor's deeper acknowledgement and understanding of himself. Some sort of a mutual nurturing occurs here; just as the actor constructs the character, the character constructs the actor. Stanislavski views acting as more than just a technique, but also an internal feeling, personal and direct, which the actor experiences in his personal life, conveying it exactly as it is "from heart to heart" through transferring emotion from past to present, and presenting it as though happening at the moment, for the first time, the actor induces a duality of experience, which involves present experience through the past. He lives the character through the self. The actor is to approach his inventory of memories in order to bring to light an experience similar in quality to the character's experience in the fictional situation within the plot. From Stanislavski's point of view, role consists of psychological and social factors, as well as physical and behavioral ones.

Following the footsteps of Stanislavski and his peers, who expanded the psychological plane to the "role" concept, a considerable part of the theater world was based upon role typology. The actor who played a role through a mask characterized a certain types of roles embodied in daily life; thus, in fact, life stories were brought onto stage (Moreno, in Fox, 1987, pp. 61–63; Landy, 1991, pp. 99–101; Moreno, 1961, p. 319; Rap, 1984, pp. 52–53; Moreno, 1953, p. 688; Moreno, 1964a, p. 39; Feingold, 1996, p. 18).

Thus, it may be inferred that first, psychology penetrated into the theater field, and only later on, theater and drama penetrated into psychology.

The social aspect

The word "role", which, as mentioned, originated from Latin, became part of the English language and other European languages. From the primary theatrical meaning, of a paper role on which the play's text was written, the word at its present meaning is attributed to the character the actor plays on stage and the description of role characteristics in relation to daily behaviors. This reveals an interesting fact: there is adherence to theatrical expression – the role is embodied, but it refers to a person's overall emotions, thoughts and behaviors, which renders the concept even more complex (Moreno, 1953, p. 689). In this day and age, "role" is defined almost similarly to the way role -lay is defined, being a functional characteristic and the individual's contribution to the group, as well as expectations in relation to a specific behavior and a position defined for the individual by the group (Bischof, 1970, p. 249).

The social interest in the concept of "role" first emerged in the 1930s in the United States, in the works of Charles Cooley (1864–1929), Ralph Linton (1893–1953) and especially George Herbert Mead (1863–1931), whose perception will be broadly addressed in comparison to Moreno's.

These schoolars explored the broad term "self" according to role theory's social perception, greatly contributing to the emphasis of the social dimension's importance to shaping personality (Landy, 1996, p. 100). Until those authors arrived on the scene, the dominant perception was a philosophical perception of the self that views personality as constant and unchanging under social circumstances, while those authors indicated the great influence of social factors within the socialization process on the shaping and development of one's personality and his becoming a human being (Ben Eliezer and Shapiro, 1989, p. 61).

George Herbert Mead's view

Mead was the first to use the expression "role taking" in order to conceptualize and demonstrate the development of the self through organization and linking of significant roles in a certain person's social setting. According to that view, the concept of "role" does not stand by itself. Rather, it is secondary in relation to the general concept of "self", which, in turn, is associated with the concepts of "mind" and "society".

Role is a process of action, which provides the social contents so as to allow a person to assimilate them and consequently develop her or his own identity. Hence, the concept "role" served as a fitting metaphor, which was immediately adopted by the theater realm, while ignoring the original theatrical meaning thereof (Landy, 1996, pp. 100–101). Mead's rule for personal identity development is based upon the dynamic tension between the "self", "role" and other concepts. Mead represented a philosophical movement which maintained that human behavior is not driven by urges or conditioning, but rather, on an outcome of his ability to judge for himself whether or not his behavior fits a given problem (Ben Eliezer and Shapira, 1989, p. 179). Mead's key idea was that a person's identity is not a firmly standing entity, but rather an incessant sequence of actions, occurring in the form of stimulation and reaction. Mead did not accept the idea which was common at that day and age among his fellow professionals, that stimulation is an external factor arousing a person's reaction. Rather, he believed that a person chooses himself from the prospective stimulations, thereby shaping on his own the environment which conveys the stimulations to him. Obviously, the main environment that conveys stimulations to the person is the one consisting of other human beings (Rap, 1984, p. 55). The self is not completely there at birth, but gradually develops through socialization and social experiencing processes, which involve assuming the role of another person. In the absence of social interaction, the body might develop, but the self will not come into being (Mead, 1972, p. 135).

Being a Social Darwinist, Mead perceived man as the final outcome of development through his ability of symbolic interaction. That ability allowed man to be an object per se, exploring his own actions through the eyes of others. Mead assumed that "generalized others", which he defined as the collective embodiment of others, are perceived as role expectations. Through a selective perception and the organizing the unique reaction of others to him, each person is involved in shaping his own form of generalizing others (Kelly, 1982, pp. 40–41).

> The individual is no thrall of society, he constitutes society as genuinely as society constitutes the individual.
>
> (Mead, 1934, p. xxv)

Mead's viewpoint was defined as social behaviorism; social behaviorism's therapeutic approach diverts focus from the imaginary, intra-mental motives and instead focuses on external behavior, which may be observed and measured. Mead emphasized both the open and hidden social action in order to understand human behavior. He determined that human behavior depended upon social factors. Society was perceived as a set of behaviors and expectations. Through constant interaction and contact with others, the self of each person emerges (Kelly, 1982, p. 40). That movement was called "symbolic interaction". It was named so by Herbert Blumer (1900–1987), who was a follower of Mead's and the founder of this theory (Ben Eliezer and Shapiro, 1989, p. 180). Symbolic interaction is based upon the idea that human beings interpret or define each other's actions; thus human interaction is mediated by use of symbols and interpretation of gestures which become symbolic, or, alternatively, by authentication and verification of the interpretation of actions taken by one person toward another (Blumer, in Rose, 1962, p. 145).

In Mead's philosophy, understanding the concept "symbol" is of great importance. We see and identify objects surrounding us, which bear social meaning for us. Those are symbols of meaning. Interactionism means that we are capable of communicating with each other through symbols, because they bear meaning that is common for all human beings. Through the self's communication with another individual, the self develops and enhances the ability to assume the other's viewpoint. Then, the other nurtures himself back to that same information regarding the self. Thus, the self becomes an object in itself. The key quality of the self is its capability of being reflective. We experience ourselves in the same way in which we experience other objects and people (Meldrum, 1994, p. 80). Hence, human behavior, is not only reactive, but also interacts, interprets and explains the behavior of another (Landy, 1996, p. 31). The communication between human beings is facilitated by mutual understanding of symbols and a consensus of understanding and shared expectations. The common meaning is the one which facilitates order within society, and the social action is the one serving the establishment of the self (Kelly, 1982, p. 40).

According to Mead, the symbolic interaction occurs through the act of assuming the role of another. When a person assumes the roles and positions of others within his social setting, he is capable of developing self-perception. Thus, a person acts toward himself in the same way others will act toward him (Landy, 1996, p. 31). Mead writes the following:

> It is only by taking the roles of others that we have been able to come back to ourselves. [. . .] The self can exist for the individual only if he assumes the roles of the others [. . .] We appear as selves in our conduct insofar as we ourselves take the attitude that others take toward us.
>
> (Mead, 1925, p. 25)

Brain

Mead thought the way in which the mind and the self develop lies within a process of actions in biological-social terms. Through the ongoing social process, the mind and the self develop through the assimilation of the gesture discourse. Mead explains that as follows: Human intelligence's development is spread throughout the long period of infancy. The infant's cry evokes a psychological reaction in the parent, where the parent adopts a protective behavior toward the infant. Thus, the infant's cry is a vocal gesture prompting the gesture, which expresses the parent's protective response. The way the terrified infant's cry sounded to him, just as it does to the mother, is psychologically similar. The child assimilates the cry and the effect of uttering thereof, namely, the mother's response. Then, he himself utters the voice the parent uttered to soothe him. In other words, the infant assumes the parent's role. Thus, children stimulate themselves in order to utter the voices they have prompted their parents to utter to them. The long period when the infant is dependent on his parent grants him an exceptional opportunity to play. Through the play itself, he assumes the roles of different people out of the social and familial groups to which he belongs (Meldrum, 1994, p. 81).

> Insofar the social situation within which the child reacts is determined by his social environment, that environment will determine what sounds he makes and therefore what responses he stimulates both in himself and in others.
>
> (Mead, 1934, p. 365)

During infancy, the child assimilates his array of roles, as well as his own self, gradually establishing integration through those varying social positions. He always conserves the ability to address himself and respond to a given approach by reactions which, in some senses, are normally attributed to others. The child reaches adulthood with the brain mechanism (Mead, 1934, p. 366).

Through the social process, the biological human, namely, an organism – becomes a rational organism, or, alternatively, a human being. Thus, the individual becomes a human creature with self-awareness and the ability to channel his actions out of awareness of his ability to render himself an object on its own. The human individual regulates his part within the social action by containing others' roles within himself. (Mead, 1934, pp. vi–xxv).

This social process, where all social figures surrounding us are assimilated within our personality, occurs through a thinking process. Thinking means a person's conversing with himself. When a person thinks an objection or criticism toward his thought and emotions occur to him, then he assumes the role of another, namely, standing outside himself, in relation to himself, yet all that occurs within him and the other may be general or impersonal, not necessarily a specific person. Hence, in Mead's eyes, the brain, similarly to the social realm, is a stage toward symbolic interaction. (Rap, 1984, p. 57).

Language

Mead emphasizes the issue of language, namely, the social relations associated with language. He referred to primary gestures as the early stage in the action of an organism who responds to another organism. The early stage serves as the foundation for a later, more developed stage of the social action, from which the primary verbal communication stems (Mead, 1972, p. xiv).

The vocal gesture bears most significance and influence on the individual. We hear ourselves speak insofar we hear others do the same, yet we cannot see our facial expressions, and normally will not observe our own actions. The vocal movement became a symbol bearing profound significance; thus the individual is aware of what he has achieved, namely, the language stage replacing the unconscious communication, using lingual symbols, rather than sign-based communication. In terms of behavior, a dialogue between the movements occurs: one is conveyed and the other is received. Hence, the communication process is a process of stimulation and reaction characterized as a gesture-based conversation.

Gestures in the human interaction consist both of the nonverbal movement component and the verbal component, which is heard. The verbal component is unique, because it is mainly based upon language. It is noteworthy that the language, though not the only tool of communication between human beings, is the still the main tool differentiating human beings from other animals. Mead maintains that only the human organism possesses the neurological ability required for establishing symbols of meaning (Mead, 1972, p. xxi). In the first stage of the child's development, his movements are spontaneous, and he utters sounds unconsciously. At the stage where he is to integrate into a wider society, not only is he required to identify himself with significant others, but with others in general, which Mead defined as the generalized other – namely, human beings who speak the same language and are subject to the same rules (Rap, 1984, pp. 57–58).

For Mead, language is an objective phenomenon indicating interpersonal communication within a group representing all forms of communicational, interpersonal symbols within a given society. The action of the individual himself is taken through language, while language, in turn, represents the existence of a certain society, and some biological abilities within the individual (Mead,

1972, pp. xiv–xxi; Kelly, 1982, pp. 42–45; Rap, 1984, p. 55). Language, therefore, is a live, symbolic means that serves people.

> Possessing a self meant that an individual could respond to one's self as another responds to it, could take part in one's own conversation with others, and be aware of what one is saying to determine what one is going to say thereafter.
>
> (Mead, 1969, in Kelly, 1982, p. 41)

Mead proved that the brain and the self are social discoveries and that language, in the sense of vocal gestures, provides the mechanism facilitating the growth of those expressions (Meldrum, 1994, p. 81).

The playful act

Mead proposed the idea according to which the social self development occurs through the playful act, which is a key factor in the child's development. Toddlers respond to others only through imitation. They imitate behavior without understanding the hidden intentions underlying it. On that basis, Mead concluded that since toddlers are unable to employ symbols, they have no self. Children first learn to employ language and other symbols through play, mostly through role playing (Anokh and Stern, 1999, p. 129). This implies that the development of the brain, self and self-awareness is a dynamic process through which infants assimilate adults' reactions and assume their roles. They get to know who they are the more they learn what society is; they learn roles meant for them, consequently learning to assume roles of others. This is the psychological-social role of play, in which children appear to fulfill a variety of social roles. All this learning occurs, and may occur only while interacting with other human beings, be it the parents or any other person who raises the child.

Moreno's interdisciplinary and psychotherapeutic aspect

As elucidated earlier, the theater component is more dominant than the theory of the self and social perception in the role concept. The theatrical source of the term bore no psychological or psychiatric meaning. It became included in the scientific index through drama and theater, as well as through technological conserve, namely, the book. According to this etymology, a role is a unit of "conserved" behavior (Moreno, 1953, p. 689).

The American school which Mead and his colleagues represented overlooked the original theatrical aspect, focusing upon one aspect only, namely, the social aspect. Moreno, on the contrary, who represented the European school in psychodrama, sociometry and interpersonal relationship, adhered to the original theatrical aspect, and, relying upon that universe, gradually developed the new perception and meaning, namely, the psychotherapeutic meaning of the term "role" (Moreno, in Fox, 1987, p. 61; Moreno, 1960b, p. 84).

In relation to the theatrical tradition and the long years of European drama, Moreno was influenced by Aristotle, who introduced the term "catharsis" (purification) in order to express the special influence of Greek drama on its audience. Moreno diverted the focus of catharsis from the observers to the patients so as to induce the sense of relief and setting oneself free, which indicated the therapeutic aspect. He developed the "role" so that it will suit therapy or psychopathological treatment. Hence, for Moreno, psychotherapy had become a dramatic technique of role play (Moreno, in Fox, 1987, p. 45; Moreno, 1964a, pp. 12–15).

The psychodramatic view of the "role" concept is psychiatrically oriented and more comprehensive. It encompasses all aspects of life, beginning with birth, and all through the individual's and society's life. The psychodramatic role theory consists of the following three aspects; physical, emotional and social. Furthermore, it allows observing individuals in real-life situations, in which they are practically involved. This psychiatric perception was extensively developed out of the clinical context as well, referring to industrial organizations, education, interpersonal relations, etc. Thus, Moreno believed that the new perception rises above the research limitations characterized by psychoanalysis and behaviorism, each focusing upon one aspect alone, either the personal or social (Moreno, 1961, pp. 519, 522).

Moreno supported interdisciplinary research of roles, which may facilitate overcoming the limitations imposed by the separate research approaches by removing the existing boundaries between them. He maintained the term "role" crosses the boundaries between sciences and is, essentially, interdisciplinary. The new role theory of knowledge and research, which he developed in the 1930s, aimed at bridging the interpretation of the term "role" by psychiatry and complementary concepts in social sciences and theater (Moreno, 1961, p. 518).

Moreno argued that most meanings associated with role and personality come from the psychodrama field, terms such as role play, role exchange, role player, outward play and, finally, the development and expansion of this day and age, namely, psychodrama and sociodrama (ibid, p. iv).

Moreno's and Mead's views: similarities and differences

Moreno and Mead discussed the social act, role theory and self's development drawing upon the same context. Both perceptions objected to Freud's assumption asserting that man is a product of his inner motives, as well as to the explanation proposed by J. B. Watson (1878–1958), who coined the term "behaviorism" to describe social behavior (Enoch and Stern, 1999, p. 18). Mead and Moreno focused upon what was then considered a unique outlook on man, which maintains that the true human interaction occurs when one person meets another. Although Moreno's and Mead's approaches stemmed from different perspectives and scopes of viewing matters, their point of intersection remained the research unit as a social act. The encounter between people at a social context is more than a mere reaction to an external stimulus, as explained and concluded by behaviorists (Kelly, 1982, p. 40). The discourse between Moreno and the behaviorist concerned the Skinnerian and Pavolvian behaviorists. At the time cognitive behaviorism (CBT), which integrates internal and external influences, did not exist. Mead and Moreno thought interaction seemed and was perceived as a creative process, where each person is shaped by and contributes to the shaping of others. Social order did not exist by virtue of any social plan to dominate it or by incidental occurrence of events, but rather, resulted from consistent assessment of social behavior and personal reaction, which was based upon assessment. When a person draws and concludes the meaning, he may react to it. The meaning of everything simply lies within the way in which people behave in a given situation in relation to an object, event, person or some experience. Both Moreno and Mead resolved the complexity of human interaction, directly focusing upon man at the context of his relations with others. According to the new interpretation they provided, social order may occur at a place where people draw close to each other, bearing similar understanding and expectations, sharing a common definition of the given situation (Kelly, 1982, p. 40). Moreno believed Mead and he were aiming at the same goal, namely, preparation for society's creative emergence and sociometric-oriented guidance (Moreno, 1951, p. 120).

In spite of the common points in their views, there was a difference in terms of their paths' focus. Mead focused upon theory, whereas Moreno focused upon the practical field. Mead was a theoretician who engaged in formulating the symbolic interaction theory. He relied upon the key components of each human interaction (symbols, roles, meaning, self), turning them into a uniform organic unit. He never withdrew from the world of theory and never practically studied interaction within a live group. In Moreno's opinion, Mead, similar to other thinkers as Freud, Dewey and Bergson, was an analytical observer, who looked upon the occurrence but did not participate in the action that was going on.

Moreno, on the other hand, focused upon the field of practice and experienced firsthand practice and training of human behavior. As opposed to Mead, he was personally involved in social groups in Vienna, observed social roles as they were being established and analyzed them within a practical framework. He attempted to establish a new methodology which would synthesize a player and an observer, a synthesis combining one theoretical model with another model, which was on the practical side, both were meant to form a model relating to human interactions in small groups. He developed a practical method known as psychodrama, which consists of all components containing Mead's symbolic interaction, but differently from the latter, Moreno's view allows more room for the emotional aspect, namely, internal influences as a crucial cause prompting external interaction. Moreno perceived role interaction as something consistently occurring, both in the here and now and in fantasy, as a reaction to interpersonal situations life brings about (Kelly, 1982, pp. 42–44; Moreno, 1960b, p. 86).

From his dramaturgical point of view, Moreno perceived man as an agent who is active in forming society. Man is both the player and the playwright of his actions. Thus, the true human interaction occurs when one person meets another as the experience originally emerges (status nascendi).

Moreno argued that if one wishes to meet others and truly know them, we must learn to see ourselves through their eyes, and they are to see themselves through our eyes (role exchange). It is because of this argument that Moreno was closer in his perception to Buber's dialogue perception, though Buber's approach is anthropological, past-oriented and describes an intellectual dialogue, whereas Moreno's perception is psychological, occurs in the immediate present and illustrates the existentialist dialogue. This approach to people and objects resulted in the development of a social method, which may be defined as the analytical-player, compared to the analytical-observer method, action research vs. research through observation. The analytical component does not disrupt the player's spontaneity and creativity, but rather, is a part of him. Spontaneity is manifested through the creative action that occurs in the here and now, rather than then and there. It is taken within the moment time unit, which addresses the present. In Moreno's opinion, it is a formal, passive, constant time unit. It is not characterized by creativity or spontaneity.

With the expanding sense of human spontaneity and creativity, we need the philosophy of the moment, which sheds light on the philosophy of the present:

> We must learn to realize that life is history in the making and that it is the status nascendi that constitutes Mead's present.
>
> (Meyer, 1974, pp. 155–156)

Moreno's social perception concerning the true encounter between human beings and the distinction of the analytical player and the analytical observer also manifests itself through his role perception, in comparison to Mead's. According to Moreno, until 1935, two role theory schools developed independently, representing opposing views: Mead's school and his school (the other social perceptions developed after 1935). Historically, those opposing views appeared in two books, which were published that year, a few months apart. Moreno's book, titled *Who Shall Survive?*, was published in March 1934, and Mead's book, titled *Mind, Self and Society*, was published in December 1934. The emphasis on the publishing date stemmed from Moreno's wish to prove that he was the first to address the role theory from the action-related aspect (Moreno, 1953, p. 689). Moreno claimed that his book was written "From the standpoint of a social Actionist", while Mead's book was written "From the standpoint of a social Behaviorist" (Moreno, 1951, p. 121).

The difference between both perceptions is highly important, because Mead developed the role-taking notion, while Moreno developed the role-play notion. Therefore, Moreno's highly significant contribution to the term "role" is related to the fact that essentially, a person is a role player. Consequently, the self develops, contrarily to Mead, who thought a person is, most of all, a cognitive being, who develops the self through the brain by means of a dramatic conception of representation, by assuming the role of the other. Hence, man is, first and foremost role taking, rather than role playing (Landy, 1996, p. 101; Moreno, 1953, p. 689, 1960b, p. 84).

Moreno's term is more active-dramatic in orientation. Moreno believed there should be a distinction between role taking, which has been fully established, which allows the individual no degree of freedom, and role playing, which allows the individual some degree of freedom, and role-creating, as the spontaneous player (Moreno, 1960b, p. 81).

Moreno's role theory begins with criticism regarding the conserved role. In his opinion, the more rigid and less modifiable the roles are, the more the roles will be ineffective, such as theater roles or social roles. The moment of creation is not free, and the performing player is allowed no freedom. Moreno observed the resistance some people bear toward several roles which were dictated in advance by society. Those people were forced to embody them in their conserved form.

A conflict arose between the conserved role and the individual, which causes behavioral disruptions, is defined as the man vs. role conflict. This conflict is much clearer and apparent in a professional actor, who must suppress his spontaneity. Moreno noticed the resistance among professional actors toward playing conserved role, which were written by a playwright, and which are imposed upon them, contradicting their views. (Moreno, 1960b, p. 84; Moreno, 1953, p. 690; Moreno, 1964a, p. 154).

The connection Moreno establishes between conserved roles and the man–role conflict stems from the acknowledgement that man is essentially a role player, and each individual is characterized by a specific range of roles which dominate his behavior. Plus, every culture is characterized by a specific range of roles imposed, with some degree of success, upon a particular group (Moreno, 1961, p. 522).

Moreno offered several explanations to people resistance to conserved roles:

1. We live in a constantly changing world; a new set of roles appears, attempting to dismiss the old ones.
2. Within a given society, one set of roles represents one cultural group, while another set of role represents another cultural group, both struggling for dominance and continued survival.
3. Just as the infant resists the assimilation of an organized language and syntax, he will resist to the set of social roles with which he copes throughout childhood and adulthood.

(Moreno, 1960b, pp. 84–85; 1956, p. 691)

The fact that role-playing technique was developed in a constantly changing world is highly significant. In Moreno's eyes, assuming roles of others, which have already been firmly established, allows no prospect for change, thus the roles are to be revived, dismissed or replaced by roles induced and required rapid refinement.

Hence, the goal was to find a way by which we would all become role changers and role players. In Moreno's eyes, role playing is probably the ultimate means for achieving that goal. The turning point came when Moreno proposed the idea of role spontaneity to counter role conservation.

To spontaneously play a role means warming up toward it and changing it in correspondence to any new situation encountered. The spontaneity element allows a person not only to improvise and learn new roles, but also to revive conserved roles or annul conserved roles which are no longer necessary, thereby forming a flexible, evolving personality. Role perception is especially important, since role play may be varied, as is role presentation and interpretation of others' gestures and symbols by means of outside information. If that does not occur spontaneously, namely, in accordance with the new situation, the outcome may be a presentation of unsuitable or irrational roles in social interactions. For that reason, Moreno argues, learning roles in the original situation is important, and if possible, in the original place where they emerged and were established, namely, in the status nascendi. The psychodramatic method he invented allowed him the following: (1) to observe the role process at the context of life itself; (2) to implement the role play and role exchange methods as a psychotherapeutic method (in deficient situations and behaviors); and (3) to explore and train for behavior at the here and now (Moreno, 1960b, pp. 85–86; 1953, p. 690).

> The objective of revolutionary role research becomes then to study roles in status nascendi and if possible in locus nescendi. The role was frequently found alien to the self as it is often to the living actor.
>
> (Moreno, 1960b, p. 85)

In the author's opinion, Mead's addressing the roles issue was only linked to their establishment in their reference groups and in the collective aspect. Mead allowed very little room for replacing a conserved role with a creative role or fantasy. Moreno, however, consistently searched for a way to establish a new cultural arrangement which could withstand and cope with conserved roles both in the personal and collective aspects. Moreno distinguished and differentiated the emotional and social factors in human behavior, also modifying deficient functioning by means of group therapy, which was based upon role playing. This is also the source of the problem in comparing Moreno and Mead in relation to the question whether a person is basically role playing or role taking.

The author assumes that when Moreno addresses role playing, he does not only mean conserved role playing, but mainly to that sensorimotor play as it occurs in the primary developmental stage; the modification of deficient functioning is conducted within the therapeutic-psychodramatic structure, where all of us may indeed be turned into role players, though that is not related to the natural development process, but more to role training.

The role as precedent to the self

As opposed to Mead, Moreno emphasized that roles emerge even before the self develops and stay with us for a lifetime. Role became a dominant preceding term, since in Moreno's opinion, even before the emergence of the self, the playful act is already present, and it is through it that the early roles are established in gradual stages, to draw the psyche's boundaries. Those roles are the pioneers of the self:

> Role playing is prior to the emergence of the self. Roles do not emerge from the self but the self emerges from roles.
>
> (Moreno, 1964a, p. ii)

Hence, Moreno hypothesized that the self is not an innate, genetic structure. Rather, it develops socially, emerging from the roles a person constructs and assumes:

> Role precedes self. That is, self is not an inborn, genetic construct. It develops socially from the roles one takes on.
>
> (Landy, 1986, pp. 70–71)

Beginning with the contradicting assumption, according to which the self precedes roles, and roles stem from it, then it might be assumed that roles are already integrated into the self, appearing according to need and necessity. Prior to their emergence, roles could assume a predetermined position. Moreno thought that in a world where the self is creative and dynamic, such a theory will be will be hard to accept. According to a view in which the self precedes roles, we are closer to past theologians' view, who assumed man is born with a psyche, which was described as the source of all feelings, emotions and thoughts arising or about to emerge. Moreno thought modern theology would benefit from viewing the psyche as a whole that develops and creates itself out of millions of small beginnings (Moreno, 1964a, p. iv).

Differently from humanistic psychology at the time, which viewed the self as whole and good, the self in the dramatic model is not constant or disconnected from a given role's context. The self evolves just as the role evolves (Landy, 1986, p. 91; Moreno, 1964a, p. iv). As stated, Moreno developed a theory which identifies three types of roles: psychosomatic roles, psychodramatic roles and social roles. For Moreno, the psychosomatic and psychodramatic aspects of the "role" concept are developmentally precedent to the social aspect of the term, and they are the ones of which the self is constructed. His view, however, remained unconvincing: on the one hand, he criticizes Mead and his colleagues, while relying upon their psychological orientation. Furthermore, Moreno proposed a dual perception of the concept of "role", both personal and collective.

> Every role is a fusion of private and collective elements. Every role has two sides: a private side and collective side.
>
> (Moreno, in Fox, 1987, p. 62)

The way language development and self development connect

The emphasis placed by Moreno on the fact that roles emerge prior to the development of the self reveals another controversy between him and Mead. Both were influenced by the movement and language issue in relation to the development of role and the self. For Mead, this issue assumed a great role in the psyche's life, living little room for research concerning pre-semantic stages. He regarded language development as a condition for symbolic interaction to occur, as well as the ability to assume the other's role, thus to the development of the self.

> For Mead the self and a society of selves are language ridden.
>
> (Moreno, 1964a, p. 157)

Moreno believes that the social perception which assumes a role emerges simultaneously to language's emergence, thus stemming from the same primary source, is mistaken and does not prove itself in reality. According to the psychodramatic role theory, the early stages of the "role" concept are not to be connected with language's emergence alone, as it begins in life's nonverbal stage. There is no reason to attribute a lesser degree of importance to areas devoid of any forms of language, categorizing them as subhuman, as Mead thought. Those silent areas coexist in every human with semantic and vocal areas and bear great potential for growth. Thus, it is impossible to restrict role theory to social roles only. Long before language develops, psychosomatic roles, which function actively, constitute an integral part of the child's world. Furthermore, Moreno thought infants were mentally inclined against the penetration of language, speech and syntactic grammar. The so-called infant language is a spontaneous language of an autistic nature, which is different from adults' syntactically organized language. It is more act-oriented than verbal, closer to the spontaneous act than the frozen word. It is devoid of meaningful gestures and symbols. Instead, emotions are linked to phonetic sounds and gestures. The basic language is characterized as an unlimited inventory of spontaneous expression, uninhibited by formal language's limitations. This is the matrix from and to which organized, syntactic language begins emerging and organizing (Moreno, 1953, pp. 32–34). Syntactic language is a later development within the cycle of life. It is preceded by the act and the player who nonverbally communicates through improvisations on the stage of life. Hence, it will be a mistake to reduce communication to reactions and counter-reactions and to link role development and interpersonal communication development process to human communication through language (Moreno, 1951, p. 121; 1960b, pp. 80–81; 1972, p. xiii; Z. T. Moreno, 1989, p. 182).

The tele phenomenon functions in all human communication planes, both semantic and pre-semantic. Thus, the "I"-and-other system does not necessarily require a language and a social universe.

Linking role and personality in Moreno's theory: reasoning

In Moreno's opinion, "ego" and "self" are unreal, subtle concepts, tending to be mysterious and meta-psychological, because they are invisible. Roles, however, are tangible and may be seen to the eye; thus working with the role concept in relation to personality constitutes a methodological challenge to him, allowing him to create a concept which removes the mystery from the self, rendering it known and tangibly expressed (Moreno, 1972, p. iii). The self is invisible and may be identified through role only; as written by the American psychologist Theodore Sarbin:

> The self is what a person is; the role is what a person does.
>
> (Sarbin [1954], in Landy, 1986, p. 91)

> The tangible aspects of what is known as "ego" or self are the roles in which it operates with the pattern of role-relation around an individual as their focus.
>
> (Moreno, 1964a, pp. v–vi)

According to this view, role is an observable behavioral unit. It is specific to a given situation and related to other people or objects associated with that situation. That means its significance as an act could not be understood out of the social context in which the role occurs. In other words, Moreno defines role as the mode of functioning one undertakes while reacting to a unique situation associated with other people (Davies, 1987, p. 114). This is the linkage to Moreno's personality model, which mainly addresses the interpersonal relations between human beings, with the role concept being the key element in this theory. Moreno emphasized that as individuals, we are mostly dependent upon others to serve as a source of support and appreciation, which contribute to maintaining one's sense of personal identity. Based upon this view, man is not perceived or observed as an isolated unit, but rather, as an organism within a wide social system, constantly engaging in interaction with his environment through his role and role structures. The concept of role provides a more accessible language, which allows better understanding of individuals, as well as interpersonal and group situations. The focus is human behavior's mode of functioning as appearing in reaction to other people or objects at a specific time and in a specific place. This view is characterized by its system approach, which considers individuals and their nets of connections (M. Clayton, 1994, pp. 122–123; L. Clayton, 1975, p. 144). "Role is a cultural unit; ego and role are engaged in constant interaction" (Moreno, 1964a, p. v).

This implies that understanding the connection and the relationships between the self and role, from Moreno's dramatic outlook, requires exploring the third party, defined as "other". In this model, the three terms may not be isolated from one another. The self, in spite of all its uniqueness, relates to the other, who represents the social universe through role. The role component, in turn, mediates the self and the other to the social universe. (Landy, 1986, p. 31).

Moreno considered the way in which a group of individuals spontaneously molds itself so that the personal roles are determined by the group and its actions as a whole. Moreno's social atom (the smallest social structure to which a person belong) may be understood as an open system of roles, which constitute the self's external manifestation, and through which the individual is involved in even larger open systems, namely, family, employment, circle of friends, etc.

The collective aspect of a predetermined social role was observed on the basis of status within a given social system. Each position within a social system entails a set of norms of expected behaviors that are socially accepted. Those norms set the boundaries to the individuals, by which he is required to function if he wishes to positively function within a given social system. Each is expected to live by her or his formal role in life. A teacher should behave as a teacher, a university student as a student and so forth. Yet an individual yearns to demonstrate and embody more roles than those he is permitted to demonstrate and play in life, and even to embody several aspects of the same role.

Stereotypical relations that are too dominant, submissive, or dependent, which may be noticed within social groups are common examples to the system's tendency to force its members to assume roles too sophisticated. Thus, there is confirmation for Moreno's role-related view as being dependent upon the dynamic social network, where one attempts to attain understanding and self-esteem (Davies, 1987, p. 115).

Moreno viewed the roles as a framework for creative changes, through which roles may be redefined over and over again. Roles' dynamics are based upon the notion that a person is multifaceted. Each role a person plays in reality reflects one side of his personality, another part of his identity. Sometimes, the roles within a person contradict one another. He is not aware of all roles and does not always accept himself with all the roles he sometimes encompasses. Roles that are not acknowledged and accepted guarantee the breaking out of interpersonal conflicts.

The self is unique to every person, and therefore distinguishes us from one another. Paradoxically, however, the individual's insight is based upon relationships with others, with the other's role being generalized and transformed in accordance with the unique way in which everybody constructs and creates mental images. Just as two theater actors do not mold the conserved role in the same way, though they say the same words and demonstrate the same basic actions exactly in the same manner, the life actor shows his own, unique version of social roles; role interpretation and presentation vary, depending upon each individual's unique characteristics (Landy, 1986, p. 92).

Finally, Moreno implements the role structure in relation to personality, since potentially it is measurable. As such, it paves the path toward empirical practice development. In his opinion, role tests bear the greatest potential for exploring personality because of the highly close interaction upon the emergence of personality, on the one hand, and the cultural context, on the other hand. All that is based upon the assumption that an individual's set of roles is subordinated to and subject to a specific culture's influence on personality; each specific cultural as assimilated by the individual and the way he interprets it. The role test is based upon the promise that roles are the most important factor defining the individual's character or social characterization. Consequently, even unique, personal roles may be linked to roles of group members or their expectations (Moreno, 1964a, pp. 161–162).

> The role is the most important single factor determining the cultural atmosphere of personality.
>
> (Moreno, 1972, p. 161)

> Roles and relationships between roles are the most significant developments within any specific culture.
>
> (Moreno, 1960a, p. 81)

As the following chapter will demonstrate, the use of the term roles, with all its aspects from a methodological viewpoint concerning personality, allowed Moreno, on the one hand, to establish his theoretical concepts, namely, spontaneity, creativity, tele, the here and now and status nascendi, while employing those concepts as the foundation stones constructing psychodrama, the therapeutic tool he invented.

Chapter 5

The personality theory viewed through psychodrama

The previous chapters presented the hypothesis of the cosmodynamic man, who operates on many spheres: personal, interpersonal, familial and social, and is involved in the dialogue with God, which is spontaneity's universal principle in both the philosophical and developmental aspects. The hypothesis aims at understanding the human organism as a being creating his own identity as a role player. Whereas Moreno's existentialistic philosophy attempted to portray the cosmodynamic man's ideal, psychodrama aims at converting philosophy into action, demonstrating the way in which that ideal may be fulfilled both concretely and practically. Moreno believed he managed to formulate a methodology in which he presents a whole new perspective regarding man, elucidating existentialistic psychotherapy's main principles. He viewed psychodrama and sociodrama as a bridge linking existential phenomenology to empirical science. Dasein philosophy became Dasein therapy (Moreno, 1959, pp. 216–217). By definition, this is therapy in action, within a dramatic framework, which justifies processes between individuals and within them, also emphasizing the transpersonal and psychospiritual.

This chapter's goal is to demonstrate how Moreno's philosophical and psychological concepts were converted and shaped psychodrama's purpose, namely, establishing a theater for rebuilding and restoring spontaneous man; a theatrical cathedral for releasing natural spontaneity and creativity, which Moreno believed are naturally inherent in every person. Moreno claimed the spontaneous self concept preceded his spontaneous theater establishment notion (Moreno, 1947a, p. 5).

Most of Moreno's theoretical points of reference were based upon life observations and were not limited to clinical experiences. Moreno's primal encounter with the role and personality issues resulted from his personal experiences of playing with the children in Vienna. He was impressed with the invention and originality demonstrated by the children while acting out the stories they had heard. Nonetheless, he realized that the more the children repeated the same story or game, the less spontaneous and intuitive they became, thereby yielding a mechanical, robot-like show. He also noticed that people become less spontaneous the older they grow. This phenomenon, involving energy storing and lack of spontaneity, is mostly common among people who suffer specific mental disorders, who repeat the same act regardless of the given situation, that is to say, memory or emotion stagnation (Z. T. Moreno, 1989, p. 179).

Later on, Moreno experienced the role issue when he began improvisation process in his spontaneity theater in Vienna, with adult professional actors. One of the actresses became ill with histrionic neurosis (a term coined by Moreno in 1920 that is common within psychiatric literature), where a conflict between her own personality and the conserved roles she was required to play was revealed. Based upon that case, Moreno concluded that powerful therapeutic potential lies within play. He began to question the essence of catharsis and its immediate effect on both actors and audience (Z. T. Moreno, 2000, p. xvi).

Following the encounter with spontaneity among children and revealing the person–actor–role conflict among professional actors, Moreno searched for a medium that would facilitate understanding the reasons underlying energy storing, manifested by cultural conservation, and also prompting the spontaneity factor to function as a healthy rather than pathological phenomenon; a medium allowing the observation of human personality through a person's roles and relationships with others. The medium is supposed to involve spiritual, mental and physical mobility of a person within society, allowing him to express himself not only verbally, but also physically. The medium which Moreno was searching for was also supposed to allow exploring and treating immediate behavior in all its space, through experiential observation of outer behavior on the one hand, and focusing upon subjective components on the other hand. It was also supposed to allow open expression and concretization of emotions and feelings, making them distinct in a clearly known universe, which may be controlled. The behavior within that universe will be visible, observable and measurable, and then subject to reintegration within the human psyche. Plus, the medium should be such that it allows one to investigate and explore the person, with all its complexity, out of the person himself, rather than through animals or defective personalities, based upon the existentialistic perception which views man as a whole entity. The patient is the main guide in the research concerning himself and constitutes his own cure (Moreno, 1959, p. 216). Finally, the said medium is supposed to explore man based upon his being in the universe, with all this world's complexity – places, objects and his relationships with others – so that a person will be able to explore the way in which he perceives the world and himself within this world, in the past, present and future, from the viewpoints of his family, friends and his own.

Those were the seeds from which the therapeutic theater, which was yielded entirely by incidence from the previously mentioned theatrical experiences, grew and developed. The more human experiences related to role-plays and real personal situations multiplied and became complex, the more the difficulty employing the term "playing" grew. The participants' commitment and circumstances of reference were so profound that the conception of a game was abandoned.

> The word 'drama' still seemed to imply a poetic fictional product and therefore the qualifying prefix 'psycho' was added.
>
> (Moreno, 1975, p. 30)

The existence of a dramatic alternative, which guides us in living fully and creatively as improvising actors on the stage of life, is eventually manifested in psychodrama – the drama of the psyche:

> It is a form of drama which releases realms of our being that were always there in our infancy but which had no proper channels for fulfillment.
>
> (Z. T. Moreno, 2000, p. x)

What is psychodrama?

For Moreno, psychodrama constituted a lifelike therapeutic model through which deficient behaviors could be modified and associated with his general views concerning man's creativity and spontaneity skills. Psychodrama represents the first organized implementation of the dramatic act for the sake of interpersonal problem solving and expansion of an individual's or group's awareness.

Essentially, psychodrama is life itself, and it addresses humanity as a whole. The occurrences are derived from real life, but they are understood through dramatic terms, as life's drama. The dramatic viewpoint constitutes a bridge connecting research fields, which is based upon the assumption that it is not only art that imitates life, but also life imitates art. However, in the author's opinion, there is one concept which guides Moreno's perception, which is attributed both to humanities and social sciences, to which the dramaturgy concept eventually leads: communication. Psychodrama's approach toward communication, with its various levels, is total. Interpersonal communication in itself is the art of encounter, or the "encounter" between two individuals, which is psychodrama's core.

Life allows merely a symbolic, intellectual encounter. The outlook of the universe is symbolic, because man, by nature, establishes and forms both personal and collective symbols. "Act" means structured behavior in symbolic terms, through which people form interactions with one another. The symbolic outlook of the universe is linked to the term "role", which is directly borrowed from the drama field, referring to that structured behavior which the individual establishes and demonstrates in a specific social context. Moreno clearly identified the representational, psychological and social power lying within the dramatic experience, focusing upon the present, which is the moment of spontaneity. Psychodrama is constructed to allow exploration and treatment of immediate behavior in all its spheres.

Moreno maintained that the encounter, which is the key concept of existentialism, was restricted to a particularly abstract philosophical meaning, following the works of Husserl and Sartre. The challenge he was facing was finding a way to induce encounter on psychodrama's stage as a consistent part of life itself, most concretely and tangibly. In other words, the question raised was how to link personal existence to the cosmos as a whole?

> The encounter is not produced in an artificial situation [. . .] when two beings coincide in the encounter, they attain the greatest truth of their lives.
>
> (Moreno and Z. T. Moreno, 1969, p. 25)

Direct encounter calls for utmost authenticity and involvement in the encounter of the self and the other in the here and now.

> Being in this world is based on the relationship of one man or woman to others and on the emotional and intellectual climates they create spontaneously with each other in the short time they are together.
>
> (Holt, 1966, p. 610)

In Moreno's opinion, the classic theater reduces the utmost expression of real life, not facilitating people's encounters, and coping with their real problems. It is characterized by some reducing of real-life patterns, while life is to be experienced to its utmost greatness. Human encounter should be turned into the exalted essence of human existence. That should be the path leading to the experience of the self through exchanging roles with the other, and fulfilling the rare, unforgettable experience of total interaction.

Hence, the encounter theater's purpose is to enhance and train human abilities to become involved in new, spontaneous and healthy encounters, with the main intention being to re-establish a new tele between people or various roles and characters by means of role ex-transition.

> The existential encounter is, in its highest form of communication, more than a collection of roles. It goes beyond psychodrama. For this kind of encounter there is no specific therapy available. For it, there is no therapy necessary. It is a form of therapy in itself. But for the forms of encounter which fall short of this experience psychodrama is the most appropriate therapy we know. No one is left out. Psychodrama enables the protagonist to build a bridge beyond the roles he plays in his daily existence, to surpass and transcend the reality of life as he lives it, to get into a deeper relationship with existence, to come as close as possible to the highest form of encounter of which he is capable.
>
> (Moreno and Z. T. Moreno, 1969, p. 29)

The notion according to which traditional drama outlines life within a microcosm, particularly the roles embodied in human interactions, was not new to philosophical views of that day and age. What differentiated Moreno from others was a dramatic integration of traditional existentialistic themes, which were linked to face-to-face encounters of people. That integration demonstrated the here and now concept, the act, moral responsibility, the role and drama of interaction. Finally, existentialism was complemented by the notion missing from Nietzsche's legacy, namely, regular social orientation.

> Encounter has reached the sociometric level, the sociology of the people, by the people and for the people; it is no longer a matter for philosophers, priests, physicians, scientists, but a matter of the people.
>
> (Moreno, 1972, pp. 212–213)

Moreno's main contribution to the new approach lay within the fact that by clearly understanding the encounter and its key dramatic nature, it became possible to develop techniques which will result in a focusing and re-embodiment of the encounter in action, not in the sense of play-acting, but rather, in the sense of doing, namely, performing an act. Moreno succeeded in understanding what other existentialists failed to understand. It was the ultimate meaning of moving into action (J. D. Moreno, 1976, p. 29).

> But there is an alternative, to step into life itself, as a producer, to develop a technique from the moment upward in the direction of spontaneous-creative evolution of society, in the direction of life and time.
>
> (Moreno, 1953, p. 11)

Moreno synthesized drama's medium and modern psychology's insights by means of the psychodramatic method. He resolved the contradiction between theatrical drama and existentialistic encounter by turning the audience and the actors into participants. He modified the conventional theater's structure and architecture; he annulled the theatrical stage, exempting the actors from relying upon the prewritten script. Instead, he included their personal lives in the script, without rehearsals, without a playwright, but with absolute spontaneity, where everybody became potential actors in dramas where scripts, situations and roles, whether imaginary or real, reflected their true problems. They were actors of their collective drama, namely, the social-dramatic conflicts in which they were involved in reality (Moreno, 1964a, p. 1). Psychodrama's theatrical element was only implied. There, everything was real, as in life itself, as an extension of their own lives. It might have been even more real than life itself, as in life, they would wear masks; that is to say, one does not present his true self in daily life, either. This is the theater where life is explored through play. This is the place designated for truth and for everybody; a theater where all people are driven, emotionally aroused, transitioning from a state of awareness to a state of spontaneity, from the real, practical world, with true thoughts and emotions, into a world of fantasy, which contains reality's potential. The value of life is measured by the value of spontaneity (Moreno, 1947a, p. 31). All that became possible in the theater of psychodrama:

> 1) By declaring the pathological normal and providing for all forms of pathological behavior a world sui generis, simply by giving the venerable theatre a psychiatric twist in the form of the therapeutic drama; 2) by giving all forms of subjective existence, including the prophetic and the deviate, a place where it can fulfill and perhaps transform itself; unencumbered by the restrictions of the prevailing culture; 3) by preparing the way for therapeutic community in which the prophetic and the deviate would find better treatment and deeper understanding and so be able to contribute to its total productivity.
>
> (Moreno, 1959, p. 215)

In this ideal play, all essential elements are presented respectively: the production process with respect to the presentation process; the spontaneous state with respect to the word, before it became conserved. The science of conventional drama, which is based upon rules and principles derived from analytical studies, as well as from an organized set of situations and dialogues, is transformed into the science of spontaneous drama, the science of here and now art, which reveals a new form of psychological rules, that are based upon the creative act itself, emerging in the status nascendi. Since the spontaneous actor is the producer and director of his own role, he must immediately integrate and establish a sequence of actions, as they emerge in the status nascendi so that they do not block or hide one another, but rather, create a total, unified wholeness, which bears meaning (Moreno, 1941, p. 216).

In its classic version, psychodrama was fully spontaneous for both the group and the director, without rehearsal or pre-meditation, occurring in the here and now, rather than yesterday or tomorrow (Moreno, 1953, p. lxxi).

In the spontaneity theater, the 'I-Thou' encounter concept, the "here and now" concept, is not a function of the past or future, but is a category in itself; the notion of a concrete situation and the here and now fulfillment at a specific setting were practically implemented. The challenge stemming from that is the idea of spontaneity and creativity as a universal behavioral process (Moreno, 1949a, pp. 203–204).

> The theatre for psychodrama stems from the theatre of spontaneity which had originally nothing to do with therapy. It introduced a new art of the theatre and the drama, as it called itself an "art of the moment".
>
> (Moreno, 1947a, p. 99)

> By whatever name we call this living and creating in the moment, psychodrama is the method of our last stand, into which we pack all our resources,

> magic and scientific, physiological, pharmacological, sociological, cultural, and cosmic, so as to successfully encounter and answer the demands of life in this moment, the here and now.
>
> (Moreno, 1964b, pp. 170–171)

> Both Freud and Jung have studied man as an historical development; the one from the biological, the other from the cultural aspect. On the other hand, our approach has been that of direct experiment, man in action, man thrown into action, the moment not a part of history but history as part of the moment – sub species momenti.
>
> (Moreno, 1945, p. 21)

In order to reunite life with its representation, the early psychodramas took place in the actual reality. Life is equal to drama, and drama is equal to life. What we lose in reality we gain by setting intermediary values of techniques serving the psyche's experience far beyond all that life brings about. Psychodrama allows us to expand this experience by means of techniques which are not implemented on a daily basis, but facilitate the highest level of existence; techniques as auxiliary-egos, auxiliary chair, double, role extransition, mirror, magic shop, the high chair, psychodramatic infant, soliloquy, rehearsal for living, etc. (Moreno and Z. T. Moreno, 1969, p. 28). Those techniques are feasible within the surplus reality framework. In psychodrama, surplus reality is an enhancement of reality through extensive use of imagination. Surplus reality is a universe without boundaries, setting a person free from the real world and creating an "as if" world.

> There is in psychodrama a mode of experience which goes beyond reality which provides the subject with a new and more extensive experience of reality, a surplus reality.
>
> (Moreno, 1965a, p. 213)

Within surplus reality's framework universal psychotherapy had been facilitated, where time, space, reality and cosmos are considered.

To begin with, psychodrama's purpose was to establish a therapeutic setting which relies upon life as a model, integrating all life models from universal things as time, space, reality and cosmos, to life's small details and trifles, and practical reality (Moreno and Z. T. Moreno, 1969, p. 23). Throughout the course of life, time is experienced in three dimensions: past, present and future. As a psychological-therapeutic concept, time has been addressed to a limited extent. Psychodrama, however, integrates all time places: past, present and future. All three are explored in a current situation, through a practical action. All time spaces are brought together, as they are in life, from functional therapy's viewpoint (Moreno and Z. T. Moreno, 1969, p. 13).

> Time represents the passage of the psyche which is forever living in the present manifesting the past, and by so doing, describing the future.
>
> (Lousada, 1998, p. 207)

The concept of "space" has been overlooked in all branches of psychotherapy as well – not semantically or psychologically, but concretely, within the therapeutic process. The space concept in psychotherapy, which is, in essence, action, was first demonstrated in psychodrama, which demands actualization of space (Moreno and Z. T. Moreno, 1969, p. 13).

Now we reach the discussion of another space of the psyche's life's unique structure. There is a reality broader than psyche's dynamics or social dynamics. This reality is the universe's dynamics.

> Motto: A science of man should start with a science of the universe. A central model of the universe hovers continuously in our minds, if not consciously than unconsciously, whether magical, theological or scientific. It influences the form, the central model man takes. An incomplete or deficient model of the universe is better than none.
>
> (Moreno, 1956, p. 359)

Moreno claimed in the first place that man is a cosmodynamic creature, rather than only social or economic. Psychopathology and psychotherapy of the cosmos allow the cosmodynamic man an opportunity to express himself in all spaces of life. Just as time, space and reality have functions, cosmos' function must integrate into the therapeutic setting. For the patient, it bears existential and experiential value. In Moreno's opinion, any therapeutic method which does not address the cosmic ramifications of human fate is a lacking, incompatible method. Within psychodrama's therapeutic process, the cosmic phenomenon may be integrated in a variety of techniques. At this point, the surplus reality technique is prioritized.

In the psychodramatic universe, anatomical and physiological differences are ignored, as well as gender and age differences. For instance, a man may act as a woman, and vice versa. Likewise, differences related to life and death are ignored. In psychodrama, there are no boundaries, but not in a sense of regression, but rather, in a sense of creative involvement. This nation manifested by creating a fictional character, a real character, an animal character or any other character. Man is not bound by actual facts, though not belittling them, leading to the thought that things transition and nothing is carved in stone or absolute. It is not a call for illusion or escaping reality, but just the opposite: this is a call for man's creativity. This is a type of surplus art channeled to cosmodynamics.

We live within a time, space and reality framework, which may be enhanced only if explored within an experimental therapeutic setting, where they are expressed and experienced, where they are practiced and reunited within a framework of psychotherapy which follows the model of life itself. Otherwise, the distinction between time, space and reality expression in life itself, and their representation within the therapeutic process, may be irrelevant.

> Thus it is imperative that we transfer these phenomena from life itself into the therapeutic setting and back from the therapeutic setting into life setting.
>
> (Moreno and Z. T. Moreno, 1969, p. 22)

Surplus reality framework may contain the cosmodynamic man hypothesis, as well as explore and enhance in behavior in all life spaces in a tangible, actual way.

> This new man may be called the "Cosmic Man". He is just as real as the animal and just as symbolic as homo sapiens, but a synthesis of both.
>
> (Moreno, 1959, p. 225)

Psychodrama: structure and components

The structure and components involved in the psychodramatic occurrences, in the surplus dramatic reality, are equivalent to life components in the actual outer reality.

The protagonist

The word "protagonist" originates from two Greek words: *protos*, which means "first", and *agnoistes*, which means "to compete", "to be a rival". At the time during ancient times in Greece, the protagonist served as the author, the director and the actor. In a later development of drama, those roles were separated and allocated to different persons. Now, the dramas were directed and rehearsed. They were no longer spontaneous, even if played only once. In the much later dramas, the protagonist performed out of the chorus, and the written drama was the source of the protagonist-chorus dialogue (Z. T. Moreno, 2000, p. 85).

The word "protagonist" may also be interpreted as "first in agony", the first to experience sorrow, suffering, struggle. Indeed, following the ancient tribal drama, the Greek classics defined the protagonist as the person whose tale of suffering is laid on the stage. The subject, the coping therewith and the purification at the drama's end represented a process undergone by each and every person in that same tribe or group (Artzi, 1991, p. 66).

The psychodrama's protagonist is analogous to the one which was common in classical Greece. He embodies all the roles, and yet is required to maintain his selfness on stage, rather than being a dramatic actor, and outline his own, private universe (Moreno, 1953, p. 82). In classic psychodrama, some of the ancient motives may be found. First, the protagonist is selected by his fellow group members – this implies that he is their chosen one, the "first" of them to represent them in a given matter (Artzi, 1991, p. 66). However, since Moreno was also influenced by the Greek theater, we may assume that he intended to imply that the psychodrama protagonist also undergoes Dionysus' journey of suffering.

The protagonist, or the psychodramatic plot's main character, is a group member who turns into the whole group's center of activity. Usually, the protagonist emerges out of some kind of a warming-up process. The protagonist is in the upper end of the warming-up stage. He is mature and prepared to explore a problem, issue or conflict, and he may explore whatever he wishes (Naharin, 1985, p. 23; Kellermann, 1986, p. 8). Once he has warmed up for the task, it is easier for the protagonist to express his daily life through action, because there is no supreme authority for him but himself. He is supposed to freely act, as things come to his mind; hence he should be granted the freedom of spontaneous expression, which is followed by the embodiment process. The verbal level is elevated and included within action's level (Moreno, 1953, p. 82). While in a spontaneous state, the protagonist presents an event out of his real-life story by means of improvisation role-plays, so that the self and roles are distinct, yet merging.

> Protagonist means man in frenzy, a madman. A theater for a madmen, a theater for psychodrama is thus a theater of the madman.
>
> (Moreno, 1964a, p. 12)

During the embodiment, the protagonist acts out his life, revealing his own universe, bringing up the true characters and experiences (even if he imagines them, they possess a core of truth). Assisted by the facilitator and the auxiliary-egos, he encounters the characters involved in his mental conflicts, as well as the parts in controversy within himself (Moreno, 1951, p. 104).

From the moment he begins embodying the significant ones in his life as he has fantasized them, not only do they lose their power but also he may now avoid wasting his energy on them. His benefit is great satisfaction, which leads him to positions he has never experienced before. The self is granted the opportunity for self-acknowledgement, reuniting all figures which might have been separated before, and, in fact, gaining some degree of power and freedom to develop all the sources of his unique personality and reach a catharsis of integration (Moreno, in Fox, 1987, p. 13).

In psychodrama, the participants usually undergo four stages: warming up, action, closure and division. At first, the protagonist is selected and he is assisted in being emotionally involved (warming up) in the production. Then, the protagonist dramatizes situations, which is defined as the action stage. Toward the end, the protagonist is assisted in forming the integration of the dramatized contents, of finding some sort of closure. Following the action, the observers are invited to share experiences with the protagonist in a nonjudgmental way and discuss the extent to which they were affected by the session (Kellermann, 1986, p. 8).

Group

As a response to the human, social structure, psychodrama offers the therapeutic group as a representation of society within its various levels. The group provides the protagonist with support and feedback, facilitating him in overcoming fears and inhibitions. If necessary, the group members assume roles of significant others or generalized others as they appear in the protagonist's life, whether through interaction or encounter. When the interactions within the psychodramatic play are in order, the group influence is compared to the basic value of the individual notion, developing his versatility and creativity, namely, learning and acquiring new roles and abandoning conserved, incompatible ones. Without the process of moderation and adoption of a new, different outlook, the individual will not find his creativity. A rigid position, namely, conserved roles, is the counter-position of creativity and does not allow the individual to integrate into any social collective.

In this work, human development has been derived through his belonging to various groups, which mold his behavior and personality. It is within those groups that individuals establish interactions with one another, developing emotions, some conscious and others unconscious (tele). The tele process between people indicates the way in which one acquires friends and partners for life or makes other emotional preferences. (Bannister, 1998, pp. 111–115)

Moreno realized that by working with tele forces in a group, people may learn new ways and modify their behavior. Interactions and tele relations which occur naturally are established, examined and re-examined at the conscious therapeutic context, as close as possible to the reality of life. The group is actively involved in the extensive help with which she provides the protagonist in establishing his tele relations with his significant others. The group fulfills another function, namely, the audience role. The audience consists of the group members who are present during the psychodrama, playing the protagonist or auxiliary-ego roles (Rabson, 1979, p. 10).

The audience fulfills an important role in relation to the protagonist, as he fulfills all auxiliary roles and assists in clarifying his social image (public opinion) by means of a spontaneous feedback. (Naharin, 1985, pp. 29–30). For the protagonist, the audience constitutes a representation of the universe. Much of the therapeutic output revealed on stage may be attributed to the presence of the audience. The presence of the audience expands the range of responses which may be produced from the patient on stage, providing the director with strategic material for analysis. The patient's behavior during the discussion of his problem and when other group members discuss their own problems bears significance, and if there were no audience, that kind of exploration would not be possible (Moreno, 1964a, p. 262).

For each individual in the group, the group serving as an audience represents the outside society, where he lives and returns, the mother society.

The stage

The psychodramatic occurrence attempts to provide a reconstruction that is as accurate as possible of the experience's original locus, as it took place in reality. Locus represents a point where a choice is made, as for therapeutic intervention. The stage is a core tool, integral to the ideal of psychodrama's objective form. The stage is not a means in itself, but rather, part of the positioning of the structure and total setting (Moreno, 1965a, p. 212; Moreno, 1964a, p. 262).

Moreno referred to psychodrama as sort of a dramatic religion, with which he was going to present humanity, hoping it would replace the conventional theater and serve as a means of expression for the spontaneous, creative and cosmodynamic man. Constructing the stage of the new theater, psychodrama was supposed to serve that purpose (Moreno, 1947a, p. 4). As in religion, in psychodrama the means provide psychotherapy with a live anchorage for total involvement.

The architectural design of the stage corresponds to the performing-related and therapeutic requirements, allowing mobility and versatility of action. The patient may perform and act on the stage, presenting his universe and significant ones. His encounter with them takes place in the presence of the audience (Moreno, 1948c, pp. 193–194).

In practice, the stage is the place where the psychodramatic evolves. The stage may be any space upon which the group and facilitator agree. The action must occur in situ, namely, in the actual place of conflict or issue (Rabson,1979, p. 17). Although psychodrama may be conducted anywhere the patients are, the ultimate solution of a deep mental conflict calls for the therapeutic theater's objective setting (Moreno, 1953, p. 82; Moreno, in Fox, 1987, p. 13). Moreno devised an idea for a special stage, which, he believed, reflected his mode of psychodramatic thinking (Artzi, 1991, pp. 63–64).

The stage is part of the psychodramatic session, paving the path toward dramatic methods for research and therapy in action, role test, role training and ideas for situations where the audience is an integral part of the psychotherapeutic process (Moreno, 1951, p. 105). The psychodramatic stage is the protagonist's exclusive territory. It is some kind of a space which allows him to set himself free and experience the true sense of freedom for the determined work time. Psychological elements underlying the psychodramatic stage offer special prospects for exploring man in spaces which have been restricted to verbal expression thus far. This exploration involves delving into a new space of fulfillment, action and analysis. Essentially, it represents the expansion of the protagonist's life space. The stage provides the patient with a multidimensional space of living, characterized by the utmost versatility possible.

Reality's space of living is usually narrow, restricting and blocking; thus the protagonist may easily lose his balance. The stage facilitates the restoration of this balance based upon the methodology of freedom, namely, freedom of unbearable stress and to experience (Moreno, 1953, pp. 53–54). The space is real and, at the same time, infinite. Its limitation relates only to the scope of our imagination. Indeed, a theatrical and psychodramatic space is essentially psychological and symbolic (Moreno, 1964a [1944], p. 263).

On the psychodramatic stage, the participant is permitted to create a special time for himself as well, connecting the past, present and future; dream and reality; fantasy and daily life (Artzi, 1991, pp. 63–64). Fantasy and reality are not contradictory, but unite within Moreno's surplus reality (Blomkvist and Rutzel, 1994, pp. 235–238). Two realities dwell side by side, and meet: daily reality (awareness) and dramatic reality (surplus, internal, psychological and symbolic).

> The stage space is an extension of life beyond the reality test of life itself: Reality and fantasy are not in conflict, but both function within a wider sphere – the psychodramatic world of objects, persons, and events.
>
> (Moreno, 1953, p. 82)

Finally, it may be stated, at least in principle, that the architecture was devised and structured following such a reasoning that any life form, physical or mental, may be embodied and illustrated (Marineau, 1989, pp. 81–83).

Scene

In psychodrama, this term is used to assist the protagonist in diagnosing the original time and place where the issue, presented here and now, occurred. The person who puts on a psychodrama brings up a scene from memory, dream or fantasy, in which his issue is manifested, and he reconstructs the scene as accurately as possible. He may also transfer from one scene to another scene that is close to it. The structure each scene forms and the transitions from one scene to another allow a person to draw closer to the original place and time of the issue's emergence. According to Moreno, the source of occurrence is highly important for the psychodramatic-therapeutic process (Artzi, 1991, p. 30).

Action principle

Moreno's experience with children's play also yielded the notion that speech alone is not the ideal route into the psyche. There is a primal, earlier level, which is found underneath language, namely, action and interaction. The theory of active, spontaneous learning among infants and children proved they experience and live their environment powerfully and passionately, and learn even before they speak or use memory, as demonstrated in Chapter 3. Hence, a philosophy was developed that action precedes words and that the human organism possesses act hunger, both physically and mentally. According to Umberto Maturata (1990, in Dayton, 1994, p. 30), the brain operates according to a closed organization principle. Every one of us is an independent, whole biological system, dominated by a closed organization principle. In cases of unresolved traumatic experiences involving pain or loss which we bear within us, the closed organization principle is damaged. We strive for a stage of closure and acceptance. If we fail to satisfactorily end a given event, we are seized by anxiety and fear. The brain attempts to impose closure and conclusion, to facilitate living, and it will be closed for better or for worse, as this is its nature. According to Moreno, in cases where the traumatic experience's indication has not been completed, there is yearning to take action. He defined that yearning as act hunger:

> Act hunger is the drive toward a fulfillment of the desire and impulses at the core of the self.
>
> (Blatner, 1973, p. 68)

As a therapy, the drama works toward symbolic fulfillment of act hunger, namely, fulfilling of passions and drives at the core of the human soul, as well as at the core of his interaction with others. The psychodramatic method offers the protagonist a safe stage, which allows him to relive the original, unresolved traumatic experiences. The re-embodiment occurs in a supportive, sufficiently safe setting to draw the protagonist out of his stagnation. The psychodramatic representation assists the clients to set themselves free from the unrealistic system and also allows the traumatic events to reconstruct in their psyche as a resolved, closed experience (Dayton, 1994, pp. 29–30). In fact, the patients put a closure to their unfinished businesses. The re-embodiment is designated to rebuild the low self-esteem, which may be explored, familiarized and reintegrated in a way that shall allow the emergence of a functioning self (Landy, 1986, p. 46).

The psychodramatic representation is conducted in a tangible, practical mode with the assistance of auxiliary-egos, which play the roles necessary for the completion of the act. At first, the auxiliary-egos become an extension of the protagonist's unrealistic system. Yet the more frequently the protagonist experiences the dramatic representation through auxiliary-egos, the easier it is for him to set himself free and relinquish them as an extension of themselves. If the need and the motive are fully satisfied through the renewed psychodramatic embodiment, then the psyche accepts the auxiliary-egos as real, allowing the patient to relive the traumatic experience, but to be empowered. Then the traumatic experience may induce reintegration into his experience as a new structuring form, which grants the experience a significant context. With that, the protagonist may carry on (Dayton, 1994, pp. 29–30).

> Act completion has value in that it validates the protagonist's emotional experiences, thus reinforcing an integration of the previously rejected and suppressed dimension of the personality.
>
> (Blatner, 1973, p. 72)

Additionally, verbal representation and practical acts are often contradictory. Moreno wished to reduce that. Patients demonstrate an incomplete perception of themselves and others – perceptions that are lacking, weak, distorted or pathological, and particularly one-way and subjective. When perceptions are clear and happy among all parties involved, a positive tele flows between people.

Accordingly, the psychodrama principle involves action. The action is rooted in a natural experience, which occurs in a social setting. The person-actor relies upon the creative and spontaneous abilities lying within him in order to complete the act, which is conducted for a certain purpose. The psychodramatic act is a trigger. It allows raising the emotions living within the psyche from the unconscious, and the brain may examine and redemonstrate the structure of the memory, which diagnoses the way in which the psyche experiences the event. The psychodrama method offers a safe stage, which allows the inner world to emerge in order to understand what has been accepted by the psyche as real. The importance of soul searching through the act lies within the fact that emotions may arise from the original experiences, from a primal perspective.

The psychodramatic method directly engages in action models of man, from the most primitive stage through the most complex level, exploring not only the language stage and below, but from action upward, based upon known psychological and physiological facts. This is a simple, practical method geared at the forces defining personality's development (Moreno, 1964a, p. 216). Since psychodrama's purpose is to arouse the patient's spontaneity through creative act, the psychodramatic treatment is conducted on the basis of reconstructing life situations, because of the relation between the creative act and matrix (mother–pattern). According to Moreno, a verbal treatment involves an abstract discussion of behavior, resulting in some loss of the matter's point. Ideally, the creative act is supposed to be observed at its locus nascendi, in vivo. If that possibility does not exist, the best prospect is to conduct a simulation that will be as close to life as possible (Kipper, 1986, p. 14).

Psychodrama allows people to simulate real life without taking a risk in case the outcome is not good, to gain experience in a nonpainful way if the outcome is not compelling.

> Psychodrama is a living laboratory for experimentation with life, with all its encumbrances, except punishment for trying new ways of living it.
>
> (Z. T. Moreno, 1969b, p. 213)

However, Moreno did not intend psychodrama to be a limited act, a unique therapy accessible to selected groups in specific situations. Rather, he simply stated it should possess universal implementation to be employed in a variety of modes and situations in order to assist the human species. Psychodrama is a therapy that suits everybody, humanity as a whole; nobody is excluded (Davies,1987, p. 110).

> The psychodrama is human society in miniature, the simplest possible setup for a methodical study of its psychological structure. Through techniques as the auxiliary-ego, spontaneous improvisation, self-presentation, soliloquy, the interpolation of resistance, new dimensions of the mind are opened up, and, what is most important, they can be explored under experimented conditions.
>
> (Moreno, 1964a, p. 177)

In psychodrama, life is taken and miniaturized into a group laboratory, replaying within a theatrical alternative. Repeating a scene or an interaction that occurred in life is permitted. Since life scenes may not be accurately reconstructed, the novelty element is naturally applied to them. It is all about re-experiencing, but this time, with transition and novelty, as opposed to the cultural conservation and theatrical drama, which permit no diversion from the original scene. By means of the psychodramatic structure and components, the actual interaction of people in roles is explored – the dynamic circling of the self, the other and the emotional flow of connections between them.

This is a group psychotherapeutic activity where the participants demonstrate, or, more accurately, spontaneously play the issues and distresses in the personal, familial or social field. The psychodramatic process is based upon the role-play principle: spontaneous, creative activity and the natural human tendency to play a role. As opposed to theater, its purpose is to express and actualize the self as an entity of character and identity and to come up with correct understanding and insight of the self and others. A person fulfills many roles throughout his life, as he does within the psychodramatic event; but at any rate, the role in its psychodramatic sense is not predetermined, similarly to the role a person plays by virtue of his life role or a theater actor's role. The script is written through the very performance, and, as a matter of fact, determines itself and is formed during the psychodramatic event. The role is not a fiction, yielded by the playwright's imagination or creation, but a psychotherapeutic process of personal and group coping, where a person plays himself out of the necessity of self-actualization and personal expression (Feingold, 1996).

The spontaneous man plays and improvises a role so that the self and the role are distinct, yet merge. The man–role relations in psychodrama are not only actor–role relations, but also an interesting encounter between a person and role-plays, creating an illusion of another "as-if" life, which constitutes a manifestation and fulfillment of experiences and emotions, combined with the self's identity and actualization.

Psychodrama is organized to assist and modify the dysfunctional experience repertoire of people by undergoing a process of new, unfamiliar experiences and feelings, which occur within the therapeutic setting. The new repertoire is supposed to yield transition and new attitudes. It is an experimental approach of reintegration to group psychotherapy. Psychodrama links present experiences with significant past experiences, some of which may have materialized, while others may have not. Plus, it offers people a unique opportunity to engage in new experiences, including hopes, fantasies and aspirations, functioning as a tangible illustration of the saying "If I could turn the clock back and start everything over". The prominent hypotheses upon which psychodrama is based are that spontaneity, creativity and the ability to let go of those in relation to others depend upon our ability to acknowledge and maintain a mutually intimate relationship, which grants that type of psychological gratification; that we may function elsewhere, at a different context without concerning ourselves with the question "What does the other think of me?"

This method's effectiveness depends upon the ability to re-create experiences which have occurred in real life in the same degree of powerfulness and intensity, and even more so. This demand is highly important, because the impact of experiences whose power and intensity are equal in value to the original experiences or stronger may suffice for instigating a significant transition in a person's repertoire.

Not only do we cope with the contents related to the embodied character (text, speech), but also with the context, since the contents alone are not effective. Other conditions are to be met, such as the total experience principle. In other words, the experience should also be manifested in the emotional dimension. Because a person is to benefit from the experience, it will be ideal to conduct it in vivo in situ.

The need to be involved in an emotional experience suits the existentialistic approach of total involvement and the protagonist's subjective perception. The total simulation, which is defined as an in vivo simulation, is the simulation through which the resemblance the real-life situation may be attained. The physical context is a precise reflection of the source. The auxiliaries and the roles they play are of those people and behaviors involved in real-life situations (Kipper, 1986, p. 50).

The following argument in itself constitutes psychodrama's novelty: treatment should occur within a context, and it is because of this argument that psychodrama is preferable to other treatments. Plus, it offers the patient an opportunity to become more closely acquainted with himself in various contexts and roles, complementing those experiences he has not had in life through techniques which fill in for what is missing in life in the time, space and reality dimension. The learning within a context is important, since various imagined situations yield different psychological processes, which, in turn, are subject to cognitive and emotional processes. Since the method is based upon the psychological simulation principle, the psychodramatic processes meet that requirement. They may powerfully copy, compete and cope with experiences of real-life situations, reconstructing that cognitive and sensorimotor process which is present in the original experience, thereby leading to a transition. Another thought relating to learning within a context stems from the ability acquired to embody a role by demand. Here, the "role" concept is important, because role is defined as behavior within a context and is associated with other people. The rationale principle in focusing, rebuilding and experiencing repertoire expansion stems from the assumption that all personality theories argue that human behavior, no matter if adaptive or maladaptive, is induced consequently to influences and experiences he has accumulated throughout his life. Every event is experienced by parts in the brains, which only later are cognitively translated and coded, and then stored, recalled and conserved as a guideline for a consecutive future behavior. Fixation in past experiences (success or failure) does not permit coping with present experiences, nor to capture opportunities which cross our paths here and now. This is part of the argument that daily life is richer in roles than a person allows himself to embody in practice. The anxiety resulting in stagnation and lack of spontaneity contributes to that (Kipper, 2004, pp. 1–7).

In real life, most of our actions, whether big or small, follow the warming-up stage. Naturally, people are role players, in the sense that their behavior is expressed through verbalization involving gestures and actions. They are natural actors because they may easily embody a set of roles that are called for them in a given situation and behave accordingly. Yet what is done easily and naturally becomes even harder to accomplish if prompted by a demand or an order, and role play is not different in this regard. A person may find it easy to scream, and even to hit while he is angry, but he will find those same actions difficult to perform if he is required to do the same in role play. It will even seem strange to him. Generally, role play in psychodrama works similarly to reality, and begins with warming up. The purpose of warming up is to provide the protagonist with the best prospects to develop effective involvement, desire and willingness to move on to the following stage, namely, the action, as well as for sufficient involvement, which will enable him to respond to and obey certain demands. Additionally, people who approach psychotherapeutic treatment seek help coping with psychopathological difficulties, and during the session, the process of coping with the problems involves concern, which is manifested by great anxiety and resistance to treatment. Warming-up's purpose is to loosen defense mechanisms, bringing them to their lowest intensity possible, thereby increasing the likelihood of a patient's involvement within the therapeutic process and its success (Kipper, 1986, pp. 82–83). Zerka Moreno maintains that when the protagonist is fully warmed up, there is no part of the self bound to remain out of action; no part is bound to engage in observation, remembering or recording the action only. If we appear to be forgetful, then the lack of memory means warming up has been completed (Z. T. Moreno, 1998, p. xii).

In the psychodrama process, everybody – protagonist, audience (group), auxiliary-egos and the director – requires warming up (Blatner and Cukier, 1998, p. 295). If any of them is not warmed up to the utmost spontaneity available to them, no task any of them assumes will be fully completed, and creativity will be at its minimum. Unsuitable warming up will yield an unsuitable psychodrama (Tauvon, 1998, p. 37). The activity in the warming-up stage of psychodrama reveals the social structure among the group members by indicating their movement and locations in space in relation to one another. Consequently to the physical and mental warming up, group members become more aware of the active psychological processes within themselves at the moment (Tauvon, 1998, pp. 41–42).

During the psychodrama, at least one person, the protagonist, is warmed up for the beginning of the therapeutic experience. He may explore any issue or problem he wishes. He is asked to be himself, rather than a dramatic player; the purpose is not to turn him into an actor, but to cause him to be more aware of himself and who he truly is (Kellermann, 1986, p. 8).

> There is no real drama until an individual acts out his own life on a stage. In Moreno's words: Play yourself, as you never were, so you can begin to be what you could have been. Be your own inspiration, your own author, your own executor, your own therapist and finally, your own creator.
>
> (Røine, 1997, p. 20)

> We have been brought up with the idea that, in test as well as in treatment situation, a minimum of involvement with other persons and objects is a most desirable thing for the patient [. . .] In the psychodramatic situation of involvement with other subjectives and things is not only possible but expected. Reality is not only not feared but provoked. Indeed, in the Psychodramatic situation all degrees of involvement take place, from a minimum to a maximum. In addition comes the principle of realization.
>
> (Moreno, 1951, p. 104)

By means of various techniques, the director allows the protagonist to express his emotions and distresses at a broader connotation. Embodiment may involve anything – memories and fears relating to events, occurrences specific of unfinished scenes, inner dramas, fantasies, dreams or preparation for risk taking in future situations. Ideally, outward embodiment in psychodrama refers to an organism's output on a whol, and overall known behavior within the therapeutic setting, through the universal language, which is the language of action (Kellermann, 1986, p. 8).

> Psychodrama is not just for recreating a disturbing experience. It is meant to do, undo, redo and reintegrate, producing closure. Subjective perceptions may be distorted in ways only others can reveal to us, therefore in that corrective interaction we can accept and integrate the correction. We are continuously processing our lives: we need to actively correct the past in ourselves and to help others to do so. Role reversal is a profound corrective, and, if used with positive tele, a true reorientation.
>
> (Z. T. Moreno, 2006b, p. 285)

In re-embodiment, the protagonist is no longer the person who passively accepts the events, but rather, controls them and open to new ideas. Through re-embodiment, he gains active control on the present, as well as freedom from the past.

> Re-experiencing the old, unsettled conflict, but with a new ending, is the secret of every penetrating therapeutic result.
>
> (Moreno, 1959, p. 108)

Moreno presented the protagonist's existential, subjective reality, as well as the surplus reality of the therapeutic space. As previously elucidated, surplus reality is based upon the idea that there are spheres that are invisible in reality, that are not fully experienced or expressed. Based upon Moreno's view, surplus reality is designated to expand reality by removing boundaries (Kipper, 1986, pp. 75).

> Surplus reality, therefore, represents a therapeutic factor that emanates from a temporary dissolution or guarded removal of both outer and internal psychological boundaries.
>
> (Kipper, 2001, pp. 142)

The developmental aspect

In its developmental aspect, psychodrama duplicates life; life is a school, a natural source of identity and role learning. The development of a personal identity as a system pattern, and fundamentally as a social network, clearly suggests that all elements which are naturally present in life when role development is concerned, and additionally, in terms of one's own identity, are present as therapeutic techniques and tools within psychodrama's framework.

Psychodrama offers individuals the opportunity to reprocess missing stages in the development by allowing them to experience and practice in a safe therapeutic setting. The main aspects in identity development stem from the psychodramatic process as a corrective, re-educating force. When the pain or trauma is released in that way, they are subject to re-structuring.

> In this sense, psychodrama recreates the ordinary. It gives us the opportunity to say what was left unsaid and in this way to correct our original experiences, it provides the pathway to bring our inner and outer reality into balance and accord.
>
> (Dayton, 1994, p. 7)

The double technique

Psychodrama defines the primal stage of infant development as the "double" stage. This is the stage where the child's self is not distinguished from the mother's or the primal caring figure's self. In life, the double emerges from the unity and integration with the mother, where the infant and the mother share an identity and where the mother serves as the child's natural double (Tauvon, 1998, p. 39). After the infant serves as his own double, relying upon his movements and gestures, the mother serves as an equivalent double. According to matrix of identity, which was presented in Chapter 3, after the infant is born, for several weeks onward, there is a unique existence where nothing is known of the infant's mental state, aside from the fact that the mother contains the infant as a physical and biological infant on and on within herself, and though there is no direct communication, the mother bears powerful influence on the child. The mother–infant relationship flows mutually. Those processes have no beginning and no end. At that stage, the infant lives in a state where the mother, other people, the infant himself and all surrounding objects belong to the only world – one wholeness.

At his beginning, the double serves as a training process for assimilating outer roles without acting out. The double should provide an echo to the self and other's echoes in relation to the self. The child is supposed to best assimilate the double. If the doubling succeeds and the assimilation is proper, then the child will undergo a primary process of integration into his own identity. He learns that he is not alone in the world; that the universe is a friendly place where his needs are noticed and fulfilled. He learns that the self is a place within himself, where he may gain stability and confidence, and that he may come and go without disappearing. A personalization process is induced in which the infant experiences himself within his body and begins viewing his body as a place where integration occurs. If assimilation is incorrect, then an identity crisis will occur. At any rate, there and then the double phenomenon first emerges.

It may be said that Moreno relied upon that natural process in order to use the term "double" (Z. T. Moreno, 2000, p. 67; Dayton, 1994, pp. 33–34; Landy, 1986, p. 92). Doubling is viewed as a developmental need and a developmental stage. As soon as the young child discovers himself capable of moving independently into space, he needs to be assured that being himself is a positive category – he requires self-affirmation. That can be transmitted by the parents through affirmative doubling and later through a noninjurious role reversal (Z. T. Moreno, 1975, p. 155).

This stage, which occurs in life itself, is highly important for the therapeutic process. In places in one's life where an identity crisis emerges, psychodrama as a corrective tool may provide a new, ideal double, which will outwardly present the protagonist's inner self. The double is an auxiliary-ego in a special role who assumes the protagonist's identity, playing the part of his inner self, developing activities which the protagonist is unable to perform. Since the double technique is one of the most powerful techniques, which allow the patient's emotions to rise to the surface, it may be defined as "the heart of psychodrama" (Blatner, 1973, p. 24). The double technique is considered a special psychodramatic intervention, bearing therapeutic power in role-play intervention. Because of its significance, it has become a key technique within psychodramatic and action techniques (Kipper, 1986, p. 155; 2002, p. 93).

Basically, the employment of the double as a therapeutic mediator is quite simple. The double simultaneously plays with the original protagonist, attempting to act as his "psychological twin" in order to serve as some inner voice, mirroring his feelings, revealing hidden thoughts and assisting the protagonist to freely and openly express them (Kipper, 1986, p. 152). The double is not supposed to be a duplicated self, but rather, an extended, more complex self. Its purpose is to prompt the protagonist's progress so that he encounters repressed conflicts, arousing his spontaneity and providing him with support and sympathy so he may feel safe and open. The double may provide a safe means of potential expansion of the crucial emotions in the protagonist's life. He becomes both the mirror and the echo of the protagonist, while reflecting his body movements and providing a nonverbal feedback to his physical expressions and verbal clues. He assists the protagonist in focusing upon his feelings and directly expresses them through words and movements (Moreno, 1987, p. 129). The double is to absorb and identify the patient's images, moods, colors and rhythm (Z. T. Moreno, 2000, p. 70). What is seen on the psychodramatic stage is two people, who are in fact the same person; the double is trained to form the same models of actions, emotions, thoughts and verbal communication which the patient generates. He is there not only as an aesthetic mediator, but also in order to delve into the patient's psyche, allowing him to influence him (Moreno, 1987, p. 129).

The double is a profound technique, which not only facilitates the protagonist's emotional expression, but also enhances his involvement in the scene (Moreno, 1953, p. 319; Z. T. Moreno, 1948, p. 463). As the figure representing the patient's inner voice, he possesses the freedom to speak and add movements and gestures as he wishes. The protagonist, on the other hand, has the prospect to transition, reject, ignore or accept whatever the double says. In cases where the patient does not accept the double's words, he may present other emotional alternatives. The double, perceived as the protagonist's supportive part, may also draw himself away a bit from the action and express thoughts out loud while the protagonist acts or speaks, and vice versa; the double may act and speak while the patient is thinking out loud so that both roles may reverse and appear alternately (Farmer, 1995, pp. 15–16).

According to classic psychodrama, the auxiliary-ego who assumes the double's role has two roles: one, to serve as the voice communicating with the therapist, namely, to act as the protagonist's extension, thereby enhancing the therapist's understanding of the patient. The double continuously aims at providing the therapist with clues and explanations regarding the protagonist's feelings and thoughts and assuring that those messages are heard. The other role is to serve as the therapist's extension, in particular, to function as another therapist or mediator through whom the therapist may provide tools which will instigate the expected transition in the protagonist.

The instructions given to the classic double include declarations that his role is to function as the inner voice and to demonstrate whatever the protagonist feels through this inner voice (Goldman and Morrison, 1984, p. 16; Blatner, 2002; Yablonsky, 1976, p. 120). Other instructions include expressing out loud the protagonist's feelings and thoughts. Although the double's task is to express feelings, in practice he expresses both feelings and thoughts.

In classic psychodrama, the protagonist sits or stands behind one side of the protagonist so as to allow him to observe the process in a clearly enough mode to provide feedback, yet be invisible by the patient, so as to assist the search for an extension or a new horizon of meaning within the existential reality which is already presented within the psychodramatic moment. A physical parallel to the protagonist and fluent, articulate speech re-create the protagonist's world, and in an imaginary way, begin expanding and presenting it in a new way. The double assists in the protagonist's effort and challenge to understand his plan regarding the world by raising life aspects with which the protagonist might cope but is still unaware of. Sometimes, the double manages to articulate whatever is already present in the protagonist's life but has not yet become conscious for him, linking to it new meaning through a dramatic act. At any rate, the double speaks while he stands by the protagonist, entering his existential reality. He blends and merges with the world's structure, which, in the current case, is the protagonist's actual reality. A tele state will occur until the point where the double occupies the protagonist's space of living together with him, with the protagonist's acknowledgement. Then, "existentialistic validity" has been achieved (Moreno, 1959, pp. 216–217).

The double technique's aim is to establish the balance in the distance between the inner and outer self (Moreno, 1987, p. 129).

> The patient represents the deeper, inner levels of experience, while the ego acts as a double, copying physical bearing in every way and representing the outer levels.
>
> (Z. T. Moreno, 1948, p. 436)

That may require a considerable effort on the double's part, now required now to initiate and start a process of establishing comparison and resemblance. The purpose is to set the double free of his personality, attempting to make him as much of a protagonist as possible, though in fact, it is difficult to impossible to achieve. A person never relinquishes himself. It is more a matter of involvement, an attempt to establish psychological unity. The protagonist, on the other hand, should speak to the double as he does to his inner thoughts. He should read in between the lines and express out loud all that has not been said. The double should take risks and say things the protagonist has not dared say. Thus, the patient and double share a task in which each member of the group is involved. It is not something that goes on in the individual's mind, but a methodic process which contributes to objective positioning (Z. T. Moreno, 1948, p. 436).

Construction of double as a therapeutic tool: the theoretical concepts involved

When the protagonist has a double on stage who truly touches his soul, their relationship resembles the primal mother–child interaction. When they reach that point, they are nearly as one. Similarly to the mother–infant tele relations, what goes on between a patient and his double is beyond mutual empathy. A process where both participants' thoughts and feelings merge, penetrating and influencing each other, is a process where tele occurs (Z. T. Moreno, 2000, p. 67). If the double experience involves transference from the patient onto the double, it will yield nothing significant other than the patient's free associations and delusions in relation to the double. Likewise, nothing of significance will be yielded if the double maintains transference relations toward the patient, unless the patient is extremely pliable so that he blindly accepts anything the double induces, which has not occurred to this point. Furthermore, the double experience may not be explained solely through empathy, which the double may hold in relation to the patient. In their relationship, several transference components may exist, as well as several empathy components.

Throughout the therapeutic process, the double presents the issues the patient raises, with far-reaching additions, while the patient inputs new aspects. This process goes back and forth, from the double to the patient, and vice versa, until all configurations of the experience have been manifested outwardly. It is true verbally, and even more deeply on the action level. Those two-way emotions, which are expressed outwardly, induce a very deep interaction. This does not apply to projected materials, but to true occurrences; hence the tele phenomenon occurs at the core of their relationship.

Moreno claimed the "double" situations in psychodrama is a clinical technique where the patient forms a mutual action with the double, providing an excellent opportunity to learn to combine empathy and transference within the framework of the tele process.

The double is summoned to step into the stage and participate in the other's (protagonist) world, not as an outer party, but as an internal one, who belongs to his world. In order to succeed, the double must enter in his imagination to the protagonist's existential plane and move, feel, act and speak out of that plane to the point where he succeeds, thereby forming an enhanced therapeutic connection between the protagonist and himself. The tele relationship grows more intense, involving body and mind, thought and speech. This connection is part of the therapeutic magic moments of psychodrama, meaning "where two meet eye to eye".

The mirror stage and mirroring technique

The next stage of personal identity development is the mirror stage. When infants first look in the mirror, they are surprised, and they laugh, with an expression of wonder on their face. It is clear that the experience is significant for them. Initially, when infants look in the mirror and do not know themselves, they think it is a stranger and are scared. Often, it may be noticed that children approach the mirror, touch it and even break it, and gradually, the expression and gestures evolve. When the child realizes that the picture in the mirror is his, it is an important turning point in terms of his growth and self-perception (Moreno, 1987, p. 131).

The mirror stage serves as an initial training for role assumption. The mirror provides external information, and is not necessarily linked to the inner voice. A mirror provides a safe transition from the double's inner world to the other's outer world, thereby providing the child with feedback and information regarding the self, on which he may rely in order to adapt to the social tapestry. At first, it seems like an external process, as an imitation of movements and sounds, thus learning the language of the other significant one in his life. In Piaget's terms, the infant adapts himself to the mother role by developing the cognitive scheme necessary in order to begin seeing himself as a separate individual. In the mirror stage, one presumes that the infant gradually learns to know himself as an individual who is separate from others and is learning to see himself through others' eyes (Moreno, 1952, p. 246).

Though imitation begins as reflection of others' behavior, another development occurs when the child goes from a functional play to a constructive play, getting to know himself as a creator (for example, building a sand castle). The child relies upon his own reactions in order to promote stimulation, thereby allowing him to establish the self. For instance, he offers himself something and buys it from himself. At this stage, the child possesses a type of thinking which is to be received from others. He takes those clusters of answers, organizing them into one unit. This is the simplest form of demonstrating the role the other fulfills in relation to 'me'. The child conducts a dialogue within himself, which is supposedly conducted between two people. In one role, he questions, and in the other role, he replies. In both states, he plays a role.

This role play is allowed because of two main elements. First, imitation's key element, which is paradoxically given as the reality element. The child attempts to act, speak and seem like a person, whether real or imaginary, forming reality-like states. Since the child's reality, identity and environment limit the prospect of an accurate imitation, another element is combined into the play behavior, namely the unreal element, the representing, the "as-if". That "as-if" element serves as an imitation aid. It allows the child to project himself into acts and states which may not be constructed in practice but only played.

Imitation is not an inner role assumption process. Rather, it is an outer act, a play preparing the child for an evolution toward a more complex relationship with other significant ones. In the deep level of role assumption, the child identifies with the mother. Not only does he imitate and play his outer acts and sounds, but also her emotions and values. Through identification, the child sees himself as his mother; the mother serves as a mirror. If the mirror is sensitive enough, it is capable of providing a safe transition from the self to a larger group or society. That facilitates the child in understanding not only the way he sees himself from inside, but also how he is perceived by others. When the mirror is sensitive and touches within, the child feels attachment at being seen and understood by external others. If the mirror reflects rough things to him and as a result he fails to become attached to his inner world, the child will develop a feeling that he is invisible and will feel unable to communicate with others or satisfied by the expectations that should come from the outside. The sense of self is gradually damaged, and the connection with the outer world becomes weaker. If the identification with the mirror is improper, the child experiences an identity crisis. In order to overcome that crisis, he must be capable of finding himself again by observing significant others, as well as to uniting, merging and containing their views and positions.

As opposed to imitation, identification is an inner dramatic process. The child does not play the mother's role, but establishes a mental image of himself as a mother, acknowledging the ability to act as a mother and play the son in his relationship with her. Both roles, son and mother, are separate yet linked. However, in the later identification stages, a process of becoming emotionally independent occurs, or the development and appearance a separate self. The latter is gradually enhanced with the other being viewed and distinguished of "I", so that "you" will become "I am not you". The self must be separate from the mother's or another person's; it comes to be the child's core, rather than part of his parents' personality (Dayton, 1994, pp. 34–35).

The mirror technique which was developed in psychodrama may specifically address that childlike developmental stage. Relying upon that technique, we outline and pull the relations' elements which the infant develops toward the mirror guiding him through his early days (Moreno, 1987, p. 131).

In the psychodramatic process, the need to see the self in action may be fulfilled through people who act as a mirror to the patient. The mirror may be a powerful technique for a protagonist who is unable to see himself from the outside within a relationship or in a scary, threatening situation. The mirror provides him with a correct point of view regarding the self's behavior in any situation or occurrence where other humans observe him. Proper assimilation in psychodrama constitutes a corrective experience to the mirror which has not been present before, or which has been "broken" in real life, thereby allowing the protagonist to establish a proper dialogue with others (Dayton, 1994, pp. 33–34).

Mirroring is a feedback method that allows the protagonist to see himself from the outside. Since we are not truly able to see ourselves from the outside, we need an external party to reflect to us who we are (Kellermann, 2007, pp. 84–85). In psychodrama, this technique is implemented when the patient is unable to present or represent himself by means of words and acts. The protagonist is removed from the stage and replaced by a group member (the auxiliary-ego), who is summoned to portray his role in a given scene. The auxiliary-ego assumes a place in the action area within the psychodramatic space, assuming the protagonist's identity and name, reconstructing the occurrence through which the protagonist has just come full circle. He represents his behavior, forming interactions with significant others in his life, whether real or imaginary. The patient sees himself "as if in a mirror", perceiving the way other people see and feel him (Z. T. Moreno, 1974, p. 92). The auxiliary-ego might exaggerate (without hurting the protagonist's feelings) one aspect or more of the protagonist's behavior. Based upon the embodiment's purpose, and upon what the protagonist should face, the auxiliary-ego may exaggerate the body language and vocal expression in order to arouse the protagonist's awareness of the contradictions and dissonances between the verbal message and the physical expression. For example, a person might say he is not angry, while his overall body position expresses restrained fury he is unable to express (Kellermann, 2007, pp. 84–85).

The mirroring technique is also effective in portraying resistance in nonverbal communication. It is stated that in resistance toward the protagonist, the mirror might exaggeratingly employ deliberate distortion techniques so as to urge the patient to progress and transform from a passive observer to an active participant, leading him toward new insights, views and fulfillment (Moreno & Moreno, 1969, pp. 240–241).

From a psychological point of view, the mirror reverses things, or places them inversely and backwardly; it diverts and distorts images. The word perverse is a word of Latin origin, whose etymology implies going backward, reversal and destruction. Consequently, the protagonist reaches a point where he sees himself mirrored from a distorted point of view. As a rule, the protagonist will react with intense resistance to that deliberate distortion. Since the image outlined on stage by the auxiliary-ego does not necessarily connect to the protagonist's image of himself, he no longer attributes that to himself, nor does he experiences the same things. The psychodramatic mirror image leads the protagonist to a surreal space where he reacts to the scene and views it through the group member's eyes. As an observer, he has been removed from the mirroring process, and therefore he may view the scene as something that does not concern him. The importance of this technique lies within the fact that it provides the protagonist with the opportunity to modify and amend the mirror. What would you want this mirror of you to be like? What should it be like? How will it be good for you? (Z. T. Moreno, 2000, p. 42).

Following the portrayal or embodiment, the protagonist is usually encouraged to respond to what he has seen or to become active again (Hollander, 1967). Mirroring may generally present how a protagonist comes up with a way of expression in a given situation, providing him with the opportunity to receive a view from afar of his behavior. The protagonist observes his own embodiment from the outside, as though he looks into a mirror. He withdraws from the scene in order to see that from afar, while the auxiliary represents him through mirroring. The psychological distance allows him a more realistic self-esteem.

When the protagonist views himself from outside, it is easier for him to understand the occurrences within the interaction and provides the insight to develop and mature from within, rather than receiving it from somebody else. The protagonist is then able to experience and feel himself, to think of himself and respond or devote himself to the mirror. The difference of viewpoints allows the protagonist to notice and better perceive the various prospects in order to continue the psychodramatic act. The act induces objective self-awareness in him, while he interacts with others (Z. T. Moreno, 2006b, p. 285).

> The purpose of using this technique is to enable the protagonist not to be personally involved in the action that he/she should see the whole situation from a distant perspective rather than an involved, individual point of view.
>
> (Z. T. Moreno, 2000, p. 40)

While looking at the mirror, we force ourselves, time and time again, to come to the insight of who we are, although we constantly transition. This mirroring process is, in fact, an inherent, crucial part of what being in the world entails, since it assists us throughout life to coordinate the mutual interaction between the outside world and ourselves (Kellermann, 2007, pp. 84–85).

The mirror technique may facilitate us in becoming more self-aware and engaging in self-exploration. Yet mirroring holds the key to something even more valuable, namely, to discover who we wish to be. No matter what we see in the mirror, we are not obliged to accept all contemporary qualities of our personality. We possess the power to transition and become somebody we will like even more. The psychodramatic mirroring allows the protagonist to view himself and objectively evaluate what he sees. The idea is to set ourselves free from a limited self-perception and become the person we are destined to be (Kellermann, 2007, pp. 93–94).

Both stages, double and mirror, are stages in the identity's development from "I" to "me" and from "other" to "I". The third stage of personal identity development, according to the psychodramatic theory, is the discovery of the other and acknowledgement of his existence. This stage lies beyond the child's narcissistic needs and aspirations. He develops awareness of the notion that the world is full of other people separate from the self. If he has received a decent double and mirror, he develops a sense of self that is sufficiently strong to enable him to establish empathy and interactions between him and them. The acknowledgement of others is followed by the ability to live as a human organism among other human organisms and take his place in society. The child learns to choose and be chosen, give and take and express tolerance to people other than himself. He learns that his viewpoint is not exclusive and that there are other viewpoints, that balance and fair play are necessary in order to live in peace side by side with other people. This stage is when the child crosses the threshold into society, as he assimilates the reflected self's double and mirror; he carries this confident awareness to the wide world, to a wider mirror who places him in the social world. Thus the social self and social roles clusters develop (Dayton, 1994, p. 35).

At this stage, psychodrama is aided by others, who are known as "auxiliary-egos". Originally, Moreno identified the following functions of the auxiliary-ego:

> **The first function** is of the player who undertakes and fulfill the roles of the significant others in the protagonist's life, who are not part of the psychodramatic process, but are essential for the therapeutic drama (they are known as "the absent ones", or "others"). Those characters may be derived from reality, imagination, or the non-human world, that is, animals, plants, or some object; from the past, present or future. The auxiliary-ego also assumes roles representing various aspects of the protagonist's life within or outside of the individual's boundaries, such as a body part, object, or emotion with which the protagonist struggles (for example, fear). In this function, the auxiliary-ego is the protagonist's extension in the drama of his life. This technique allows the auxiliary-ego to openly express the protagonist's inner world, explore it and facilitate him in modifying it. The process allows the protagonist a so-called dramatic re-birth on the psychodrama stage.
>
> (Moreno, 1951, pp. 104–105)

Once the auxiliary-ego is on stage, he is to act in favor of the protagonist, and play for him the absent character or significant other, based upon the information he has been provided by the protagonist. However, in order for the character embodied by the auxiliary-ego to be present and of influence, he is to expand the role based upon his own assumptions, including unexpected behaviors. He may transition his behavior and render it radical, reverse roles with the protagonist, act as a mirror for presentation and assist the patient in forming a personal reality on stage, while providing him with dramatic means in order to demonstrate his dilemma and focus upon it. Nonetheless, in these role relations, the auxiliary-ego should separate himself from the role of the person he is supposed to embody, in order to assist the protagonist.

> The auxiliary-ego can take good advantage of the gap between himself and the person to be aided. As only a part of his ego is sent in the process of unification, a part of it is free to act on behalf of the other person beyond what he can do for himself [. . .] The function of the auxiliary-ego is therefore to attain unity with a person, to absorb the patient's wishes and needs and to operate on his behalf without being able, however, to become identical with him.
>
> (Moreno, 1964a, p. 240)

One way or the other, no matter how close the auxiliary-ego comes to the ideal, unity will never be complete because of the diverse organic and psychological limitations (Kellermann, 1986, p. 240). In that sense, the mother is the ideal auxiliary-ego to the infant she carries in her womb during pregnancy and for whom she cares and nurses immediately after birth. The mother is an example of an instinctive auxiliary-ego, yet the organic and psychological gaps become even more prominent after birth, until the final psychological separation (Moreno, 1964a, p. 240).

As opposed to the significant other in life, in psychodrama the auxiliary-ego assists the protagonist in expressing his hidden emotions, anxieties and dreams, encouraging him to find prospects of new spontaneous acts. Stretching the limits of the patient's perception expands his experience of self and cultural atom, prompting a cleansing release of emotions to the extent of catharsis or renewed insight. In life, the other is perceived by the protagonist from only one viewpoint and dimension. In psychodrama, he is perceived and viewed also as the patient thinks he sees and perceives him and as the auxiliary-ego presents him.

Usually, the auxiliary-ego embodies for the protagonist the absent character or the individual with whom he is in conflict. The technique grants the protagonist a psychodramatic opportunity to experience what has been absent from his life and modify previous relationships. For instance, instead of the repulsive, rough parent, the auxiliary-ego will play the role of a communicative, accepting and understanding parent, the one the protagonist wishes for. The fulfillment of the wish made in a controlled setting calls for a surplus reality framework: a new, comprehensive reality, an extension of the existing reality (Moreno, 1953, p. 85). In places where the protagonist experiences intense ambivalence with regard to a significant person in his life, it may be wise to ask the same auxiliary-ego to play both roles so that the protagonist may realize there is some sense of integration with the other. Thus, a solution for a past incident may be understood and accepted as something that has already happened and cannot be transitioned. Role reversal with the modified ego or with the ideal facilitates resolution and acceptance (Rabson, 1979, pp. 99–103).

The protagonist is provided with the opportunity to work on the original drama until a more satisfactory solution is found. Aside from the presentation of himself (as he is, has been, should have been, wishes to be, etc.), the protagonist also assumes the roles of the other personalities in the drama while presenting them to the group. The director or protagonist may modify the auxiliary-ego if the way in which he embodies the role if they feel the way in which he embodies it is not authentic enough. The drama usually begins with an external presentation of a fundamental, hidden and unresolved struggle which recurs for the protagonist from within. Holmes (1992) claimed the psychodramatic process may be viewed as a theatrical expression of the inner object relations in the protagonist's private world. Typically, those conflict patterns have been assimilated throughout the early family life. Hence, the auxiliary-egos express and demonstrate the protagonist's inner life.

In any scene, the auxiliary-ego may play any party in that dual relationship. The object relationship consists of two parts: the self and the other. Thus, when the director asks the protagonist to assume another role, they will play the counter-side of those relationships as they see it in their minds. For that reason, the auxiliary-ego usually plays a double role, as he outwardly expresses the self and the other on the psychodramatic stage (Holmes, 1998, p. 133). Thanks to this process, the protagonist brings conflicts that have been hidden within him to awareness. Once they are openly expressed, he may directly encounter them, and then he gains a sense of insight, strength, and empowerment.

While the protagonist encounters the conflict through connecting to the modification of the presented situation, he also modifies the conflict within him. He becomes acquainted with new prospects, from which he chooses the best one for him, which has seemed unattainable thus far. The new outlook is attained through action, while he actively forms the drama of himself, hence the mental and physical acts become one (Farmer Chrise, 1995, pp. 13–15).

The second function of the auxiliary-ego is to serve as a therapeutic mediator, and its purpose is to draw the protagonist's perception of himself closer and establish it, since without it, the protagonist will be withdrawn from the situation and fail to be involved (Z. T. Moreno, 2006a, p. 198).

> While the absent one is represented, **the third function** is a special social research's. Its purpose is to explore and assess the protagonist's perception of role relations with the absent person.
>
> (Z. T. Moreno, 2006a, p. 198)

The auxiliary-ego's work is to assume a role of a specific person, or any role the protagonist requests. He succeeds when the patient accepts him in his role (Moreno, 1946, p. 259).

The auxiliary-ego as a social author in psychodrama serves as the director's extension. He does not function as an observer, but as an active mediator. Thus, he represents a new tool in social exploration.

The three stages of which the development of the self consists, both in life and in psychodrama as portrayed earlier, also elucidate the linkage to the roles issues. The double stage begins as a role-containment stage. The mirror stage serves as an initial training toward role assumption. The auxiliary-ego stage portrays the social role play. The following stage of identity's development, according to the psychodramatic model, is associated with the role reversal issue. Role reversal represents the phenomenon of plays, which began with the early mother–infant interactions. Those plays develop gradually, partly through imitation and partly through inquiry, exploration and expansion of the acts which formed the initial mother–infant interaction, where the infant categorizes and classifies social relations. At their climax, those plays demonstrate the main lines of harmony and conflict within the parent–infant relationship (Lousada, 1998, p. 205). This is the stage of intensive communication between two people or more (Moreno, J. L. and Moreno, Z. T., 1696, p. 26).

The ability to properly reverse a role was observed by Moreno and Zerka Moreno (1959) as a key factor in the child's social growth and development. This process was also perceived as a diagnostic factor from which sensitivity and social skills may be learned and taught. Children naturally implement role play and role reversal. The philosophy underlying the world's transformation, namely, turning one organism into another, is deeply rooted in infants' imaginations as soon as they begin gazing directly at the world. The more roles a child plays in his life, the more enhanced his ability to reverse roles will be.

After age four, children spontaneously implement role reversal technique. They use their parents as neutral auxiliary-egos, as they are untrained in role reversal (Moreno & Z. T. Moreno, 1959, p. 156). According to Zerka Moreno in Kellermann (1986), role reversal's importance is not limited to interpersonal socialization with others, but also to personality integration. The key purpose of role reversal is not to engage in external reality alone, but also in the inner reality, in order to achieve an integration of the self. This is the stage where the physical, emotional and social self are supposed to connect in order to form a complete self. Role reversal enhances the strength and stability of the child's ego, with ego being defined as "identification with oneself" at this context (Moreno & Z. T. Moreno, 1959, p. 156).

According to Moreno's theory, unity and integration precede separation; first appears the important revelation of the sense of self, and only then is the infant able to place himself in somebody else's shoes (Tauvon, 1998, pp. 41–42). Without an adequate development of the ego, role reversal will be difficult to grasp. An adequate sense of self is essential for feeling the separation from another person (Lousada, 1998, p. 205). The ability to reverse roles is enhanced in correspondence to personality's development, and particularly following the abandoning of the egocentric stage, as well as the separation from the original shared identity and the absolute separation of "I" from "you" (Moreno, 1972, p. 63; Tauvon, 1998, p. 39). This process occurs at once in the other world (of the matrix of identity), where the child discovers himself in relation to the outer world of people, animals and personification of objects and exalted organisms. This also corresponds to what was later on argued by Moreno (1964) and also by Zerka Moreno (1975), namely, that throughout their social growth, children are required to learn to overcome three crucial stages. They must learn to reverse roles with (1) organisms inferior to humans, such as animals; (2) nonhuman objects; and (3) superior, authoritative organisms, such as parents, teachers, God, or the devil (Kipper, 1986, p. 176).

The preliminary assumption is that at the stage where the mirror has established itself, the infant gradually learns to acknowledge and identify himself as an individual separate from others. The matrix of identity is broken, and the child may transition from his own position to another, being able to play the role of another person and resume his own (Moreno, 1952, pp. 246–266). Role reversal reflects the separation into two objects, namely, mother and child, as they split in the infant's mind (Holmes, 1992, p. 60). At this stage, the infant realize he may initiate interactions and control the boundaries of his psyche.

> It is in this arena that the mental, emotional and psychical boundaries in the infant's psyche can be punctured.
>
> (Lousada, 1998, p. 223)

> At the role reversal stage, the infant actively positions himself in a part of the other's person, playing his role. Only upon completing that role, is the child able to assume his own, full identity.
>
> (Tauvon, 1998, p. 39)

> The feelings engendered in the infant can be overwhelming and need a holding environment to contain their natural ego defense mechanisms of splitting, projection and introjections.
>
> (Lousada, 1998, p. 222)

Attaining personal identity and sense of self also indicate freedom from the auxiliary-ego, namely, the mother or mother replacement (Moreno, 1972, p. 63). Role reversal reduces the child's dependence upon his parents until he is set free from being dependent upon the significant figures in his life (Moreno & Z. T. Moreno, 1959, p. 156). Role reversal may facilitate the separation process of children from their parents and vice versa, thus resembling a resumed presentation of the separation and individuation process (Kellermann, 1994, p. 266). The actual role reversal stage emerges when the self is sufficiently whole and separate so that the individual may become his own master and deal with others, since it is only then that he can truly stand in the other's shoes. A person who is capable of reversing roles is in a position allowing him to balance between his needs, passions and aspirations and others'. He acknowledges the fact the people do not live with themselves, in a vacuum, but in connection to others. It is more than mere empathy. It is also the ability to feel and experience, for a moment, in a position outside himself. Role reversal does not entail being swallowed up by the other's self, but to willingly put oneself into the other's shoes and see through his eyes, to see the world from his point of view and acknowledge the fact that this is a journey – both inward and outward, a momentary hopping into the other's world. Thus, at the role reversal stage, the self has adequately developed and adapted so that he may endure that temporary journey outside himself. This is an ultimate coaching act, not necessarily aimed toward another person, but in the sense of weighted solidarity within the self. Role reversal allows people to see life and themselves from different viewpoints, held by all significant and generalized others (Dayton, 1994, p. 36).

Role reversal technique

Role reversal is a primary technique and a fundamental theoretical principle in the psychodramatic method. The key philosophical assumption emphasizes its value in expanding and enhancing empathic awareness of the other, as well as intensifying sensitivity to the self and interpersonal relations. Moreno highly emphasizes role reversal, both as a learning technique for children and adults and as a therapeutic individual and social groups' therapy. In some sense, role reversal is the core of role theory as cited by psychodrama and sociodrama (Bischof, 1970, pp. 251–252). It is known as "the engine of psychodrama" (Lousada, 1998, p. 205). Role reversal may be implemented at the beginning of the embodiment stage in psychodrama, for warming-up purposes or in order to draw information necessary for the auxiliary-ego (Rabson, 1979, p. 83). Role reversal provides the other group members with a more complete picture of the protagonist's view of the significant ones in his life. Dramatizing those people also allows the protagonist to experience the world from the other's point of view, understanding the other's role (who is being played at the moment by auxiliary-egos), and from that position, experience the therapeutic expression's impact (Holmes, Karp, and Watson, 1994, p. 11; Lousada, 1998, p. 211). Often, role reversal is implemented for the sake of a therapeutic transition as an integrative technique, after an effective climax or catharsis have been achieved through action (Rabson, 1979, p. 83).

The technique itself is incredibly simple: Two people reverse their roles for a short time stretch. For example, a daughter reverses roles with her mother; a husband with his wife; a student with a teacher; and so on. Roles involved in role reversal as those mentioned earlier are usually complementary roles within internal, mutual dependency; they are both inverse and aim at unity. Each party is encouraged to understand the counter-party's view in order to find a way for a common existence (Kellermann, 1994, p. 265). At any rate, within psychodrama's framework, role reversal's meaning has obviously been expanded to include non-complementary roles as well, such as psychosomatic, psychodramatic and spiritual, which, in Moreno's opinion, combine together to form the ego's apparent aspects (Moreno, 1953, p. 75). Those aspects may be re-established within the other person, and I, myself, may form the other's aspects within myself. This technique involves reflection of human behavior within the social context (Rabson, 1979, p. 44).

In role reversal technique, both parties involved actually reverse physical positions, receiving the other's design, mannerisms and psychological and mental state. At psychotherapy's context, role reversal will always involve the protagonist as one of two parties reversing roles. During the session, the protagonist may reverse several roles with the auxiliary-ego, as necessary (Kipper, 1986, p. 160). As a technique, role reversal provides a concrete means for a metaphoric process of "walking in the other's shoes". In role reversal technique, the individual is involved in an interpersonal situation with significant others (Rabson, 1979, p. 83).

> Role reversal is the technique which brings the most insight, resolution and hope, and is therefore heralded as the most important intervention of psychodrama.
>
> (Lousada, 1998, p. 211)

Role reversal is one of psychodrama's key components, since it allows us to explore life and ourselves from different viewpoints. The protagonist goes beyond observation and forming empathy with the auxiliary-ego. Rather, he tangibly experiences what being the other is like. Not only does this experience allows him to better understand the other, but also see himself from the other's eyes. Psychodrama's primal purpose is to reveal the inner world, bringing to consciousness all that has been unconscious. Such expression and concretization of inner representation facilitate experiential learning.

The process is mostly nonverbal, but physical in nature. Another goal is to understand and explore ourselves through that new consciousness, viewing the given situation from a multitude of viewpoints, which automatically enhances our spontaneity, facilitating the performance of our own roles. A person's failure to reverse roles implies weak personality which is not sufficiently whole to leave its own permanent identity. When the individual is capable of being in the other's shoes, true role reversal occurs. Everybody is disabled while walking the path of life, having one pair of eyes for a limited view of things. Psychodrama, by nature, provides an opportunity for actual practice of leaving the self, moving other places and returning to ourselves. Role reversal allows us to speak – not for the other, but as the other person.

Throughout the psychodramatic process, the practice of this technique always occurs in the here and now, employing I-you speech. In other words, there are two independent individuals who see each other in order to gain an outlook from each other's viewpoint, undergoing each other's experiences. Role reversal calls for specific techniques which one must master in order to benefit from another person's point of view (Dayton, 1994, p. 69).

Psychodramatic role reversal allows the protagonist to view reality through the other's eyes, as well as to feel and experience the other's role. While embodying the role and speaking through it, the protagonist enters a psychologically complicated field. He offers his view of the way he is perceived by the other, presenting the comments implying the relationship as a whole. When an individual becomes part of a whole, the other parts of the whole seem to affect all other parts' behavior and experience. Role reversal allows the patient to think, feel and play interactions, rather than merely discussing them (Williams, 1989–206).

Though role reversal technique seems quite simple (Kipper, 1986, p. 161), a more thorough investigation reveals that intra-personal and interpersonal process occur therein, which involve at least three independent stages: (1) emphatic role assumption, (2) action reconstruction and (3) role feedback.

When two individuals try to enter one into the inner world of the other, they employ their emphatic skills – emotional, cognitive and behavioral – so as to assume the other's role and to play him or her for a while. That type of role assumption may begin by a superficial imitation, mirroring or character shaping, so as to eventually embody the other's role in a more thorough whole way, which involves deep identification and containment. Similarly to empathy, role reversal begin with a perception of sensation of subtle clues of the others, and is yielded through employing certain mental abilities, such as memory, fantasy, one's awareness of emotions and thoughts within the other's role. The first stage of role reversal broadly relies upon intra-=personal experience, involving very little of the feeling the other person experiences inside (Kellermann, 1994, pp. 266–268). Yet while empathy is one of the basic principles of role reversal technique, Moreno emphasized that technique alone may not explain the process, which, as mentioned, involves concepts as "spontaneous state", "warming up", "tele" and "cluster of roles", all of which are vital for a more thorough and broad explanation. Second, whether it is true or not, individuals involved in role reversal attempt to subjectively reconstruct and report what they have felt in the other. According to Moreno, the person who assumes the other's role not only feels, but also does; he also constructs and reconstructs a present or absent figure in a specific role relation. Role reversal involves a response which is not only based upon the way in which I feel you, but also on how I feel about the way you feel me, and so forth. In the third stage, namely, role feedback, the individuals are asked to mirror themselves based upon the other person's reaction and mutual interaction. "The observing self" must inspect and notice "outside" behavior, even if he is embodying his own role, as well as when he is the other's role. When people become emotionally involved with each other, they are required to observe the act very closely and continuously record, while warming-up for the role, what the role arouses in them, and how they, in turn, affect the role (Moreno, 1964a, p. 259). Role feedback process requires distinguishing between "me" and "myself", as well as an ability to sustain them both in the present, mirroring the experience through the observing self (Kellermann, 1994, pp. 266–267).

Moreno thought a perfect role reversal with another person was impossible. Nobody can assume the other person's side in an absolute way, and no one possesses a total perception of another human organism (Z. T. Moreno, 2000, p. 14). The psychodramatic techniques succeed at coming as close to that point as possible. Psychodrama, by nature, allows the person to practice withdrawing from himself in order to feel and experience other selves and restore himself, yet even then, he will never be able to fully perceive or conceptualize the other person's emotions, feelings, views and motives, and even less so, to re-create them. We all differ from one another in our ability to place ourselves in another person's shoes, as well as in the skill of reinducing the feelings of the other person involved in the action. those who in life demonstrate rigid, undeveloped self, which is neither spontaneous nor creative, may benefit from role reversal training in psychodrama, where they may acquire an enhanced, developed and stable self (Bischof, 1970, pp. 251–252).

The role reversal technique is more effective the closer two individuals are psychologically, socially, and ethnically, such as mother-child, father-son, husband-wife (Moreno & Z. T. Moreno, 1959, p. 157).

In psychodrama, role reversal is conducted with the assistance of the auxiliary-ego according to the total involvement technique, so that the person is able to see himself from the other's point of view. "Perception" is the key word here; the protagonist enters the scene with his mono-dimensional perception, and if he properly reverses role, a transition in his perception should occur. The main learning is of a new viewpoint which transitions the way in which the protagonist views the situation. He may now later his view in terms of new learning (Z. T. Moreno, 2000, pp. 14–15).

The four psychodramatic techniques presented earlier – double, mirror, auxiliary-ego and role reversal – allow the reconstruction of the infant's stages of development, and if necessary, to treat, modify and enhance deficient behaviors. Moreno summarizes that as follows:

> And so we may say that the double, the mirror and the reversal are like three stages in the development of the infant which have their counterpart in the therapeutic techniques which we can use in the treatment of all human relation problems but also in treating mental patients. When you practice these methods, I hope you'll realize that they did not spring out of role playing in a sort of naïve way, but that they are profoundly related to the dynamics of human growth and the reason for their profound effectiveness is due to the kind of relations that they have. Thus the utilization of these techniques has helped to further a theory of the infantile self and a basis for its empirical verification.
>
> (Moreno, 1952, p. 246)

Training for role play, spontaneity and creativity

The whole personality and role doctrine as cited in this work is based upon one point of departure: the roles, as taught and played in life, and consequently, personality as it develops are subject to modification through the psychodramatic method. Psychodrama is Moreno's unique way of developing and enhancing role-play skills, and is directly related to the theory. Training refers to two goals – spontaneity training and role repertoire expansion (Kipper, 1996, pp. 8–9).

> By means of my role theory, which is increasingly becoming the lingua franca of behavioral science, and the techniques of role playing we become better able to provide a plausible empirical presentation of life as it is lived, in the form of psychodrama.
>
> (Moreno and Z. T. Moreno, 1969, p. 28)

Psychodrama was a leap forward through the experimental theater into the realities of the lead actor's unique life experiences, transitioning from the relative security of the foretold role to the sensitive center of needs, fears, frustrations and expectations lying in the core of our personality. For Moreno, the roles a person plays and must play are attempts at self-fulfillment, but they often arouse frustration. In his perception, the questions of how we accept our roles and how we feel about them are equally emphasized. If in life a role naturally develops, and in theater the role is played, then role plays within psychodrama call for a great diversity of roles into the play, providing a golden opportunity to practice those roles which we failed to perform or fulfill in our lives, or those roles that life has not granted us, though they exist in imagination and fantasy.

In that sense, psychodrama constitutes a new method for learning of roles and developing role-play skills within psychotherapy groups, serving as a frame of reference for roles measurement. It provides an experimental framework, free of boundaries set by given a given community or culture. The roles are learned in their status nascendi, namely, in their original form and place of establishment, before our eyes. The artist does not hide himself behind his creation, but allows that to see the role's process of creation or coming into being, step by step. Not only does it open a new path for learning of in vivo roles from their moment of creation, it also allows a scientific frame of reference and role measurement means. Some roles are formally shaped ("lawyer", "criminal"), whereas others are shaped by psychological states ("the eater"), but it is only through a psychodramatic process the way in which they are spontaneously shaped may be witnessed (Moreno, 1987, p. 93).

> Psychodrama is a method of diagnosis as well as a method of treatment. One of its characteristic features is that role-acting is organically included in the treatment process. It can be adapted to every type of problem, personal or group, of children or adults.
>
> (Moreno, 1964a, p. 177)

Role theory provides a better presentation of life. When it is experienced through psychodrama, human life is designed as a drama in many ways. The roles we fulfill in society are not a part of our existence unless we construct them as ours. It is easier for us to speak of them than speaking of the essence of our being or our imagination. Whatever happens on the psychodramatic scene is life itself, and what takes place in life's scene is psychodrama (Sarro, 1966, p. 140). This is the point to state that the expression "life is a theater" is often erroneously interpreted. The resemblance of the roles played in life and the roles played on stages is artificial, and to be more accurate, they bear a different meaning. In life, our suffering is real, as well as the hunger and anger sensations. This is the difference between reality and fiction or as Buddha, as cited in Moreno, stated: What is terrible to be, is lovely to see (Moreno, 1947a, pp. 42–43). Role assumption is being in a role in life itself, within the compelling relational context, for instance, being a mother, father, policeman, etc. Role play refers to a person's ability to imitate, accurately copy another person's role (person, animal, body organ) and his own role. Role play means "playing the role" out of choice, in a selected setting, for exploration, experiencing and development purposes, as well as for the sake of role training and alteration (Moreno, 1953, pp. 722–723).

Moreno indicated that role play is spontaneously present in children's behavior, thus he considered it a basic force of self-development and basic learning strategy (Kipper, 1986, p. 146). The skill in role play is also essential for proper communication and social self's development. The ability to play collective role is important for the personality and adaptation. Role-plays in daily life are authentic and original, serving further functions beyond fulfillment and satisfaction. This is another effort in complementing communication through adaptation to cultural and social norms, and through protection from exposure in place where such exposure threatens inner balance (Kipper, 1986, p. 93).

Role-playing is a natural phenomenon that is practiced by children in the process of growing; therefore, it forms part of the normal repertoire of roles that are performed and enjoyed by everyone. The client who plays roles in therapy may provide insights concerning roles that are played elsewhere by others or by himself or herself. The therapist and other clients (if present) can also gain insight or add their interpretation in the role-playing session. Role-playing also allows the client to practice alternative roles (rather than simply talk about them). *It is also inherently a "dramatic" technique [. . .] which implies that the client may have "peak experiences" when deeply involved in role-playing. These experiences can also lead to insights or to the reliving and resolving of painful episodes from the client's past* (Biddle, B. J., 1979, p 329).

One of the basic assumptions of role theory is viewing the person as simultaneously developing in numerous planes. Additionally, psychopathology does not only mirrors distortions of various personality aspects, but usually represents manifestations compensating for one personality fact, first and foremost deficiency of the other's development. Viewing the person from the role theory's viewpoint will demonstrate the training of human ability through a wide range of roles which may balance one another (Blatner, 1973, p. 125). A role-play situation contains an important component which the verbal-therapeutic situation tends to omit. This component emphasizes real life's characteristics, namely, the behavior which often occurs under conditions where the self's control on the environment is not whole. As opposed to real life, where a given decision regarding an action leads yields the outcomes with which the player must live for a certain time, in simulation situations the outcomes and conclusions may be easily pronounced. If the client does not like them, they may be thrown away. There are at least two advantages to that. First, when the outcome is not compelling, the patients tend to be more open and spontaneous. Second, seeing patients acting in a tangible, real way in an actual situation enhances the credibility of what they may say of their own behavior (Kipper, 1986, pp. 64–65).

Moreno believed psychodrama was the medium in the experiential behaviorist's simulation of clinical role play. The term "behavioral simulation" refers to re-creation of a situation presenting people who mutually act with their surroundings.

Role playing was described as the tangible manifestation through which the behavior component of the method expresses itself (Kipper, 1986, p. 65).

Role play and role training

Role play and role training are similar terms, which sometimes even merge. Role training allows the participants to acquire and outwardly try out social skills and role-related behaviors. The participants train applying practices for participations in future situations (for example, job interview) and the training facilitates their transition from one role to another (for example, from a patient who is hospitalized to a community member). Role training assists in expanding the behavioral repertoire and the individual's range of reactions; hence it enhances the ego's functioning and the concept of self, adding it versatility and adaptability.

Role training's purpose is to assist the individual in playing his life roles in a more proper, satisfactory way. Similarly to role play, role training is a versatile technique that may be processed. It also forms the action part in the psychodramatic session (Kipper, 1986, p. 77).

We human beings are role players, blending private and collective elements in our outward behavior. This explains why everyone is capable of experiencing the role process on the stage. We are also expected to live up to our official (expected) role in life, and this can undermine our cravings to embody far more roles or more varieties within the same role. This usually produces some sort of anxiety (Blatner and Cukier, 2007, p. 298).

On the psychodrama stage, a person may receive a certain feeling of what it means to speak and act in different ways, within a different role, receiving feedback while he performs the role. In daily routine, the person is limited in terms of the number of roles and situations which he experiences, but personality's potential strengths are infinite; we live only part of the roles our personality may contain, and the vast majority remains unexploited and undeveloped. Throughout the therapeutic process, the individual may experience countless roles and situations. Role play techniques, as drama plays are very effective in creating new roles. When we undertake a variety of roles, improvising them in real time, we actually release the stored energy in new ways which real life does not necessarily allow or provide us. In his work with patients, Moreno discovered that their warming-up process in life covers only a narrow range of their personality when they are in a pathological state. Yet in the therapeutic, artificial warming up, a wide range of their personality gets ready for action (Moreno, 1964a, pp. 223–224).

Plus, role training allows us to deal with difficult, painful roles in the here and now; roles in which we are blocked, that leave emotions trapped and hurt. In daily life, we embody roles for various reasons. When we explore a given role, we explore the reasons, the needs, hidden fears and marginal benefits that lead us to play it. From psychodrama's point of view, psychological health stems from our ability to express, both inwardly and outwardly, the ensemble of roles (active involvement when the role is concerned). (Dayton, 1994, pp. 19–21).

In that experimental setting, a person may be trained for a given role by learning various modes of fulfilling it. Thus, everybody may learn the most effective means of coping until he may exhaust his and others' satisfaction to the fullest (Tyson, 1966, p. 223).

There are many advantages to the method, compared to training for adaptation through real-life experience, particularly in the formative stage in a person's life. First in real situations the individual usually faces difficulty learning from mistakes. His apprehension might make him repeat that erroneous behavior when he encounters another occurrence, which makes his learning slower, so as to overcome that mistake. Second, for many individuals, real-life situations prompt emotional perseverance if the behavior in a given role appears to be successful, which results in their clinging to the existing reality. Third, in real-life situations, even if the individual achieves perfect compatibility with a certain role, life can turn that role into a single path, blocking prospective new situations or development of other skills.

> As a developmental technique spontaneity training is thus superior to life training. Through training of individuals for conduct in possibly arising situations in a variety of roles and functions they may have to assume towards a variety of persons in the possible roles they may assume, the subject learns to meet life situations more adequately, the training makes him more resourceful and versatile. The possibility can be envisioned of directing man's evolution with the aid of "stegrife" (spontaneity) techniques into avenues which differentiate and enlarge the spontaneous base of his heritage, his ability to be spontaneous, his spontaneability. Spontaneity research has disclosed that spontaneity is not a mystic and irrational factor, but a capacity with which all men are endowed and which can be tested and trained [. . .] These considerations have led me to the development of a "spontaneity theory of learning".
>
> (Moreno, 1953, p. 535)

A psychodramatic role play is a form of experimental and experiential learning, and learning is a key aspect of a psychotherapeutic program.

The connection between role playing, catharsis, spontaneity and creativity

There is a mutual relationship between role play spontaneity, creativity and catharsis.

Play is about spontaneity; playing means to warm up toward an emotional state leading to a spontaneous state. It is a profound transformation activity, whose initial goal is involvement. When we play with people, we feel them and ourselves in a new way. Role play is the way to induce true spontaneity, from which stems the creativity which a person needs for proper existence in order to struggle against the cultural conserve.

The spontaneous person embodies an improvised role in such a way that the self and role are separate yet merged. In other words, the actor is aware that he plays a fictional role, yet he plays the role with awareness and commitment, just like children who play in daily life, living two parallel realities. Plus, two time frames are addressed, past and present, though spontaneous embodiment involves focusing upon the moment of experience, here and now.

When a person stores his ability to play a role, he is unable to modify familiar behavioral models, thus he loses the benefit of future spontaneity and creativity, as well as the ability to cope with transitions. Transitions may occur in a person's life at any given moment, for many reasons and resulting from various experiences. Those transitions result in an imbalanced atom, thus they influence others, simultaneously and at the same time (Moreno, 1987, p. 47).

Moreno argued that human brain functions as memory and intelligence are not constructed to prepare them to deal with the unexpected, while spontaneity is a brain functions designated to teach people how to deal with unexpected occurrences and situations. Unexpected situations are states where intelligence or memory may not assist, or states where intelligence or memory is not powerful enough to guide us through (Moreno, 1947a, p. 40).

> Taken by surprise, people are frightened or stunned. They produce false responses or none at all. It seems that there is nothing for which human beings are more ill-prepared and the human brain more ill-equipped than for surprise.
>
> (Moreno, 1947a, p. 6.)

The moment of surprise and transition may trigger concern, which is the opposite of spontaneity, leading to proper control of the situation (Z. T. Moreno, 2000, p. 85). Concern may go in two opposite directions. It may begin with an aspiration to withdraw from an old situation with no sufficient spontaneity to do so, or it may swiftly stabilize and be fixated, since the person has withdrawn an old situation, where he may not return, but has not yet found himself in a new situation which will restore his sense of confidence and balance, thus he is up in the air and experiences a feeling of vacuum and loss of control (Moreno, 1953, p. 336). Moreno, considered the moment of surprise as a moment of transition which is necessary for the person to perform a creator's role (Z. T. Moreno, 2000, p. 8).

> The fact that man is capable of action means that the unexpected can be expected from him, that he is able to perform what is infinitely improbable.

> And this again is possible only because each man is unique, so that with each birth something uniquely new comes into the world.
>
> (Arendt, 1958, pp. 177–178)

Thus, playing means being able to take initiative and do the unexpected. To act, play and be free, in that sense, are synonymous concepts. Spontaneity enables us to feel free, control life situations and surprises encounter or face new situations with new, adequate responses, out of awareness that nothing will be the same as before (Z. T. Moreno, 2000, pp. 117–118).

Spontaneity grants a person a feeling that he is free to act in according to the situation, and that he can control it. In order to adequately cope with transitions and maintain balance within the social and cultural atom, each person is to gather the necessary amount of spontaneity in accordance to the extent of transitions that have occurred for him (Moreno, 1987, p. 47). Moreno emphasized the spontaneity training issue so as to restore the power allowing the creative state and the maximum innovation ability (Nehnevajsa, 1960, p. 717). One of the ways in which this effect maybe induced within a person is a mental catharsis, which causes relief and release from anxiety with no obligation to transform the outer situation. In that way, a large amount of energy, which would otherwise be wasted on the effort to transform reality, is maintained.

> The wider the range of disequilibrium, the greater becomes the need for catharsis.
>
> (Moreno, 1987, p. 47)

Moreno wished to promote the use of improvisation techniques in a group setting, believing it would increase spontaneity and creativity and assist in developing an anti-mechanic position toward our time (Moreno, 1972, p. 31).

The theater of spontaneous man aims at contributing to the development of spontaneity as a vital dimension of an individual's response to his life situation (Bobula, 1969, p. 57).

> Psychodrama is a complete psychotherapeutic method originally created by J. L. Moreno on the basis of his theory of personality development and group behavior [. . .] It was first introduced as a form of group psychotherapy, but it can also be used in individual therapy, the treatment of dyads, families, and large groups.
>
> (Kipper, 1982, p. 5)

Chapter 6

An integrative and critical discussion and analysis of Moreno, personality theory and psychodrama

This book has explored Moreno's personality theory and its affinity to psychodrama in both the theological-philosophical and developmental aspect. The goal of the five preceding chapters was to provide a comprehensive view of Moreno the individual, his theories and the therapeutic method he established. This chapter will provide a critical and integrative discussion of the basic assumptions cited in each of those previous chapters. One of the key basic assumptions was that the philosophical, psychological and therapeutic aspects rely upon the same principles, namely, spontaneity, creativity, warming up, cultural conservation and tele. The great challenge in figuring when the theory ends and therapy begins is a consequence of the fact that Moreno, in his discussion of the three aspects concerned, applied the same concepts. That induced great confusion, which affected his work. In this study, the author attempted to distinctly apply those concepts, in the following order: Chapter 1 presented the concepts as manifested in Moreno's life; Chapter 2 explained those concepts in their philosophical-theological aspect; Chapter 3 elucidated the way in which those psychological concepts may be implemented in all personality development's dimensions and their connection to the role concept; Chapter 4 clarified that the implementation of the role concepts, with all its aspects, as a methodological point of reference in relation to personality, laid the foundations for the theoretical concepts, on the one hand, and served as the foundation for psychodrama as a therapeutic tool on the other hand. Finally, Chapter 5 provided an explanation as for the way in which Moreno's philosophical and psychological concepts shaped psychodrama's therapeutic aspect. Plus, a methodology was formulated to present a new, complete perspective of the human being which clarifies existentialistic psychotherapy's key principles.

The author demonstrated that rather than being five different parts of a puzzle, this work's chapters stands in itself, but respectively to the others, discussing the principles of spontaneity, creativity, warming up, cultural conservation and tele from a different perspective and relying upon different basic assumptions.

Moreno's personality theory, with its implementations in group settings, is both psychological and sociological. At psychodrama's context, it is represented theoretically and practically.

Review

The research upon which this book is based begins by relating Moreno's life story, relying upon another basic assumption which maintains that the relationship between the theoretical principles and the therapeutic, practical implications stems from Moreno's biography. Moreno's philosophy concerning personal development parallels his own life.

Accordingly, the chapter portrayed Moreno's own history and personal development as means of elucidating his scientific and technical contribution, and as an overview of his philosophical-religious and ethical belief. The key concepts in Moreno's work were explored, considering they stemmed from Moreno's psychological nature and the complex dynamics of his psyche, which received their interpretation in an academic work, while adhering to the frame of reference provided by his existentialistic vision.

Moreno claimed to have been the lead actor in his own psychodrama. Therefore, his life story, his familial association and key figures in his life justify his worldview more than anything else. Thus, he became the living model of his own theory. This study explored the way in which Moreno chose to present himself, tracing the path of his life, starting with the tale of his birth and his given name, through his childhood and adulthood experiences, involving God plays, which we are permitted to attribute to the category of "creativity", the term underlying the psychodramatic theory, to Moreno's continuous need to be a God-playing human.

> The embodiment of the I-God was practiced by me in life, long before it took psycho dramatic form.
>
> (Moreno, 1969, p. 21)

Moreno's God-play and the primal experience with the creator convinced him that creativity was the core of human interactions. Meanwhile, he presented his ideas regarding God and their application to human behavior. Psychodrama itself evolved from Moreno's belief that it assists people in discovering and expressing the sources of creativity and potentiality lying within them, elucidating divinity's workings in the cosmos.

Later on, we learn of the way in which Moreno perceived himself as part of his "social atom", of the relationships with significant ones in his life, namely, his father, mother, Rabbi Bejerano and characters who served as role models to him, such as Jesus and Socrates. Plus, we learn of his personal and family crises, the search for identity and the necessity to amend and modify his social atoms and to find a solution in constructing a broader, alternative family model. Hence, we understand his idea, as well as the theory and practice he proposed, in relation to a child's development, which is embodied by the "spontaneous man" perception. Among other things, he presented psychodrama as "social atom's modification work" so as to assist people to transition beyond emotions and views which might inhibit spontaneity.

Moreno was a man of vision, possessing tremendous powers of creation, who was leading an extremely intensive life. Even as a young boy he examined the theoretical aspects of any topic which he found interesting and would often imbue it with new ideas, finding ways to be actively involved in it.

Throughout his career, Moreno strove to establish a new way of life which will elevate and enhance the creativity concept through action and encounter between human beings.

Moreno believed that in the authentic encounter process, people feel more alive and free in their creativity. The authentic experience conveys the feeling that the interaction has achieved a new understanding of the relationship with another person.

Moreno himself demonstrated the encounter concept through several existentialistic actions. When he took interest in social issues, an interest which never ceased, he mainly focused upon society's rejected groups. He did not just voice his opinions on the given matter, but would go out to work in Vienna's suburbs with those groups. The work with prostitutes served as the basis for group psychotherapy and movements addressing personal potential fulfillment. Working with children provided the foundation for the spontaneity theater, psychodrama and the birth of the spontaneity and creativity concepts. The identification and concern with immigrants resulted in the establishment of an immigrants' absorption center at the house of encounter which he established. In the observations he conducted in a refugee camp in Mitterndorf, Moreno engaged in resettling of prisoners of war, and later on, at the Hudson School, he focused upon placement and reorganization of new girls.

Based upon his experience in the "Encounter House" establishment and his work in Mitterndorf, Moreno concluded that a "creative revolution" may occur only if social structures could be reorganized, especially structures mirroring interpersonal choices, so as to provide utmost support for each individual's creativity.

Moreno's way of integrating thought and practice is evident through the development of the psychodramatic matter. In this context, it is difficult to know whether the idea preceded the act, or vice versa, since while he was processing his idea, he had already been involved in an experimental theatrical activity. He also developed his own psychodrama theaters, where he served in several roles: director, therapist, group facilitator, actor and teacher.

The introduction of Moreno's life story and his involvement in religion, drama and society provides a perspective justifying his personality's components and his sources of motivation. Three main motives that require special attention as motivation factors are the "idée fix" concept, the "falling Gods" concepts and the" normal megalomania" concept.

The idée fix concept is of French origin and means moderate obsession, not in its pathological sense but as in the sense of a guide through a vision. This is the source of creativity and the laboratory where Moreno's ideas had been developed since he worked with the children.

Moreno's psychobiography offers assumptions as for idée fixe's psychodynamics. First, in the "God Play" tale, where it was stated that in the heat of the play, the child Moreno forgot about reality and tried to fly. But in the nonplayful world, ruled by the laws of gravity, the child hits the floor, breaking his right arm; the pleasure principle and the reality principle manifest themselves in a conflicting way. Even then, as a child, Moreno demonstrated the resoluteness not to submit himself to the laws of gravity. Despite his falling, he attempted to fly, to find a way to turn his dreams, fantasies and play into reality. Moreno believed that in a symbolic sense, the ideas of "fallen gods", spontaneity and the birds' flying are quite similar.

In his opinion, flying like a bird is human beings' dreams; if not by means of actual wings, then by means of artificial wings. Likewise, if we cannot be God, then that may be materialized at least through theater. The common source of all three ideas is the yearning to actualize the concept of divinity through science or any other method, assuming this idea is attainable. (Moreno, 1947a, p. 84). starting with the revelation that theater offers a means for experimentation, to adoption of established theatrical tools designated for spontaneity training, group psychotherapy and sociometry. (Blatner, 2002).

Moreno's unique view of God facilitates in elucidating the concept of psychodrama, in light of the paradoxical relationship between divinity and humanity, involving connection and separation. Psychodrama is interpreted as the solution for man's yearning to be God, who walks hand in hand with the recognition of his humanness.

According to this theology, psychodrama's ambitious goal is to reconnect man with the inner God, which receives the image of spontaneity and creativity. Those dynamic connections and separations between the individual and the cosmic world are examined in accordance with the present relationship between them and the psychodramatic child development theory, normal megalomania, role reversal and surplus reality. Psychodrama is a method which was designated for people who have fallen because of their dreams. Each fall of theirs confirms their separation from God and the fact that they are mortal, rather than immortal (Kraus, 1984, p. 48). Through a therapeutic process, psychodrama helps those "fallen angels" back on their feet, channeling toward the fulfillment of their dreams and hope. The prescription curing from such a fall is to engage in psychodrama and re-play God.

In order to understand Moreno's personal psychodrama, his full identification with God, he must be viewed as a replacement, as a substitute for humanity as a whole.

Moreno allows himself "to be God", namely, to be creative and spontaneous. Meanwhile, he allowed everybody to be the same.

In the psychodramatic world, the fact of embodiment is central, axiomatic, and universal. Everyone can portray his version of God through his own actions and so communicate his own version to others. (Moreno and Z. T. Moreno,1969, pp. 21–22)

Epilogue: general assessment of Moreno

Just as Moreno's life covers a wide range of activities, from theater to therapy, from quantitative analysis of interpersonal relationships to direct experimenting with God, so do his theoretical contributions and practice cover a similar range. The main themes in his life are reflected by the theoretical contribution in his research and mode of treatment. Moreno could have been considered one of the greatest, innovative intellectuals of the 20th century for his well-known contribution in psychodrama group psychotherapy and sociometry, but because his work challenged existing concepts in psychology, psychiatry and sociology, Moreno as a person, and his methods were often a ground for controversy.

This research demonstrates and justifies the main reasons for that:

A ***Misunderstanding Moreno and his work.*** Moreno developed his psychodrama theory in a nonorganic manner. He proposed a set of theoretical ideas, which were philosophically justified, but was not always precise about providing a psychological explanation of the way those ideas connected. What he wished to convey and the way in which he expressed it were clear to him, but not necessarily clear to or accepted by the rest of the world. Therefore, the theory remained a mere collection of discrete thoughts, which do not assemble to become a methodical, well-set theoretical framework.

B ***Moreno acted against academic conventions.*** The theological basis of Moreno's theories was not accepted in the social sciences and the medicine fields. Moreno did not clarify himself, which resulted in a difficulty of accepting him, thereby excluding him from the mainstream scientific realm of the day. Most of his key ideas, including the research methods he proposed, stemmed from his theological-existentialistic view. One of Moreno's main arguments was that psychodrama addresses primal, immediate behavior, rather than facts as intelligence, hereditary data or other hidden factors. Thus, in psychodrama's case, the "existentialistic" validity is concerned, and it is to be distinguished from scientific validity (Moreno, 1968, p. 3). Consequently, psychodrama as proposed by Moreno may not be proved through linear thinking, but rather, through an existentialistic research method. This is a theory which engages in heuristics to a greater extent than prediction. For a long time, the lack of reliable measurement instruments posed challenges in putting Moreno's theoretical hypotheses to an empirical testing, and perhaps making it impossible. That problem disrupted the ability to demonstrate the validity of psychodrama's theoretical basis (Kipper and Christoforou, 2006, p. 31).

C ***Moreno's complex personality.*** Moreno did not attempt to be a conformist and play the role he was expected to fulfill by the culture in which he lived. Therefore, his original view was totally misunderstood even in the religious and scientific circles. His philosophical view encompassed both logical positivism and religious existentialism. The contradictions and duality it contained were difficult to accept. Thus, Moreno wrote the following, in response to the criticism directed at him:

> I was literally playing two roles: the role of a religionist and the role of a scientist [. . .] The two roles ran paralleled, one complementing the other. This was in accord with my position that science and religion are like the two ends of a stick. There is no conflict between them.
>
> (Moreno, 1953, p. xxxviii)

Aside from the earlier described position, Moreno maintained an ambivalent relationship with his colleagues in psychiatry. Berger maintained that Moreno's interpersonal issues with the academic establishment did not stem from his ideas, but rather, from his arrogance. (Berger, 1990, p. 213). In the author's opinion, Moreno's greatest failure was in justifying his own behavior. Rather than attempting to contend with the giants of his generation, like Freud and Marx, Moreno preferred to present himself as better than them. According to Moreno's justification and ambition, the superiority of his contributions should be constructed by the following order: (1) personality theory, which is superior to that of Freud's – psychodrama; (2) a social theory which is superior to Marx's – sociometry; and (3) a cosmic theory, which is more exalted than the Bible, the Koran and Buddha's speeches – *The Words of the Father* (Bischof, 1970, p. 235).

Moreno's complex personality caused people to focus more upon his behavior and rather less on the statements he made in relation to the psychodrama processes. The opposition to the man resulted in the opposition to the theory as well. Consequently, there was a failure to understand psychodrama not only as a therapeutic process, but also a method founded upon theoretical principles.

D When Bratesco revealed the historical truth about Moreno's biography in 1975, many felt cheated and there was a scandal. Very few tried to understand the legend associated with Moreno's birth in symbolism and surplus reality perspective. In the author's opinion, if Moreno is examined by psychoanalytical measures, he might be considered a pathological liar, but if he is examined by the principles underlying the psychodrama method, then adding biographical motives in the discussions conceptualizes the surplus reality idea, which, as previously seen, is an enhancement of the actual reality through extensive use of imagination. Exaggeration by the psychodramatic method is like a magnifying glass; in order to see the small details, the true story must be exaggerated. Not only does psychodrama exaggerates and intensifies, it also includes things that did not take place in reality and sometimes ignores the accurate facts so as to identify whatever underlies them. In psychodrama, adding a fictitious dimension is not only possible, but justified.

When Moreno developed the concept of "surplus reality", he viewed that addition as a means for a person to make his life better and more agreeable for him. This surplus reality involves proper use of imagination, spontaneity and creativity to create a psychodramatic and poetic truth, as opposed to historical truth. Thus, it is important to understand that when Moreno refers to a historical truth, he is interested in developing the ability to transform a historical truth into something much more poetic or psychodramatic. Moreno did not lie; he used another channel to tell the truth in a way that was both symbolic and inducing reality-rooted satisfaction. Moreno clearly made that distinction prior to employing this technique (Marineau, 1989, p. 172).

In order to understand Moreno's thinking, it is important to know the previous concepts existing in the field in which he acted. The religious concepts, which are incapable of containing the pantheism of Moreno's position; the preceding concepts of psychoanalysis, which viewed Moreno's personality from a psycho-pathological point of view; sociologists' prejudice, who refused to associate the trans-personal approach with science; theater's prejudices, where God was perceived as just another role or actor, who refused to see the God in man.

There are different schools by which Moreno was judged and through which his work was assessed. However, if psychodrama was not respected by the academic establishment initially, in the past fifty years Moreno's ideas and methods have spread worldwide not only as a confirmation of his findings, but also of the fact that he assisted in introducing a new type of thinking. In that sense, we witness how those ideas range from the private to the general. The research portrayed in this book demonstrated Moreno's influence on the group psychotherapy movement, existentialism and therapeutic techniques in psychotherapy and psychodrama, as well as the conceptual development in those areas. On a whole, Moreno was the lead actor, active in the key revolutions of social sciences.

More than any other psychiatrist, Moreno was responsible for the transition from individual therapy to understanding psychological life's interpersonal components. His main concern with spontaneity and creativity corresponded to his emphasis on behavior and his preference of action to the word.

Moreno succeeded in raising man's social organization from a status of a literary and philosophical issue, as perceived in the 1930s, to a status of an experimental issue, as it would be later on. The techniques he developed induced conditions allowing others to continue the search for fundamental characteristics of a social organization and laws to be considered in regards to them.

No matter how appreciated or unappreciated Moreno is, his work was without a doubt, first and foremost, original. He invented a new science and did not borrow ideas of other disciplines to be integrated into his own. Moreno's techniques found their way into human potential fulfillment movements and into a variety of action-oriented therapies, as well as into the therapeutic community. Moreno anonymously published many books; hence many of his ideas were taken from him and transformed, and their exclusivity and precedence were denied him.

Moreno made many contributions, yet they are to be examined according to the rapid changes occurring in the world in which we live, rather than as finished works. In the author's opinion, Moreno's work should be the foundation upon which the rest of the psychodrama method is further constructed. All Moreno's insights – philosophical, theological and scientific – are to be brought together and integrated into one, coherent image, as though from the viewpoint of Moreno himself. Thus, a full image of Moreno and his work will be formed, serving as a basis for its continued development. That was the purpose of this book and, hopefully, it has been achieved.

The death of Moreno – the universal man

A series of small strokes confined Moreno to his bed. Thousands of students and professionals came to visit him. When his disciple Yablonsky came, Moreno told him it was not a time for sadness.

> I have lived a full life. I've done my job. It's time for me to go on to something else.
>
> (Moreno, in Yablonsky, 1976, p. 284)

Moreno refused medical treatment and did not allow medical intervention to artificially extend his life. He preferred to submit to the cosmic forces which gradually diminished his existence (Murray, 1976, pp. 16–20). Moreno died on 14 May 1974, after nearly eighty-four years of a productive, creative life.

Perhaps, of Moreno's thousands of sessions, the writing he requested on his tombstone was to be remembered most.

> Here lies the man who brought joy and laughter into psychiatry.
>
> (Moreno and Z. T. Moreno, 1969, p. 258)

> Fellows, those are *The Words of the Father*, this is a commitment to humanity, it is necessary to form a true human family. *The Words of the Father* are: I created you, you should keep on creating, creating yourselves; you should work to achieve humanity's final configuration, for the sake of peace, because creativity is absent and cannot exist if one kills another. I leave you psychodrama, group dynamics, sociometry, group psychotherapy, but you are to live all that. Do not leave it all in dead books. You are to live that all in order to find a solution. *The Words of the Father* are [a continuation of] the Old and New Testament. This is the will of our time.
>
> (Moreno, 1969c, p. 143)

Bibliography

Anokh, J. and Stern, P. (Eds.). 1999. *Introduction to Sociology*. Tel Aviv: Open University. [HEB].

Allport, Gordon W. 1950. *The Individual and his Religion: A Psychological Interpretation*. New York: The Macmillan Company.

Allport, Gordon W. 1955. *Becoming: Basic Consideration for a Psychology of Personality*. New Haven: Yale University Press.

Allport, Gordon W. Discussion of the first lecture in Moreno, J. L. 1959. *Psychodrama: Volume 2: Foundations of Psychotherapy*. Beacon, NY: Beacon House, pp. 15–16.

Arendt, H. 1958. *The Human Condition*. Chicago, IL: University of Chicago Press.

Artzi, E. 1991. *Psychodrama*. Tel Aviv: Dvir. [HEB]

Atkinson, R. L. et al. 1996. *Introduction to Psychology: Volume Two*. Translated from English by S. Kedem. Tel Aviv: Ledorey. [HEB]

Auerbach, S. B. 1972. *Pages of Israeli Thinking*. Jerusalem: Jewish Zionist Organization. [HEB]

Aulicino, J. 1954. Critique of Moreno's Spontaneity Theory. *Group Psychotherapy*, 7 (1984), pp. 148–158.

Baim, C., Burmeister, J. and Maciel, M. (Eds.). 2007. *Psychodrama: Advances in Theory and Practice*. London: Routledge.

Balint, M. 1968. *The Basic Fault*. London: Tavistock.

Bannister, A. 1998. The Group. In Karp, Holmes and Tauvon (1998), pp. 111–115.

Barbour, A. 1968. Sociometric Meaning in Interpersonal Relationships. *Group Psychotherapy*, 21 (1968), pp. 193–201.

Barbour, A. 1994. A Reexamination of the Tele Effect. *Journal of Group Psychotherapy, Psychodrama & Sociometry*, 47 (1994), pp. 114–126.

Beith, R. (Ed.). 1992. *Personality: Theory and Research*. Tel Aviv: Open University. [HEB]

Ben Eliezer, U. and Shapira, Y. 1989. *Elements of Sociology*. Tel Aviv: Am Oved. [HEB]

Berg, P. S. 1984. *The Key to the Wisdom of Kabbalah*. Jerusalem: Kabbalah Research Institute. [HEB]

Berger, M. M. 1990. J. L. Moreno's Autobiography: More than Meets the Eye. *Journal of Group Psychotherapy, Psychodrama & Sociometry*, 42 (1990), pp. 213–220.

Berlin, I. 1974. *Carl Marx*. Tel Aviv: Zmora Bitan. [HEB]

Biddle, B. J. 1979. *Role Theory: Expectations, Identities, and Behaviors*. New York, NY: Academic Press.

Bischof, L. J. 1964. *Interpreting Personality Theories*. New York, NY: Harper & Row.

Bischof, L. J. 1970. *Interpreting Personality Theories*. New York, NY: Harper & Row.

Blatner, H. A. 1973. *Acting in Practical Applications of Psychodramatic Methods*. New York, NY: Springer Publishing Company.

Blatner, H. A. 1991. Role Dynamics: A Comprehensive Theory of Psychology. *Journal of Group Psychotherapy, Psychodrama & Sociometry*, 44 (1991), pp. 33–40.

Blatner, H. A. 1994. Tele. In Holmes, Karp and Waston (1994), pp. 283–296.

Blatner, H. A. 2000. *Foundations of Psychodrama: History, Theory, and Practice*, 4th edition. New York, NY: Springer.

Blatner, H. A. 2002. *Moreno's 'Idee Fixe'*. Available at: www.blatner.com/adam/pdntbk/ideefixe.htm.

Blatner, H. A. and Cukier, R. 2007. Appendix: Moreno's Basic Concepts. In Baim, Burmeister and Maciel (2007), pp. 293–306.

Blomkvist, L. D. and Rutzel, T. 1994. Surplus Reality and Beyond. In Holmes, Karp and Waston (1994), pp. 235–257.

Blumer, H. 1962. Society as Symbolic Interaction. In A. M. Rose (Ed.), *Human Behavior and Social Processes*. New York, NY: Houghton-Mifflin.

Bobula, J. A. 1969. The Theater of Spontaneous Men. *Group Psychotherapy*, 22 (1969), pp. 47–65.

Bonney, W. C. and Scott, K. H. 1983. An Exploration of the Origin of Role Formation via Psychodrama and Personal Construct Theories. *Journal of Group Psychotherapy, Psychodrama & Sociometry*, 36 (1983), pp. 47–53.

Buber, M. 1923. *Ich und Du*. Leipzig: Insel Velag.

Buber, M. 1937. *I & Thou*. New York, NY: Scribner's.

Buber, M. 1963. *The Life of Dialogue*. Jerusalem: Bialik Institute. [HEB]

Bustos, D. M. 1994. Wings and Roots. In Holmes, Karp and Waston (1994), pp. 63–76.

Clayton, L. 1975. The Personality Theory of J. L. Moreno. *Group Psychotherapy and Psychodrama*, 28 (1975), pp. 144–157.

Clayton, M. 1994. Role Theory and Its Application in Clinical Practice. In Holmes, Karp and Watson (1994), pp. 121–144.

Cooly, C. 1902. *Human Nature and Social Order*. New York, NY: Scribner's.

Davies, M. H. 1987. Drama Therapy and Psychodrama. In S. Jennings (Ed.), *Dramatherapy: Theory and Practice for Teachers and Clinicians*. London: Routledge, pp. 104–124.

Dayton, T. 1994. *The Drama Within Psychodrama and Experimental Therapy*. Deerfield Beach, FL: Health Communications.

Ellenberger, H. F. 1958. A Clinical Introduction to Psychiatric Phenomenology and Existential Analysis. In R. May, E. Angle and H. F. Ellenberger (Eds.), *Existence: A New Dimension in Psychiatry and Psychology*. New York, NY: Basic Books, pp. 92–126.

Enoch, J. and Stern, P. (Eds.). 1999. *Introduction to Sociology*. Tel Aviv: Open University. [HEB].

Farmer, C. 1995. *Psychodrama and Systemic Therapy*. London: H. Karnac.

Feingold, B. 1996. *Why Drama: Education and Theater*. Tel Aviv: Achiav. [HEB]

Fox, J. (Ed.). 1987. *The Essential Moreno: Writings on Psycho drama, Group Method and Spontaneity by J. L. Moreno*. New York, NY: Springer Publishing Company.

Freud, S. 1915. Instincts and Their Vicissitudes. In James Strachey et al. (Eds.), *The Standard Edition of the Complete Works of Sigmund Freud*, 24 volumes. London: The Hogart Press & the Institute of Psychoanalysis (1953–1974), vol. 14, pp. 109–140.

Freud, S. 1933. *New Introductory Lectures on Psycho-Analysis*. London and New York: Pelican Freud Library (P.F.I.).

Freud, S. 1938. Psychopathology of Everyday Life. *The Basic Writings of Sigmund Freud*. New York, NY: Random House.

Fromm, E. 1961. *Marx's Concept of Man.* New York, NY: Frederick Ungar Publishing. Available at: www.marxists.org/archive/fromm/works/1961/man/index.htm.

Goldman, E. and Morrison, D. 1984. *Psychodrama: Experience and Process.* Dubuque, IA: Kendall/Hunt.

Greenberg, I. A. 1974a. *Moreno's Psychotherapeutic System: An Evaluation.* New York, NY: Behavioral Publications.

Greenberg, I. A. (Ed.). 1974b. *Psychodrama: Theory and Therapy.* New York, NY: Behavioral Publications.

Hare, P. A. and Hare, J. R. 1996. *J. L. Moreno.* London: Sage Publications.

Haskell, M. R. 1975. Moreno's Image of Man. *Sociometry*, 38 (1975), pp. 156–160.

Haworth, P. 1998. The Historical Background of Psychodrama. In Karp, Holmes and Tauvon (1998), pp. 15–29.

Heidegger, M. 1962. *Being and Time.* Edited and translated by J. Macquarrie and E. Robinson. New York, NY: Harper & Row.

Hollander, C. 1967. The Mirror Technique as a Psychodramatic Encounter. *Group Psychotherapy*, 20, pp. 103–112.

Holmes, P. 1992. *The Inner World Outside: Object Relations Theory and Psychodrama.* London: Routledge.

Holmes, P. 1998. The Auxiliary Ego. In Karp, Holmes and Tauvon (1998), pp. 130–159.

Holmes, P. and Karp, M. (Eds.). 1991. *Psychodrama: Inspiration and Technique.* London: Routledge.

Holmes, P., Karp, M. and Watson, M. (Eds.). 1994. *Psychodrama Since Moreno: Innovations in Theory and Practice.* London: Routledge.

Holt, H. 1966. Existential Group Analysis. In J. L. Moreno, A. Friedemann, R. Battegay and Z. T. Moreno (Eds.), *The International Handbook of Group Psychotherapy.* New York, NY: Philosophical Library, pp. 609–612.

Horvatin, T. and Schreiber, E. (Eds.). 2006. *The Quintessential Zerka.* London: Routledge.

Howard, M. N. 1963. Psychotherapy and Anxiety: A Sociometry Study. *Group Psychotherapy*, 16 (1963), pp. 1–7.

Jennings, H. H. 1960. Sociometric Choice Process in Personality and Group Formation. In J. L. Moreno (1960a), pp. 87–112.

Johnson, P. E. 1974. Interpersonal Psychology of Religion: Moreno and Buber. In Greenberg (1974), pp. 443–451.

Kahn, S. 1964. *Psychodrama Explained.* New York, NY: Philosophical Library.

Karp, M., Holmes, P. and Tauvon, B. (Eds.). 1998. *The Handbook of Psychodrama.* London: Routledge.

Keen, J. J. 1967. Religious Behavior and Neuroticism, Spontaneity, and World Mindedness. *Sociometry*, 30 (1967), pp. 137–157.

Kellermann, P. F. 1994. Role Reversal in Psychodrama. In P. Holmes, M. Karp and M. Watson (Eds.), *Psychodrama Since Moreno Innovations in Theory and Practice.* London: Routledge, pp. 261–276.

Kellermann, P. F. 2007. Let's Face It: Mirroring in Psychodrama. In Baim, Burmeister and Maciel (2007), pp. 83–95.

Kellermann, P. F. 1986. *Therapeutic Aspects of Psychodrama.* Stockholm: University of Stockholm.

Kelly, G. A. 1995. *The Psychology of Personal Constructs.* New York, NY: Norton.

Kelly, G. R. 1982. Theoretical Applications of Symbolic Interactionism and Psychodrama. *Journal of Group Psychotherapy, Psychodrama & Sociometry*, 35 (1982), pp. 39–45.

Kipper, D. 2007. *My Personal Conversations With the Author in 2007.* [HEB]

Kipper, D. 2009. *My Personal Conversations With the Author in 2009.* [HEB]

Kipper, D. 2010. *My Personal Conversation With the Author in 2010.* [HEB]

Kipper, D. A. 1967. Spontaneity and the Warming-up Process in a New Light. *Journal of Group Psychotherapy*, 20 (1967), pp. 62–67.

Kipper, D. A. 1982. Behavior Simulation: A Model for the Study of the Simulation Aspect of Psychodrama. *Journal of Group Psychotherapy, Psychodrama & Sociometry*, 35 (1982), pp. 1–17.

Kipper, D. A. 1986. *Psychotherapy Through Clinical Role Playing.* New York, NY: Brunner/Mazel.

Kipper, D. A. 1996. The Emergence of Role Playing as a Form of Psychotherapy. *Journal of Group Psychotherapy, Psychodrama & Sociometry*, 49 (1996), pp. 1–16.

Kipper, D. A. 2001. Surplus Reality and the Experiential Reintegration Model in Psychodrama. *International Journal of Action Methods: Psychodrama, Skill Training and Role Playing*, 53 (2001), pp. 137–152.

Kipper, D. A. 2002. The Cognitive Double: Integrating Cognitive and Action Technique. *Journal of Group Psychotherapy, Psychodrama & Sociometry* (2002), pp. 93–106.

Kipper, D. A. 2004. *The Experiential Reintegration Approach to Group Psychotherapy or Why Role Playing?* Available at: www.hebpsy.net/community.asp?id=36&cat=article&articleid=339.

Kipper, D. A. and Christoforou, A. 2006. The Spontaneity Assessment Inventory (SAI), Anxiety, Obsessive-Compulsive Tendency, and Temporal Orientation. *Journal of Group Psychotherapy, Psychodrama & Sociometry*, 59 (2006), pp. 33–34.

Kipper, D. A. and Hundal, J. 2005. The Spontaneity Assessment Inventory: The Relationship Between Spontaneity and Nonspontaneity. *Journal of Group Psychotherapy, Psychodrama & Sociometry*, 58 (2005), pp. 119–167.

Kraus, C. 1984. Psychodrama for Fallen Gods: A Review of Morenian Theology. *Journal of Group Psychotherapy, Psychodrama & Sociometry*, 37 (1984), pp. 47–65.

Landy, R. J. 1986. *Drama Therapy: Concepts, Theories and Practices.* Springfield, MA: Charles C. Thomas.

Landy, R. J. 1991. The Dramatic Basis of Role Theory. *The Arts in Psychotherapy*, 19 (1991), pp. 29–41.

Landy, R. J. 1993. *Person and Performance: The Meaning of Role in Drama Therapy and Everyday Life.* London: Jessica Kingsley.

Landy, R. J. 1996. *Essays in Drama Therapy: The Double Life.* London: Jessica Kingsley.

Lindqvist, M. 1994. Religion and the Spirit. In Holmes, Karp and Watson (1994), pp. 191–209.

Lindzey, G., & Byrne, D. (1968). Measurement of social choice and interpersonal attractiveness. In G. Lindzey, & E. Aronson (Eds.), *The Handbook of Social Psychology*, 2nd edition, Vol. 2. Reading, MA: Addison –Wesley.

Lousada, O. 1998. The Three-layered Cake, Butter With Everything. In Karp, Holmes and Tauvon (1998), pp. 205–227.

Marineau, R. F. 1989. *Jacob Levy Moreno, 1889-1974: Father of Psychodrama, Sociometry & Group Psychotherapy.* London & New York: Tavistock/Routledge.

Marineau, R. F. 1994. The Cradles of Moreno's Contributions. In P. Holmes, M. Karp, & M. Watson (Eds.), pp. 81–94.

May, R. 1958. The Origins and Significance of the Existential Movement in Psychology. Contributions of Existential Psychotherapy, In R. May, E. Angle, & H. F. Ellenberger (Eds.), *Existence: A New Dimension in Psychiatry and Psychology.* New York: Basic Books, pp. 3–36; 37–91.

Mead, G. H. 1925. Genesis of the Self and Social Control. *International Journal of Ethics*, 35, pp. 251–273.

Mead, G. H. 1934. *Mind, Self and Society*. Chicago: University of Chicago Press.
Mead, G. H. 1969. Play, the Game, and the Generalized Other. In L. W. Walter (Ed.), *Sociological Theory: An Introduction*. Chicago, IL: Aldine Publishing Company.
Mead, G. H. 1972. *Mind, Self and Society*. Chicago: University of Chicago Press.
Mead, G. H. 1980. *The Philosophy of the Present*. Chicago, IL: University of Chicago Press.
Meiers, J. I. 1947. Three Word Histories Important in Psychodrama. *Sociatry*, 1 (1947), pp. 239–242.
Meldrum, B. 1994. A Role Model of Drama Therapy and Its Application with Individuals and Groups. In S. Jenning et al. (Eds.), *The Handbook of Drama Therapy*. London: Routledge, pp. 75–92.
Meyer, A. 1974. Spontaneity, Elementalism and Holism. In Greenberg (Ed.), *Psychodrama Theory and Therapy*, pp. 133–156.
Moreno, J. D. 1971. Philodrama and Psychophilosophy. *Group Psychotherapy & Psychodrama*, 24/1–2 (1971), pp. 24–31.
Moreno, J. D. 1976. Psychodrama, Phenomenology and Existentialism. In L. R. Wolberg and M. L. Aronson (Eds.), *Group Therapy 1976: An Overview*. New York, NY: Stratton Intercontinental Medical Book Corp., pp. 26–33.
Moreno, J. D. 1994. Psychodramatic Moral Philosophy and Ethics. In Holmes, Karp and Waston (1994), pp. 97–111.
Moreno, J. L. 1920. *The Words of the Father*. Beacon, NY: Beacon House.
Moreno, J. L.1934. *Who Shall Survive?* Washington, DC: Nervous and Mental Publishing Co.
Moreno, J. L. 1937. Inter-Personal Therapy and the Psychopathology of Inter-personal Relations. *Sociometry*, 1 (1937), pp. 9–80. Reprint in Moreno (1964a), pp. 177–232.
Moreno, J. L. 1941. The Philosophy of the Moment and the Spontaneity Theatre. *Sociometry*, 4/2 (1941), pp. 205–206.
Moreno, J. L. 1942. Sociometry in Action. *Sociometry*, 5 (1942), pp. 298–315.
Moreno, J. L. 1943. Sociometry and the Cultural Order. *Sociometry*, 6/3 (1943), pp. 299–344.
Moreno, J. L. 1945. The Application of the Group Method to the Classification of Prisoners: A Round Table Conference at the Annual Meeting, American Psychiatric Association Philadelphia, Pa., May 31, 1932. *Sociometry*, 8/3–4 (1945), pp. 15–39.
Moreno, J. L. 1946. Sociogram and Sociomatrix. *Sociometry*, 9 (1946), pp. 348–349.
Moreno, J. L. 1947a. *The Theatre of Spontaneity*. Beacon, NY: Beacon House.
Moreno, J. L. 1947b. Note on the Spontaneity Theory of Birth. *Sociatry*, 1 (1947), p. 127.
Moreno, J. L. 1947c. *The Psychodrama of God: A New Hypothesis of the Self*, revised edition of *The Words of the Father*. Beacon, NY: Beacon House.
Moreno, J. L. 1948a. Experimental Theology. *Sociatry*, 2 (1948), pp. 93–98.
Moreno, J. L. 1948b. Spontaneity Training & Experimental Theology. *Sociatry* (1948), pp. 170–172.
Moreno, J. L. 1948c. The Spontaneity Theory of Learning, Revision of the Experimental Method in Science and the Philosophy of Education. *Sociatry*, 2 (1948), pp. 191–196.
Moreno, J. L. 1949a. Origins and Foundations of Interpersonal Theory, Sociometry and Microsociolgy. *Sociometry*, 12 (1949), pp. 201–217 [reprinted in Moreno (1951): 5–10, pp. 201–219].
Moreno, J. L. 1949b. Sociometry and Marxism. *Sociometry*, 12 (1949), pp. 106–143.
Moreno, J. L. 1950. Hypnodrama and Psychodrama. In *Psychodrama Monographs*, no. 27. Beacon, NY: Beacon House, pp. 1–10.
Moreno, J. L. 1951. *Sociometry, Experimental Method and the Science of Society: An Approach to a New Political Orientation*. Beacon, NY: Beacon House.

Moreno, J. L. 1952. Psychodramatic Production Techniques: Role Reversal, the Mirror Technique, the Double Technique and the Dream Technique. *Group Psychotherapy*, 4 (1952), pp. 243–273.

Moreno, J. L. 1953. *Who Shall Survive? Foundation of Sociometry, Group Psychotherapy and Sociodrama.* Beacon, NY: Beacon House.

Moreno, J. L. (Ed.). 1956. *Sociometry and the Science of Man.* Beacon, NY: Beacon House.

Moreno, J. L. 1959. *Psychodrama: Volume 2: Foundations of Psychotherapy.* Beacon, NY: Beacon House.

Moreno, J. L. 1960a. *The Sociometry Reader.* Glencoe, IL: The Free Press.

Moreno, J. L. 1960b. The Concept of the Encounter. *Journal of Existential Psychiatry*, 1 (1960), pp. 144–154.

Moreno, J. L. 1961. The Role Concept, a Bridge Between Psychiatry and Sociology. *American Journal of Psychiatry*, 118 (1961), pp. 518–522.

Moreno, J. L. 1962a. Role Theory and the Emergence of the Self. *Group Psychotherapy*, 15 (1962), pp. 114–115.

Moreno, J. L. 1962b. The 'United Role Theory' and Drama. *Group Psychotherapy*, 15 (1962), pp. 253–254.

Moreno, J. L. 1963a. Behavior Therapy. *American Journal of Psychiatry*, 120 (1963), pp. 194–196.

Moreno, J. L. 1963b. The Actual Trends in Group Psychotherapy. *Group Psychotherapy*, 16 (1963), pp. 117–122.

Moreno, J. L. 1964a. *Psychodrama: Volume 1.* Beacon, NY: Beacon House.

Moreno, J. L. 1964b. The Third Psychiatric Revolution and the Scope of Psychodrama. *Group Psychotherapy*, 17/3–4 (1964), pp. 149–171.

Moreno, J. L. 1965a. Therapeutic Vehicles and the Concept of Surplus Reality. *Group Psychotherapy*, 18/4 (1965), pp. 211–216.

Moreno, J. L. 1965b. The Sociometric Approach to Personality. In S. W. Sahakian (Ed.), *Psychology of Personality: Readings in Theory.* Chicago, IL: Rand McNally & Co.

Moreno, J. L. 1966. The Roots of Psychodrama – Autobiographical Notes: A Reply to Sarro. *Group Psychotherapy*, 19/3–4 (1966), pp. 140–145.

Moreno, J. L. 1967. *The Psychodrama of Sigmund Freud.* Beacon, NY: Beacon House.

Moreno, J. L. 1968. The Validity of Psychodrama. *Group Psychotherapy*, 21/1 (1968), p. 3.

Moreno, J. L. 1969a. The Viennese Origins of the Encounter Movement, Paving the Way for Existentialism, Group Psychotherapy, & Psychodrama. *Group Psychotherapy*, 22/1–2 (1969), pp. 7–17.

Moreno, J. L. 1969b. The Concept of the Here and Now, Hic et Nunc, Small Groups and Their Relation to Action Research. *Group Psychotherapy*, 22/3–4 (1969), pp. 139–140.

Moreno, J. L. 1969c. Las Palabras del Padre. *Group Psychotherapy*, 22/3–4 (1969), p. 143.

Moreno, J. L. 1972. The Religion of God-Father. In P. E. Johnson (Ed.), *Healer of the Mind: A Psychiatric Search for Faith.* Nashville, TN: Abingdon Press, pp. 197–215.

Moreno, J. L. 1974. The Creativity Theory of Personality: Spontaneity, Creativity and Human Potentialities. In Greenberg (1974), pp. 73–84.

Moreno, J. L. 1975. Mental Catharsis and the Psychodrama. *Journal of Group Psychotherapy, Psychodrama & Sociometry*, 28 (1975), pp. 5–32.

Moreno, J. L. 1977. Foundations of Sociometry. *Journal of Group Psychotherapy, Psychodrama & Sociometry*, 30 (1977), pp. 1–12.

Moreno, J. L. 1985a (copyright Zerka T. Moreno and Jonathan D. Moreno). *The Autobiography of J.L. Moreno, M.D. Moreno Archives.* Boston, USA: Harvard University.

Moreno, J. L. 1985b. *Psychodrama, Volume 1.* New York, NY: Beacon House.

Moreno, J. L. 1989. Autobiography. *Journal of Group Psychotherapy, Psychodrama & Sociometry*, 42 (1989), pp. 1–73.

Moreno, J. L. and Moreno, F. B. 1956. Spontaneity Theory of Child Development. In J. L. Moreno (Ed.), *Psychodrama: Volume 1.* New York, NY: Beacon House.

Moreno, J. L. and Moreno, Z. T. 1955. The Discovery of the Spontaneous Man With Special Emphasis Upon the Technique of Role Reversal. *Group Psychotherapy*, 8 (1955), pp. 103–108.

Moreno, J. L. and Moreno, Z. T. 1969. *Psychodrama: Volume 3: Action Therapy & Principles of Practice.* Beacon, NY: Beacon House.

Moreno, J. L., Moreno, Z. T. and Moreno, J. D. 1964. *The First Psychodramatic Family*. Beacon, NY: Beacon House.

Moreno, Z. T. 1944. Role Analysis and Audience Structure. *Sociometry*, 2 (1944), pp. 205–221.

Moreno, Z. T. 1948. The Double Situation. *Sociatry*, 1 (1948), pp. 436–446.

Moreno, Z. T. 1959. A Survey of Psychodramatic Techniqes. *Group Psychotherapy*, 12 (1959), pp. 5–14.

Moreno, Z. T. 1966. Sociogenesis of Individuals and Groups. In Moreno, Friedemann, Battegay and Moreno (1966), pp. 231–241.

Moreno, Z. T. 1969a. Moreneans: The Heretics of Yesterday and the Orthodoxy of Today. *Group Psychotherapy*, 22/1–2 (1969), pp. 1–6.

Moreno, Z. T. 1969b. Practical Aspects of Psychodrama. *Group Psychotherapy*, 22/3–4 (1969), pp. 213–220.

Moreno, Z. T. 1971. Beyond Aristotle, Breuer, and Freud: Moreno's Contribution to the Concept of Catharsis. *Group Psychotherapy and Psychodrama*, 24 (1971), pp. 34–43.

Moreno, Z. T. 1975. The Significance of Doubling and Role Reversal for Cosmic Man. *Group Psychotherapy and Psychodrama*, 28 (1975), pp. 55–60.Moreno, Z. T. 1989. Psychodrama, Role Theory, and the Concept of the Social Atom. *Journal of Group Psychotherapy, Psychodrama & Sociometry*, 42 (1989), pp. 178–187.

Moreno, Z. T. 1998. Preface. In Karp, Holmes and Tauvon (1998), pp. xi–xv.

Moreno, Z. T. 2006a. The Function of the Auxiliary Ego in Psychodrama With Special Reference to Psychotic Patients. In Hovartin and Schreiber (2006), pp. 197–199.

Moreno, Z. T. 2006b. In The Spirit of Two Thousand: Plenary Session Address to the American Society of Group Psychotherapy and Psychodrama. New York, March 21, 2006. In Horvatin and Schreiber (2006), pp. 275–288.

Moreno, Z. T. and Blomkvist, L. D and Rutzel, T. 2000. *Psychodrama, Surplus Reality and the Art of Healing*. London: Routledge.

Murray, N. 1976. Psychodrama: Post-Moreno. In L. R. Wolberg and M. L. Aronson, (Eds.), *Group Therapy 1976: An Overview.* New York, NY: Stratton Intercontinental Medical Book Corp., pp. 16–20.

Myerson, G. 2005. *101 Key Ideas in Existentialism.* Translated from English by B. Herman. Kfar Monash: Ofarim. [HEB]

Naharin, E. 1985. *The Stage Has Replaced the Couch.* Tel Aviv: Cherikover. [HEB]

Nehnevajsa, J. 1956. Sociometry: Decades of Growth. In J. L. Moreno (Ed.), Sociometry and the Since of Men. New York, NY: Beacon House, pp. 48–95.

Northway, M. 1967. *A Primer of Sociometry*, second edition. Toronto: University of Toronto Press.

Nolte, J., Smallwood, C. and Weistart, J. 1975. Role Reversal With God. *Group Psychotherapy and Psychodrama*, 28 (1975), pp. 70–76.

Oman, J. B. 1974. A Theology for Psychodrama: In Memory of Jacob L. Moreno. *Group Psychotherapy & Psychodrama*, 27 (1974), pp. 48–55.

Power, J. P. 1975. Moreno and the God Controversy. *Group Psychotherapy and Psychodrama*, 28 (1975), pp. 164–167.

Rabson, J. S. 1979. *Psychodrama: Theory and Method.* Cape Town: Department of Sociology, University of Cape Town.

Rap, U. 1984. *Play World: Behavioral Sciences Lessons.* Tel Aviv: Ministry of Defense. [HEB]

Røine, E. 1997. *Psychodrama: Group Psychotherapy as Experimental Theatre – Playing the Leading Role in Your Own Life.* Translated by A. Zwik. London: Jessica Kingsley Publishers.

Seeman, H. 1982. A Methodology for Existential Psychotherapy: Psychodrama. *Journal of Group Psychotherapy, Psychodrama & Sociometry*, 35 (1982), pp. 70–82.

Shatil, J. 1994. *Psychological Energy's Enigma: Psychological Energy's Significance in Psychological and Religious Personality Theories.* Tel Aviv: Ramot. [HEB]

Sigad, R. 1981. *Existentialism.* Jerusalem: Bialik Institute. [HEB]

Sorokin, P. A. 1956. Remarks on J. L. Moreno's 'Theory of Spontaneity-Creatvity'. In Moreno (1956), pp. 374–382.

Spence, K. 1956. *Behavior Theory and Conditioning.* New Haven, CT: Yale University Press.

Sprague, K. 1994. Stepping Into the Cosmos With Our Feet on the Ground. In Holmes, Karp and Watson (1994), pp. 11–35.

Stanislavski, C. 1936. *An Actor Prepares.* New York, NY: Theatre Arts Books.

Stanislavski, C. 1949. *Building a Character.* New York, NY: Theatre Arts Books.

Tauvon, B. K. 1998. Principles of Psychodrama. In Karp, Holmes and Tauvon (1998), pp. 30–45.

Taylor, S. 1998. The Warm-Up. In Karp, Holmes and Tauvon (1998), pp. 47–57.

Tyson, H. A. 1966. The Acts According to Moreno. *Group Psychotherapy*, 19, pp. 220–230.

Williams, A. 1989. *The Passionate Technique: Strategic Psychodrama With Individuals, Families and Groups.* London: Routledge.

Winnicott, D. W. 1989. *Playing and Reality.* New York, NY: Routledge.

Winters, N. L. 2000. The Psychospiritual in Psychodrama: A Fourth Role Category. *Journal of Action Methods*, 52 (2000), pp. 163–171.

Wolberg, A. R. 1973. The Contributions of Jacob Moreno. In L. R. Wolberg and M. L. Aronson (Eds.), *Group Therapy 1976: An Overview.* New York, NY: Stratton Intercontinental Medical Book Corp.

Yablonsky, L. 1968. Psychodrama and Sociometry: An Appraisal. In I. A. Greenberg (Ed.), *Psychodrama and Audience Attitude Change.* Beverly Hills, CA: Behavioral Studies Press, pp. 239–248.

Yablonsky, L. 1973. Humanizing Groups Through Psychodrama. *Group Psychotherapy and Psychodrama*, 25 (1973), pp. 7–15.

Yablonsky, L. 1976. *Psychodrama Resolving Emotional Problems Through Role-playing.* New York, NY: Basic Books, Inc.

Yablonsky, L. and Enneis, J. M. 1956. Psychodrama: Theory and Practice. In F. Fromm-Reichmann and J. L. Moreno (Eds.), *Progress in Psychotherapy*, vol. 1. New York, NY: Grune and Stratton.

Zeleny, L. D. 1956. Validity of a Sociometric Hypothesis: The Function of Creativity in Interpersonal and Group Relations. In Moreno (1956), pp. 439–449.

Zuretti, M. 1994. The Co-unconscious. In Holmes, Karp and Watson (1994), pp. 213–229.

Index

act hunger 99–102, 146–147
action, science of 21
action method 21; –oriented coaching group 1
alienation 3, 14–15, 89
Allport, Gordon W. 6, 86, 94–95
ancient Greece 91, 116, 142; drama/theater 142–143
ancient Rome 116
anthropology 22, 89, 116, 126
anti-semitism 31, 43
Anusim 29; *see also* Jews
archetype(s) 29, 86, 92
Aristotle 79, 124
Asia Minor 31
atheism 2, 7–8
Austria 38, 42, 46; Army 46; Bad Voslau 47, 51; Mitterndorf community 46–47, 179; *see also* Vienna

Bach, Johann Sebastian 80
Balint, Michael 103–104
Beecher, Beatrice 51
Beethoven, Ludwig van 78–79
behaviorism 5–6, 124–126; social 120; time cognitive behaviorism (CBT) 125
behaviorist approach 4, 6
behaviorists 125; experiential 173; Pavlovian 125; Skinnerian 125; social 126
Bejerano, Rabbi 35, 178
Bergson, Henri 58–59, 69, 75, 80, 125; creativity principle 58; The Waves of Thought 58
Berlin, Germany 38
Bible 35, 39, 55, 78–79, 81, 182; book of Genesis 35, 47–48; New Testament 55, 184; Old Testament 184
Black Sea 30
Blumer, Herbert 120; *see also* symbolic interaction
Bosporus 30
Bridge, Florence 51
Buber, Martin 7, 62, 88–89, 126; *Daimon* 85, 88; *Ich und Du* (*I & Thou*) 88
Buddha 20, 26, 39, 78, 90, 171, 182
Buddhism 8

capitalistic society 13–15
catharsis 8–9, 22, 50, 74, 124, 135, 163, 167, 174–176; of integration 143; mental 176
Catholic Church 117
Christ 11, 55; scientific 20
Christianity 8, 29, 31, 33, 35
closed organization principle 146–147
cognitive approach 2
collective unconscious 86
Columbus, Christopher 31
communism 15, 31, 43; communal society 15
conscious, the 112–113
conservation(s) *see* cultural conservation(s); role(s); social conservation(s); technological conservation(s)
conserve(s) *see* cultural conserve(s); technological conserve(s)
Cooley, Charles 118
Cosmic Man 29–30, 48, 142; *see also* cosmodynamic man
cosmodynamic man 134, 141–142, 145
cosmodynamics 18, 141
creativity 1–2, 6–7, 10–11, 15, 17–22, 25–28, 38, 41–43, 45, 48–50, 52, 54–61, 63–70, 72, 75–82, 84–85, 98–99, 110, 126, 133, 134, 136, 139, 141, 144, 150–151, 170, 174–176, 177–180, 183–184; conserved 81; creative act

57–61, 79; creative circulation 81; creative revolution 82; creativity neurosis 11, 15, 60; freely flowing 81; vs. libido 17
cultural atom 163, 176
cultural conservation(s) 18, 64, 68, 72, 74, 77–82, 84, 87, 135, 149, 177
cultural conserve(s) 2, 27, 43, 64, 68, 73, 79–80, 175

Democritus 115
determinism 16, 58, 69, 73, 86; historical 16
Dewey, John 90, 125
Dionysus 143; journey of suffering 143
divinity 8, 10–11, 26, 32, 34, 38, 45, 47, 52, 78, 178, 180; *see also* divinity concept
divinity concept 9, 27, 35, 47, 49
dream hunger 102

egalitarianism 12
Einstein. Albert 64–65; theory of relativity 64
empathy 10, 92–94, 96, 105, 157, 161, 166–169; mutual 157
encounter 8, 11–12, 21, 26–27, 38–39, 43–48, 50, 84–91, 125–126, 136–138, 143–145, 149, 155, 164, 174, 176, 179; concept 39, 91, 139, 179; definition 21, 85; existential 137; groups 44, 52; I-thou 1, 88–89, 91, 139, 165, 168; man–God 8, 88; theater 137; *see also* interpersonal relations theory; role exchange
energy conservation principle 19, 62–66, 77
England 116
English (language) 51, 88, 116, 118
Europe 7, 49, 52
existentialism 2–4, 31, 137–138, 183; dialogical 12; intellectual 12; religious 181
existentialistic-humanistic psychology 7
existential(istic) movement 2, 6–7, 43, 85
existential(istic) perception/view 2, 8, 19, 40, 54, 135; theological- 181
existential(istic) philosophy 1, 3–4, 11, 61, 134
existential(istic) psychology 4–7
existential(istic) psychotherapy 6–7, 134, 177
existential reality 156
expressionism 40, 42

faith healing 94
"falling Gods" concept 179
Fascism 49
Feuerbach, Ludwig 88
France 116
free will 7, 67, 69
French (language) 33, 85, 116, 179
Freud 13, 16–20, 22, 35, 38, 49, 62–64, 69, 86, 93, 106, 124–125, 140, 182; meeting with Moreno 19–20, 35; Oedipal complex 86; repetition-compulsion principle 19; *see also* libido; psychoanalysis

Gandhi 20
God 7–12, 18, 19, 32, 34–42, 44–45, 47–52, 54–58, 78, 88–90, 111, 117, 134, 165, 178–181, 183; cosmic 55–56; nature of 55, 57; "Thou God" 55; *see also* divinity; divinity concept; Godhead; "I-God" principle; 'I-Thou' encounter concept; Jesus
Godhead 54–57; perception 55
God play 178, 180
Goethe, Johann Wolfgang von 60
Greek (language) 17, 21, 77, 91, 115, 117, 142
group dynamics 184
group psychotherapy 1, 15, 46, 53, 149, 171, 176, 179, 180–181, 183, 184; movement 183
group therapy 1–2, 12, 21–23, 39, 94, 128, 167; movement 2; *see also* group psychotherapy; tele

Ha'ari 62
Hebrew (language) 31, 35
Heidegger, Martin 3, 7, 11, 25–26; dasein 25–26, 134
here and now concept 7, 12, 19, 43, 50, 60–61, 68–69, 72, 74, 75, 80–81, 85, 94, 112, 126, 128, 133, 137–140, 146, 151, 168, 173, 175
Hitler, Adolf 43
Holy Trinity 117
House of Encounter 12, 179
"human potential exhaustion" movement 1
Husserl, Edmund 4, 137

"idée fixe" concept 44–45, 179–180
identity 31–32, 39, 90, 101–105, 110, 119, 132, 134, 149, 153–154, 158–160, 166, 168, 178; crisis 154, 159; development 119, 153–154, 157, 161, 164; and

identification 159; and imitation 158–159; Jewish 38; personal 38, 109, 119, 131, 153, 157, 161, 166; shared 165; *see also* matrix of identity
"I-God" principle 10–11, 34, 41–42, 49–50, 56–57, 59, 61, 178
International Council of Group Psychotherapy 53
interpersonal relations theory 85, 87
interpersonal theory 8, 27, 86, 88, 90
'I-Thou' encounter concept 1, 88–89, 91, 139, 165, 168

Jaspers, Karl 9
Jesus 11–12, 20, 26, 33, 35, 39, 41–43, 45, 55–56, 87, 90, 117, 178; Christ 55–56
Jews 29, 31, 38; People of Israel 39; Sephardic 29, 32, 35
John, St. 60
Judaism 8, 33
Jung, Carl 9, 29, 86, 92, 140; *see also* archetype; collective unconscious

Kelmer, Chaim 31, 44
Kierkegaard, Søren 3, 5, 11–12
Koran 182

Latin (language) 69, 116–118, 160
libido 17–19, 42, 63–64, 89
Linton, Ralph 118
Lipps, Theodore 93
locus nascendi 30, 58–59, 107, 128, 148
logical positivism 181

Mahler, Gustave 38
man: as cosmodynamic person 13, 17–18; as psychodynamic person 13, 17; as sociodynamic person 13, 16; *see also* Cosmic Man
Marx, Karl 13–16, 18, 49, 182
materialism 9, 49; economic 49; psychological 49; technological 49
matrix of identity 28, 102–114, 154, 165; cosmic 103; familial/family 103, 114; genetic 103–104; identity related 103; maternal 103, 104–105; social 103, 105–106, 113–114; theory 28
May, Rollo 91
Mead, George Herbert 109, 118–130; and language 122–123; *Mind, Self and Society* 126; and playful act 123; *see also* behaviorism; role(s); symbolic interaction
megalomania 20, 34, 37, 40, 48, 56, 110–111; normal 40, 42, 104, 111, 179–180
Moreno, Jacob Levy 1–2, 7–28; anonymity concept 31–32, 41, 44; and children 44–45, 49, 51, 134–135, 146, 179; and the creative act 57–61; and cultural conservations 77–82; *Daimon* 85; Das Testament des Vaters (*The Words of the Father*) 41–42, 51, 56, 88, 182, 184; *Einladung zu einer Begegnung* (*Invitation to Encounter*) 85; and encounter 85–90; and God 54–57; and human development 99–103; and immigrants 179; life story of 25, 27, 29–53, 178–180, 182, 184; and matrix of identity 103–114; "My Epiphany Holiday" 39; name of 31–32, 52; parents 32–38, 178; personality of 181–182; personality theory of 177, 182; and prostitutes 45–46, 179; and psychic energy 61–66; and psychodrama 134–176; and refugees 46–47, 179; and religion of encounter 44; and roles 112–115, 116, 123–133; *Sociometry: A Journal of Interpersonal Relations* 85; and spontaneity 66–77, 84; and tele 90–97; "Theatre of Spontaneity" (*Das Stegreiftheater*) 51; and warming up 82–84; *Who Will Survive?* 85, 126; and women 50–51; *see also* creativity; divinity concept; encounter; group therapy; here and now concept; "I-God" principle; interpersonal relations theory; megalomania; personality theory; psychodrama; role play(ing); self-development theory; sociometry; spontaneity; tele; warming up
Moreno, Jonathan 52
Moreno, Zerka 30, 42, 51–52, 76, 93, 151, 165

Nachman of Breslov, Rabbi 62
Napoleon 80
National-Socialist movement 43
Nazi Germany 51; Nazis 31, 43
neurosis 6, 14–15, 71; compulsive 86; creativity 11, 15, 60; existentialistic 6; histrionic 135; spontaneity 15
New York: Beacon 53; Brooklyn 51; Hudson 46, 179; New York City 51, 53
Nietzsche, Friedrich 3, 5, 7–8, 10–11, 80, 138; atheism 2
nihilism 7, 40

October Revolution 9, 16, 43; Bolshevik leaders of 43
other, the 3, 85–89, 91–92, 109, 112–113, 120–122, 127, 130, 132–133, 137, 149–150, 157–159, 161–164, 166–170, 172

pantheism 183
Peirce, Charles 75–76
personality 4–7, 13, 17–18, 25, 48, 49, 56, 58, 60, 62–63, 73–74, 77, 80, 82, 84, 86, 92, 95, 97, 99, 102–103, 110–113, 116–117, 119, 122, 124, 128, 131–133, 134–135, 143, 144, 147, 148, 156, 159, 161, 168, 170–173, 177, 179, 182, 183; development of 25, 77, 90, 98–99, 110, 112, 148, 161, 165, 176, 177; integration of 165; theories 90, 151; *see also* personality theory
personality theory 13, 16–18, 23–24, 28, 61, 82, 90, 115, 116, 177, 182
phenomenological philosophy *see* phenomenology
phenomenology 4, 25, 134
philosophy of existence 2–3; *see also* existentialism
Piaget, Jean 158
Planck, Max 65
Plato 78–79
play principle 22; role- 149; *see also* role play(ing)
pragmatism 75
projection 91, 93–94, 96, 166
psychiatry 1, 9, 13, 85, 89, 124, 181–182, 184
psychoanalysis 5, 6, 18–22, 25, 31, 35, 62, 86–87, 90, 94, 124, 183; psychoanalytical approach 4, 6, 17, 62; psychoanalytic theory 16–19
psychodrama 1–2, 9, 12, 19–20, 23–24, 26–27, 30, 35, 39, 44, 46, 48, 50, 52–53, 66, 75, 76, 89–90, 100–101, 123–125, 129, 133, 134, 136–174, 176, 177–178, 180–184; double technique 153–158, 161, 164, 170; of "Fallen God" 36, 45; God-play(s) 36–38, 42, 45, 48, 58; mirror stage/mirror technique 157–166, 169–170; protagonist 12, 26–27, 48, 50, 137, 142–144, 151–157, 159–164, 167–168, 170; scene 48, 146, 155, 160, 163, 170; stage in 36, 137, 145–146, 157, 159, 162, 164, 173; theater of 53, 139, 179; and therapeutic group 144–145; and total experience principle 150; *see also* encounter concept; psychodramatic method; role(s); role reversal; surplus reality; warming up
psychodramatic method/process/theory 9, 21, 23–25, 27–28, 29, 45, 72, 75, 76, 83, 102, 128, 130, 138, 147–150, 153, 159, 161–163, 167–168, 170–171, 178, 182
psychological simulation principle 150
psychology 5–7, 22, 24, 54, 59–60, 62, 74, 86, 91, 118, 138, 181; behaviorist 5; children's 51; developmental 74; existentialistic 4–5, 7; existentialistic-humanistic 7; humanistic 129; social 24–25, 96; *see also* behaviorism; behaviorist approach; psychoanalysis
psychopathology 54, 70, 75, 93, 116, 141, 172
psychotherapeutic process 145, 149, 174, 176
psychotherapy 1, 6, 19–20, 22, 25, 45, 53, 87, 90, 93–95, 124, 140–142, 145, 167, 171, 183; existentialistic 6, 134, 177; play-based 22; *see also* group psychotherapy; psychotherapeutic process

religion 1, 3, 8–10, 12–13, 20, 29, 33, 43–44, 48, 54, 60, 75, 76, 81, 85–86, 145, 179, 182; dramatic 145; of encounter 44; primitive 20; universal 9
religious behavior: theories of 86
robot(s) 5, 70, 76–77, 80, 82, 134; robot pathology 27
role(s) 114–115, 116–133, 136, 138–139, 143–144, 149–151, 158–159, 166, 168–174; assumption 113, 158, 164, 169, 171; audience 48, 50, 87, 124, 135, 138, 144–145, 151; auxiliary-ego 26, 101, 140, 144, 147, 149, 151, 154–155, 159–160, 162–168, 170; clusters 113–114, 169; conservation 77, 128; conserved 109, 127–128, 133, 135, 144; -creating 127; creative 128; cultural 109; development 131, 153; ex-transition 137, 140; man–role conflict 127, 135; psychodramatic 106, 111–112, 124, 129, 168, 174; psychosomatic 106, 108–109, 112, 129–130, 167; psychotherapeutic meaning 124; social 94, 98, 106, 112–114, 123, 125, 127, 129–130, 132–133, 162, 164; spiritual 167; spontaneity 128; taking 119, 127–128; in theater 116–119, 123, 127, 133, 135,

149; *see also* role concept; role exchange; role learning/training; role play(ing); role relations; role reversal; role theory
role concept 28, 123, 131, 177
role exchange 85, 124, 126, 128, 137
role learning/training 112–113, 129, 144, 145, 153, 164, 171–174
role play(ing) 22, 25–26, 29, 37, 76, 116, 118, 123–124, 127–129, 134, 135, 143, 149, 151, 154, 158, 164–165, 170–175
role-play principle 149
role relations 95–96, 109, 162, 164; actor–role 149; formal 95–96; man–role 149; nonformal 95
role reversal 1, 152, 154, 162–170, 180; feedback 169, 173
role theory 1, 115, 119, 124, 126–127, 130, 167, 170–172
Romania 29–31, 33; Bucharest 29, 32, 35
Russia 16
Russian Revolution *see* October Revolution

safeguarding mysticism principle 62
Sarbin, Theodore 131
Sartre, Jean-Paul 3, 7, 10–12, 137
secularization 7–8, 49
self, the 1, 10, 21, 23, 27, 32, 37, 40, 49, 53, 54–56, 69–71, 83, 89, 92, 96, 100, 102–107, 109–115, 116, 118–121, 123, 124, 127–132, 137, 143, 147, 149, 151, 154–155, 158–159, 161, 163–170, 172–173, 175; alienation from 15; -awareness 121, 161; differentiation of 102, 110; emotional 165; integration of 165; physical 165; selfness 85, 142; social 123, 162, 165, 172; theory of 123; *see also* role relations; self-actualization; self-development theory
self-actualization 6, 14, 89, 149
self-development theory 18, 22, 24, 27–28, 40, 98, 102–114, 116; *see also* megalomania
Shakespeare 78; *Hamlet* 78
Sing-Sing prison 46
social atom 23, 60, 96, 115, 132, 176, 178; definition 115
social conservation(s) 72
Social Darwinism 119
socialism 16, 43
sociodrama 19, 24, 124, 134, 167
sociology 1, 22, 138, 181
sociometrics 17, 47
sociometric theory 47
sociometry 1–2, 8–9, 12, 17, 22–23, 26, 29, 47–48, 52–53, 60, 85, 89–91, 95, 96, 103, 107, 123, 125, 180–182, 184; *see also* social atom; sociometrics; sociometric theory
Sociometry Institute 53
Socrates 11–12, 20, 43, 87, 178
Sorokin, P. A. 78–79
Spain 29, 31
Spence, Kenneth 5
spontaneity 1–2, 10, 17–22, 25–28, 38, 42–43, 45, 48–50, 54–57, 59–61, 63–78, 82, 84–85, 87–88, 95, 96, 98–101, 103–104, 106, 108–114, 126, 128, 133, 134–135, 136–139, 148, 150–151, 155, 169, 174–176, 177–180, 183; adequate 68; definition 66–67, 77, 99; high-degree 67; and "I-God" principle 61; vs. libido 17; pathological 67–68, 70; vs. roboticism 80; spontaneity neurosis 15; stereotypical 67–68; theater of 49–50, 135, 139, 179; training for 72–74, 76, 170, 174, 176, 180; *see also* spontaneity factor
spontaneity factor 66, 99–101, 109–111, 135
Stanislavski, Constantin 117–118
status nascendi 88, 101, 103, 126, 128, 133, 139, 171
surplus reality 26, 140–142, 146, 153, 163, 180, 182–183
symbolic interaction (interactionism) 119–122, 125, 130; theory 125

technological conservations 78, 87
technological conserve(s) 68, 80, 123
tele 2, 18, 23, 27, 54, 63, 90–97, 98, 102–103, 105–106, 109, 131, 133, 137, 144, 148, 152, 156–157, 169, 177; definition 91, 94, 103; telic sensitivity 92, 105; vs. transference 23, 90–91, 93; *see also* matrix of identity
Tertullianus 117
therapeutic dream 19, 35
therapeutic play 49, 76
therapeutic relationship 23, 94–95
therapeutic theater 49–50, 76, 135, 145
therapy: family 1; gestalt 1; *see also* group therapy; psychoanalysis; psychodrama; psychotherapeutic process; psychotherapy
transference 21, 23, 27, 87, 90–91, 93–96, 157; counter- 93–94; definition 93

transitions 146, 175–176
transpersonal approach 63, 134, 183
Trotsky, Leon 43
Turkey 31, 34; Istanbul 34

unconscious, the 17, 74, 102, 112–113, 148
United States 51, 52, 118
universality 8, 29, 40–41; *see also* "I-God" principle

Vienna 12, 22, 31, 35, 38, 40, 41, 43, 45–47, 49–51, 85, 125, 134–135, 179; Augarten park 45; prostitution in 45–46; University of 31, 47

warming up 2, 17, 21, 27, 37, 42, 54, 67, 73, 80–84, 98–101, 107–108, 110, 128, 143, 151, 167, 169, 173, 177; definition 82; starters of 83–84, 99–100, 105, 107, 115
Watson, J. B. 124; *see also* behaviorism
World War I 46, 49
World War II 3, 74

Zarathustra 11

For Product Safety Concerns and Information please contact our EU representative GPSR@taylorandfrancis.com
Taylor & Francis Verlag GmbH, Kaufingerstraße 24, 80331 München, Germany

www.ingramcontent.com/pod-product-compliance
Ingram Content Group UK Ltd.
Pitfield, Milton Keynes, MK11 3LW, UK
UKHW011012180926
475701UK00004B/698
* 9 7 8 0 3 6 7 4 8 8 2 0 8 *